# In My
# LIFETIME

# In My
# LIFETIME

Early life and career of Police Captain Herbert Smith

## Herbert Smith

iUniverse

**IN MY LIFETIME**
**Early life and career of Police Captain Herbert Smith**

*Copyright © 2014 Herbert Smith.*

*All rights reserved. No part of this book may be used or reproduced by any means, graphic, electronic, or mechanical, including photocopying, recording, taping or by any information storage retrieval system without the written permission of the publisher except in the case of brief quotations embodied in critical articles and reviews.*

*iUniverse books may be ordered through booksellers or by contacting:*

*iUniverse*
*1663 Liberty Drive*
*Bloomington, IN 47403*
*www.iuniverse.com*
*1-800-Authors (1-800-288-4677)*

*Because of the dynamic nature of the Internet, any web addresses or links contained in this book may have changed since publication and may no longer be valid. The views expressed in this work are solely those of the author and do not necessarily reflect the views of the publisher, and the publisher hereby disclaims any responsibility for them.*

*Any people depicted in stock imagery provided by Thinkstock are models, and such images are being used for illustrative purposes only. Certain stock imagery © Thinkstock.*

*ISBN: 978-1-4917-3635-7 (sc)*
*ISBN: 978-1-4917-3636-4 (e)*

*Library of Congress Control Number: 2014910030*

*Printed in the United States of America.*

*iUniverse rev. date: 10/08/2014*

# PART 1

# PROLOGUE AND DISCLAIMER

Memoirs; def: A report or record of happenings that are based on the writer's personal observation and knowledge or special information. (Webster's Unabridged Dictionary)

Being in the dark about my family's background and history, I decided to write some things down from my memory before they were lost in antiquity.

I am writing these memoirs for the benefit of any descendants Nettie and I may have, and also for the benefit of the descendants of my brothers and sisters.

After getting this work published, I intend to get a copy to each of nephews and nieces, so they can perhaps pass the information along to their descendants.

The things I have written are from my own knowledge, and from talking to friends and colleagues.

Hopefully, I have indicated in each instance wherein I have either been personally involved, or have stated the information was told to me.

On occasion, I have deliberately left out the names of people involved out of respect for the families.

It has not been my intention to embarrass anyone in this writing, and if I have done so, I apologize.

As I am finishing this up, please be advised that I have passed my 83rd birthday and am thankful that my memory is still fairly accurate, and my typing fingers still supple.

I want to the reader to know that I remember many stories from my police work which I chose to not write.

# REMEMBERING THINGS PAST
# THE MEMOIRS OF WILLIAM HERBERT SMITH
## THE EARLY YEARS

For quite some time I have given some thought to putting down on paper the events of my life, not that my life was too much different from most other folk. At least I know it was very different from my siblings.

I was born in the pre-stock market crash of 1928, on or about the twelfth of November. In another segment the "on or about" will be explained. That segment is entitled "You Have Got To Be Kidding Me! Right?

The location of my birth was at or near the town of Harrisonburg, Louisiana, in the Parish of Catahoula. I have been told all of the offspring of my parents were born at home. My father's name was William Henry Smith.

My mother's name was Versa Purnece Wright Smith.

Papa and Mama were married in or near Jena, Louisiana on January 2, 1907. Papa was 22 years old and Mama was 18. It was said that Mama considered herself an "Old Maid."

I am fortunate enough to have a black and white wedding photograph, taken, I suppose, shortly after the wedding ceremony. They are standing in a yard and are not even holding hands. The photograph or a copy thereof will be included in these writings.

I do not know what kind of work Papa was doing at that period in his life, but to be frank, he looks kind of scruffy. During that period of time the timber industry was a big thing in that part of Louisiana. Perhaps he worked at a sawmill, because I remember him talking about incidents which occurred at a sawmill.

Papa's family came from a clan of poor people. I knew of none of his kinsmen who owned real estate.

On the other hand, Mama's people were the Wrights of Jena and they were people of property. One of her kin owned the Wright Hotel in Jena and her brother owned and operated a shoe repair shop in Jena. She had several nephews who were either in the banking business or had their own businesses.

One of my sisters told me Mama had told her of the first time she saw Papa. She told my sister "That is the prettiest man I have ever seen." I do know Papa had the clearest blue eyes and maybe that is what Mama fell in love with.

In referring to the children of Papa and Mama, I will not use any vital statistics, like dates of birth and so forth.

The first born was Alphonse Smith, and then came Claudia Mae, then Mildred Marie, then Homer, then Joseph David, then Leslie Henry, then Walter Silas, then William Herbert, and lastly, Quitman Thomas, God giving Papa and Mama a family of seven sons and two daughters.

Included with these writings will be a group picture of Papa and his seven sons.

During the most of the early history of our family, their living was made by share-cropping. Apparently, this life style was very popular during this period in the South. Share-cropping was an arrangement between a land owner and a "tenant farmer" who worked the land on "halves" or some other percentage of the farm's product. I do not know when Papa and Mama began this way of making a living, but I do know they did it until about 1939. I can remember living at four different places from the time I started to school until we moved "to town" in 1939. In those days a child starting to school had to be six years of age by the time school started. We were living near Manifest, Louisiana, on the "Little" place. I was sent off to school there at Manifest. I did not go alone. I had at least two older brothers who were still in school. Since my birthday was in November, I was not six years old when school started. So I was sent home to wait another year. That meant I was nearly seven years old when I started to school the next year at Harrisonburg, Louisiana. Yep, you guessed it. We moved again during that next year. My younger brother

Pete was in the same boat, because his birthday was in November also. He was almost exactly two years younger than me.

We lived at Manifest two different times. The first time I recall, we lived off the main highway on the "Little" place. It belonged to a man named Little. There was a creek which flowed nearby from which we got our water, including drinking water. I remember my folks talking about the water tasting like bath powder. Later, when talking to one of my older brothers, he revealed the Little family lived upstream from us and their daughters swam in the creek.

That area was low country where we lived and was subject to flooding when backwater came up. There were lots of Mayhaw trees in that area. Mayhaw berries were good for making jam and jelly, if you had the money to buy the sugar.

I recall one time the water came up while the berries were ripe and we all waded out into the backwater to gather these berries. Papa would shake the tree and Mayhaws would fall. They floated, so all we had to do was scoop them up and put them in buckets.

When the Mayhaws got ripe and there was no backwater, Papa would spread sheets on the ground under the trees. He would shake the tree and Mayhaws would fall on the sheets, where we would gather them.

Papa and Mama never owned any real estate until about 1940 when we moved to Jena.

We lived at various places as Papa tried to find a good farm to work. We did not have a vehicle, not even a wagon. Most of our stuff was kept in boxes. I suppose Papa would find a friend or relative with a vehicle, a wagon or truck, to move us. I do not recall riding in a truck to move, except maybe on the move to Jena in 1939.

The first place I recall was there near Manifest, Louisiana where the creek water tasted like bath powder. I was about six years old when we lived there. We had to ride a school bus to school. The seats were long benches from front to back, four rows. Boys sat on one side and the girls sat on the other side.

There was this one boy who was always picking at me. One morning he started in and I had had enough of him. I took a swing at him and connected. The next morning he came to school with a black eye. He left me alone after that.

The next place was the Johnson place near Harrisonburg, Louisiana. We lived in two different houses there on that place. In 1936 we lived in a house quite a distance from the main road. In 1937 we moved to another house closer to the main road.

It was at this last location that Papa had to get some help with his crop. A black family came to help out. I guess the landowner made arrangements for them to help us.

They had this young boy about my age and I got into my first footrace with this fellow. I was pretty fast on my feet in those days. I went barefooted all the time and I could move on. Well, that black kid left me in the dust. I just thought I was fast.

These houses were in the flood zone also. The land was very good for farming. I am sure you have heard the saying, "He is in tall cotton!." The cotton Papa grew that year was tall, the reason for the saying was, tall cotton was easier to pick because stooping was not necessary.

These houses were definitely low-income types. The floors were plain boards with cracks and knot holes. Splinters in the feet were a common occurrence.

The one I remember most was near the main highway. I would say the house was probably fifty or seventy-five yards from the blacktop road.

While we lived there I remember hearing the grownups talking about a levee breaking and a flood was coming, which meant backwater. They said the water would first appear in a drainage ditch at the back of the place where we lived. Pete and I kept watch on that ditch. Sure enough, before long the water in the ditch began to rise. It kept coming up until it overflowed the banks. It started running through the grass of the pasture. Me and Pete kept backing up as the water followed us. It ran us right up to the house. It kept rising until it was nearly in the house! When the wind blew, waves would wash up on the front porch. Papa, at one point, said if it rises another inch we'll have to leave the house. It stopped rising, but water surrounded the house everywhere.

We had a little flat-bottomed boat which I guess belonged to the landowner. My older brothers used the boat to get out to the main road. They would have to take our dog out to the road for his daily "exercise." The rest of the time he stayed on the front porch.

I don't remember having any livestock, but if we did, Papa took it out to the road while the water was up. We might have had one old cow. The chickens roosted in the barn, which had a hay loft.

I know now that there is always a danger from snakes, rats and other varmints seeking shelter in houses during a flood. I do not recall having that kind of problem at that house.

After some time, I don't know how long, the water began receding and before long everything returned to normal, except our well had to be pumped out by hand to purify the water.

That was the last year we lived in the low farming country. Our next place was back near Manifest, Louisiana, but we lived on the side of a hill, which is another story.

# WILLIAM HENRY SMITH

My dad, William Henry Smith, whom I refer to throughout these writings as Papa, was born February 27, 1885 at or near Summerville, Louisiana. Summerville is a small community between Jena, Louisiana and Olla, Louisiana.

Papa was not a large man. I would guess his height at about five foot seven inches and probably weighed in the neighborhood of one hundred fifty to one hundred sixty pounds. This was his probable size when I was working with him in the 1940's. Papa quit farming in 1939 when he was 54 years age.

Papa apparently knew the basics of carpentry. After he and Mama bought the place near Jena, he set about remodeling it. From him I also learned the basics of carpentry. He could use a framing square to cut angles, which I could never do.

He went to work and learned to mix, pour and finish concrete. Later he learned to lay bricks and cement building blocks. I helped him build more than one cement block house in Jena. I know that one of them is still there to this day (2012).

I always thought it was amazing that he could set out to learn a new trade at the age of 54. I retired from the Police Department at the age of 54.

In these writings I tell some stories about Papa. He was always the man in charge.

From about the age of thirteen, I was taller than Papa. He had his bluff in on me, though. I was careful to walk carefully and watched my tongue when I was around him.

Papa smoked quite a bit. He smoked and rolled his own cigarettes. His preference was Prince Albert tobacco. As he got older he suffered from hardening of the arteries. I learned later in my life that nicotine causes this condition of the arteries. To my later dismay, for his Christmas present I would buy him a one pound can of Prince Albert tobacco. We did not know the evils of nicotine in those days.

As far as I know, Papa never paid any money into social security. The contractor we worked for in Jena always paid us in cash. When Papa finally got unable to work and had to retire, there was no social security. As far as I know, he and Mama drew a State Old Age Pension from the State of Louisiana. Papa never talked about their financial problems, but Mama did. She did not, however, ever say where their income came from.

Mama and Papa were always watching their expenditures, because their income was not much. Papa had a large ash tray near where he sat. When a smoker rolls his own cigarettes, the tobacco is loose in the paper. The smoker has to keep drawing on it to keep it burning. Papa would smoke his cigarette down pretty close and lay the butt in that ash tray where the fire would go out. Over time he would get quite a collection of these butts in that ash tray. I was there one day and he took that ash tray, stripped the paper off all those butts, crumbled up the remains of all those butts, put it his tobacco can and proceeded to roll himself another cigarette. There is no telling how many times some of the tobacco had been recycled. It is also no telling how strong that nicotine was he was inhaling. The last few times I visited him and Mama, I could not sit close to him, because of the strong nicotine smell he exuded. No wonder he had hardening of the arteries.

When I joined the U. S. Navy in 1950, they and Pete were still living at their place near Jena, Louisiana. While I was in the Navy, they sold this place and moved to Pineville, Louisiana, where they bought a small, two bedroom house. Even after selling the Jena place, the still had to borrow some money to buy the place in Pineville.

They never said as much, but I figure they moved to Pineville to be closer to a good hospital.

In April of 1959, we got a telephone call that Papa was in the hospital in Alexandria. Having some vacation time coming, we loaded up and headed for Louisiana. We decided to go to the hospital and visit Papa before we drove on over to Pineville. Papa seemed in good spirits. When I asked how he was doing, he said he guessed he was going to die, because someone had already sent him some flowers. There was a bouquet of flowers in the room. We stayed with him for a while, but because it was getting late and we had the three boys with us, we left, telling him we would be back in the morning.

The hospital called us the next morning to tell us Papa had passed away during the night. With his big family, Mama, seven sons and one daughter, he died alone. I regret that to this day.

Papa died on April 4, 1959 at the age of seventy-four. He had worked very hard all his life and provided for a large family, seeing all of them grown.

Papa is buried at Jena, Louisiana, next to the love of his life. Jena is where they were married in 1907.

*William Henry Smith*

# VERSA PURNECIE WRIGHT SMITH

My mother, Versa Purnecie Wright Smith, was born January 28, 1889 at or near the community of Blade, Louisiana. Blade, I am not sure the place is even there anymore, is, or was East of Jena, Louisiana In my writings I refer to her as Mama.

Mama came from a family of nine kids also. Her family consisted of eight girls and one boy.

Mama's family was business people and property owners. One relative owned the Wright Hotel in Jena. Her brother Walter had his own shoe repair shop in Jena. Some of her nephews worked in the banking business there in Jena.

I do not know how Mama and Papa met. My sister Claudia told me Mama had told her of the first time she saw Papa. Mama said Papa was the "prettiest man" she had ever seen.

Mama and Papa were married on January 2, 1907 in Jena, Louisiana. Mama was eighteen years of age and Papa was twenty-two years of age.

I do not know where they set up housekeeping at first, or what Papa did for a living.

That is one of the main reasons I decided to write my memoirs. I want any descendants of my family to know something about my life.

Their first child, a boy was born January 21, 1909 in Harrisonburg, Louisiana. I presume they moved to Harrisonburg after they were married.

Mama and Papa had nine children, seven sons and two daughters. All the children reached maturity. Mama and Papa lived to see all their children reach maturity, and all of them married.

After my brother Quitman died, his wife found some old papers he had kept secreted amongst his private property. One of the things she found was a handwritten letter from Mama to Papa, dated May 30, 1918. In the letter, a copy of which is included with my brother Joe's write-up, it is revealed she is at home in Jena, Louisiana, alone with five children, the youngest of which was my brother Joe, who was about two months old. Papa apparently was in Orange, Texas working and Mama wanted him to come home.

A check with the history of this country revealed that in the year 1918, over a half million people in the U. S. died from the flu. Why Papa and Mama's family escaped this pandemic can be attributed only to God's will.

I know Mama had a hard life, and she was tough. My sister Claudia told me she and Mama were going shopping in Natchez, Mississippi. Claudia opened the passenger side door for Mama and helped her into the car. Mama, trying to get herself settled into her seat in the car, using her right hand and grasping the door frame. Claudia, not knowing Mama's hand was in the way, slammed the door on Mama's hand. Claudia opened the door when Mama cried out. Mama's fingers were flattened. Claudia rushed her to the hospital, with Mama holding her injured right hand and crying. The doctor at the emergency room examined her hand and got her to flex her fingers. Everything seemed to be alright, with no broken bones. Mama kept telling the doctor she had a weak heart. The doctor finally told Mama there was nothing wrong with her heart, after having a car door slammed shut on her hand and surviving. Mama, at the time, was probably about seventy-five years of age.

Once, while living in Pineville, after Papa died, Mama fell off her front porch. Luckily, she fell into some shrubbery and broke no bones.

We decided it was not safe for her to live alone, so we got her into a nursing home in Alexandria. It was while she was living there she fell. It is not known if her hip broke and she fell, or it broke from the fall.

One of Mama's sisters was bedridden for a long time due to a broken hip. Mama did not want to be bedridden. She authorized the doctors to operate on her hip and put pins in it. In recovery she had a stroke and never regained consciousness.

Papa preceded Mama in death. Mama passed away on February 26, 1970 at the age of eighty-one. I was with her when she passed away, talking to her all the time, hoping she would regain consciousness.

Mama is buried at Jena, Louisiana next to Papa, the love of her life.

*Wedding Photo of Papa and Mama*

# ALPHONSE SMITH 1-2-1909 TO 2-1990

Alphonse was Papa and Mama's first born. He came into this world at or near Harrisonburg, Louisiana.

Mama often talked of Al later in her life. I know that, Al being her first born must have been special to her. She said that when he was an infant he got sick and cried a lot. Whether he ran a fever, she never said, but she did say that when he "got well," he could not use his right arm or hand. I am not sure that thermometers were available in those days. She probably had to judge by just feeling of him.

I can only surmise that he contracted the disease poliomyelitis, commonly called polio. He lost practically all use of his right arm and hand. In those days I don't think anyone knew about a disease called polio. Children became crippled and no one knew why.

Tragically, in those days children with disabilities were looked upon with ridicule and were often bullied by other children. I know it was a hard life for my brother Al, because I truly believe that Papa felt the same way about him. I do remember Papa not showing any affection toward me or any of the other children in our family. As far as Al was concerned, Papa did not "cut him any slack," as the saying goes. Al worked right alongside Papa as if he was not disabled.

I remember watching Al plow a field with a team of horses. He looped the reins around his neck and would guide the plow mainly with his left arm and hand. He would reach up and pull the reins with his strong left hand while steadying the plow with his withered right arm and hand.

Al's left arm and hand became very large and strong.

Al did have the opportunity to attend public schools. He did not, however, graduate from high school. In those days there were only eleven grades. The story, as I understood it from my older sister, Al made it through the tenth grade and lacked one year being able to graduate. He did not, however, have shoes to wear to school, at least presentable ones. He wanted a pair of new shoes to wear to school because he believed that seniors should be able to wear good shoes. I suspect that all the other seniors had new or least good shoes to wear. Well, Al, not having good shoes to wear, never went back to school. He did not graduate. Remember,, he was probably subject to teasing and ridicule about his arm and having to wear sorry-looking shoes was the icing on the cake. I do not know what the situation was about the family's finances at that time. Maybe they just did not have the money to buy a new pair of shoes.

Somewhere along in Al's life he learned to draw. He could also letter and paint signs. All of this was with his left hand and arm. Mama said that when people learned he could paint signs, he would get small jobs for which he was paid. He painted signs for stores and business places. Apparently he began to save a little of his money.

He learned of a correspondence course that was available in radio repair. He enrolled in that course. He was taught the basics of radio repair. Radio was brand new. I remember him building a "crystal" set with which he could pick up radio broadcasts. The correspondence school furnished him with the parts he needed to build this basic receiving set. This included an earphone (just for one ear) over which a person could hear the radio broadcast. It was said that he could listen to speeches made by one Huey P. Long over his little crystal set.

He made radio his career. He worked for a time at the Western Auto Store in Jena, Louisiana and later for Montgomery Ward in Alexandria, Louisiana. He subsequently opened his own radio repair shop in Pineville, Louisiana. Then he got the opportunity to go to work for the U. S. Army at Fort Polk, repairing military two-way radios. He was employed there when he finally retired.

I do not know how old Al was when he retired, but he was probably sixty-five.

Several years after he retired he suffered a stroke which took the use of his good left hand and arm.

Doctors in Alexandria believed they could relieve the pressure on his brain and ease the effects of the stroke by removing the blood clot.

The operation was not successful and his left side remained paralyzed. In addition, he started having seizures. His wife, who was disabled also, could not care for him at home and was forced to place him in a nursing home. There, they had to keep him sedated most of the time to prevent the seizures,

Al stayed in this nursing home until his death in 1990 at the age of 81.

My brother Al was a remarkable person. He was a devout Christian and very active in his church while he was able. My brother Walter told me that Al told him he became saved and accepted the Lord Jesus Christ as his savior one day while he was plowing in the field. He overcame his physical disability and lack of a complete formal education to become a successful business man.

I know that one day I will see Al again in Paradise. He will have two good strong arms to hug me with.

Al and Mary had one son. His name is Terry Edgar Smith

Terry and his wife Sharon have no children.

# CLAUDIA MAE SMITH JONES

Papa and Mama's second child was a girl, born on May 26, 1911, at or near Winnsboro, Louisiana. They named this baby girl Claudia Mae.

Since Papa and his small family lived on a farm, Claudia grew up having to do chores around the house and work in the fields. She told me one time, when we were talking about the family, that she was 17 years old when I was born. She was old enough to help Mama take care of me in my infancy. Papa and Mama had five other children between her birth and mine.

I do not know how far Claudia progressed in school, but she did not graduate from high school. Claudia could read and write very well. She was very perceptive and exhibited a good deal of knowledge, which I gathered was from doing a lot of reading.

Her life on the farm was very hard. I do not know when Claudia married, but I think it must have been in the late 1930's. That would make her age at that time about 25 or 26. When she did marry, she married a neighbor's son, Lucius Jones.

Their first child was a boy and they named him Donnie. Unfortunately, Donnie got sick and died when he was about two years old.

Claudia and Lucius had four more children, three girls and one boy; Marie, Dorothy Faye, Larry and Patricia. But Claudia never got over losing that first child.

Claudia said one time when she was a teenager she was at their house and some guests came to visit. She was wearing rubber boots at the time because she had been working outside. When Papa brought the visitors in, unannounced, she was standing behind the bed, which was in their living room. She did not want come out from behind the bed and let the visitors see her wearing those rubber boots. She stood behind the bed for the whole time the visitors were there.

Claudia was pretty short, probably no more than 5 foot 2.

While she and Lucius were living in Natchez, Mississippi and he was working at Armstrong Tire and Rubber plant, I visited with them quite often. As a matter of fact, I was staying with them when I had a summer job working for the Coco Cola Bottling Company, a story I tell about in another segment.

Claudia and Lucius were blessed with quite a number of grandchildren, great grandchildren and I am sure, some great-great grandchildren.

Claudia was a Christian and lived a long life. She passed away on December 28, 2005 at the age of 94. She is buried alongside her husband Lucius in Natchez, Mississippi.

# MILDRED MARIE SMITH SCARBOROUGH

Papa and Mama's third child was another girl, born April 27, 1914 at Jena, Louisiana.

I am sure that she also had to work indoors and outdoors, because the family was still farming.

I know very little about Mildred's early life. I do not know where she met L. V. Scarborough, or when they got married. I do know that she had at least one miscarriage and one child that did not live very long. It was Claudia who told me these things about her sister Mildred.

I remember seeing a photograph of my sister Mildred, probably taken after she was married. She was holding what appeared to be a .22 rifle and her dog, a Spitz, was beside her.

Mildred and L. V. had one son named Lynn, born October 3, 1938.

Lynn grew up to be a big man, probably over six feet tall.

Mildred became ill with leukemia and passed away in 1947 at the age of 33. She is buried at the Pine Grove Cemetery, near the small community of Whitehall, Louisiana.

Papa and Mama raised Lynn and he became like another brother to me and Pete.

As far as I know, Mildred never remarried.

# HOMER SMITH

Papa and Mama's fourth child was another boy. They named him Homer. He was born on July 18, 1916, at Jena, Louisiana.

Homer was another farm hand. Now Al had some more help in the fields.

At some point in Homer's life he became interested in playing music. It might have been because Papa could play the harmonica and the fiddle. Homer taught himself to play the guitar and later on he learned to play the fiddle.

At our home, when he wasn't working in the field, he would practice on his guitar. If he missed a chord he would say out loud, "Wait a minute," and he would start over again. He would do it until he got it right.

As he and the other boys grew up, they all learned to play string instruments, except me and Pete.

They played at dances and at store openings in Harrisonburg and maybe at weddings, I am not sure.

Our last year on a share-cropper farm was 1939. Still living at home were Al, Homer, Leslie, Walter, me and Pete. Mama had to cook and care for five grown men and me and Pete. I was eleven and Pete was nine.

That was the year that Papa decided to quit farming and move to town. Walter told me Papa held a family meeting at which he said, "We are moving to town and it is every man for himself." Of course the town was Jena, Louisiana.

By this time Al was qualified to repair radios. Papa, Homer, Leslie, and Walter went to work for a man who laid bricks and poured concrete. Joe had gotten married and moved away.

After we moved to Jena, Homer would go to town, have a seat in Nick's Café and listen to the Juke Box. He had a notebook and a pencil. He would copy down the words of a favorite song he wanted to learn. I'm not certain how many nickels he would put in the Juke Box, but it probably was not many, because he did not have many. When he ran out of nickels, he would have to wait until someone else would play that tune before he could continue jotting down the words. He would keep at it until he had the whole song down on paper. After that he could pick the melody on his guitar and sing the words of the song. The other members of the Smith String Band would learn from Homer.

Homer met and fell in love with Maxine Eric Wright. (No relation to Mama's people) Maxine Eric was born on May 6, 1925 in Baskin, Louisiana. She and Homer were married on May 29, 1942 in Jena, Louisiana.

Their marriage produced six children; Brenda, Sandra, Gregory, Robert, Homer and Robin.

Eric's family was members of the Church of Christ, a church which did not believe in musical instruments in their church.

Homer began his studies in that denomination and eventually became an ordained minister in the Church of Christ.

He basically quit playing any kind of musical instrument.

World War II started in December 1941. Leslie and Walter entered the military service to serve their country. I think Homer received a deferment because of an injury he received when he fell from a scaffold while working to build the movie theater in Jena.

The Smith Brothers String Band ceased to exist.

Homer pastored many churches in Louisiana. Eric told me he started many Churches of Christ in Louisiana.

My brother Homer died March 12, 1993 in Baton Rouge, Louisiana, where he is buried. Homer was 77 years of age.

# JOSEPH DAVID SMITH

Papa and Mama's fifth child was another boy. Little Joe was born on March 25, 1918 at Jena, Louisiana.

I am not sure what kind of work Papa was doing during this period of time. He might have been share-cropping, but the area around Jena was not suited for large farms. It is mostly hills forested by pine trees.

I found out just recently (in 2006) that Papa apparently was working in Orange, Texas in the early part of 1918.

Through my sister-in-law, Elizabeth Smith, my brother Pete's widow, I came into possession of an old handwritten letter which Mama had left with Pete. The letter was from Mama to Papa, addressed to 'Henry Smith, Orange, Texas.' The date of the letter was May of 1918. Papa was in Orange, Texas and Mama wanted him to come home to Jena, Louisiana. A postscript to the letter stated to Papa, "You need to come home, because we have to name the baby." A quick check of my records revealed that the baby was my brother Joe, who was born in March. The letter was dated in May of 1918. Joe was some two months old and had not been named. A typed version of this letter is included herewith.

Joe was the first of the boys to get married. He married at an early age; I heard that he was all of seventeen. He married a young lady who was fifteen, Perlia Mullins.

Joe and Perlia had three children; David, Jo Ann and Lester.

Joe joined the Masons and became a 32$^{nd}$ Degree Mason. He was a welder and auto mechanic by trade. Even though Joe and Perlia had three children, Joe was drafted into the U. S. Army during World War II., and served a short time before he was discharged.

My brother Joe died in January 1976 at the age of 58. He is buried at Pineville, Louisiana.

*In My Lifetime*

May The. 30. 1918

Mr. Henry Smith.

    My dear husbin it is with much pleasure I seat myself this lonly night to answer your most kind and welcome letter I just received and was truly glad to hear from you and to hear you got there without getting hurt for I have bin botherd about you ever since you left this leaves us all up but not well little Homer is sick again he taken the fever the same day you left here but he is a little better to night Claudia is very sick and cant hardly sit up I have had the tooth ache all day I hope this will find you well for I cant rest day or night I am afrad you will get sick over there but if you do you must come home at once Henry I sure do wish you were here to night with me you don't no how lonely I am. I cant hardly stay here this way You must come home to stay or move right away for I am nerly crazy here without you rite and tell me when you are coming or if you aim to move over there for I am miserble here this way I had rather be with you than have all the money in the world for ther isnt iny thing on earth iny pleasure to me when you are gone Henry I don't no much to rite for I have bin right here by my self ever since you left there never iney one comes to tell me iney thing I am afraid I am going haft to have the doctor with Claudy and Homer if they don't get better but I will try to do the best I can till you can come home Henry you must rite and tell me all about that place and about house rent before we move for I sure do dred that move I dred that move I hope you will be satisfied and stay well what time you are there rite and tell me when you aim to come home and how long it will take to make the trip from over there

    Well it is about bedtime it is now 11 o'clock so I guess I had better close for this time by asking you to rite by return mail and let me no how you are so by by rite soon to the one that loves you the best

Verse Smith

Henry you must rite me a name for the little baby if you don't aim to come home and be shure to put my letters where no one cant see them or burn them so by by come soon

*Herbert Smith*

(Author's Note: The unnamed baby Mama was referring to in this letter was my brother Joseph David Smith, DOB 3-25-18. The date of Mama's letter was 5-30-18. Joe was some two months old and had not been named. We can only surmise that Mama was not willing to pick a name without Papa's help.)

# LESLIE HENRY SMITH

In September 1920, Papa and Mama had their sixth child, another boy. Leslie Henry was born at Holly Grove, Louisiana.

Now my parents had four sons and two daughters. I am presuming that Papa was still employed as a share-cropper. Share-cropping was a popular occupation during that period of time. The reason I know this is because after I grew up and began to talk to other people about their family histories, I learned quite a few of them grew up in share-cropping families. Then I did not feel so bad about what our situation had been. Also, they came from large families like myself.

I do not know how far Leslie Henry made it in school, but I do know he did not graduate from high school.

When I was in the first grade at Harrisonburg, Louisiana, Leslie Henry was going to school there also. Being some eight years older than me, he must have been about fifteen years of age.

In another segment I told the story about what I remembered from the first grade. One thing I recalled was getting into a game of marbles and losing all my marbles to an expert marble player named Oodie Boothe. Not to worry, I went looking for my big brother Leslie Henry. I told him what happened. He located Oodie and got my marbles back.

Talking to my brother Walter one time when we were dredging up old memories, Walter told me when visitors came to the house when we lived on the farm, Papa would make Leslie Henry go to be back yard and stay there until the visitors had left. Walter had no idea why Papa would do such a thing. Apparently, Leslie Henry had a habit of doing something that Papa thought was unsightly, so he kept him out of sight.

When we moved off the farm in 1939, Leslie Henry was about 19 years old. He started doing some construction work like Papa, Homer, and Walter and later me.

In December 1941 World War II started. Leslie Henry was drafted into the U. S. Army in 1942. I do not know where he went through training. He served his country in the South Pacific. I do not know if he saw any action. I do remember him talking about having to drive military trucks as his unit moved from one location to another.

The war ended in 1945 and Leslie Henry was discharged. He came home to Jena, Louisiana and started looking for work. The government (tax-payers) paid out a weekly stipend for recently discharged military personnel. I think this lasted about six months and I do not remember how much it was.

Leslie Henry and my brother Walter, also a recently discharged military man (U. S. Navy) pooled a little money and bought a 1939 Oldsmobile, yellow in color. Gasoline was very cheap then, so they, and sometimes me and Pete, hit the highways and byways in that yellow Oldsmobile.

The fact that I went with them a lot and missed school, I tell about in another segment.

Well, the tax-payer money finally stopped and Leslie Henry had to find a regular job.

I do not remember what he did right away, but he eventually was hired at the Armstrong Tire and Rubber Company at Natchez, Mississippi. Leslie Henry worked there until he turned sixty-five and retired.

Leslie Henry met and married Tommie Estelle Reed. Leslie and Tommie were blessed with three children: Roy Randall Smith, Suzanne Smith and Dwight Smith.

My brother Leslie Henry passed away August 11, 1990 at the age of 70 years. He is buried at Whitehouse, Texas.

# WALTER SILAS SMITH

On April 25, 1922, along came another boy for Papa and Mama. I think maybe Mama was growing tired of looking at all those male bottoms; but there were more to come. Walter Silas was born at Holly Grove, Louisiana.

As is the case with my other older brothers, I remember very little about what Walter told me about their younger years. I know that when he got old enough he worked in the field just like Papa and the others, including my sisters.

Walter said it was a tough life. The living quarters for the family was always crowded, because the places where Papa decided to live were not always easy and comfortable.

When we moved off the farm in 1939, Walter was about 17 or 18 years of age. He did not finish high school either. I do remember him saying that he quit school in the fifth grade. That would have made him about 11 or 12 years of age when he quit school.

Walter had part of one of his front teeth broke off. He was self-conscious about that and tended to cover his mouth with his hand when he smiled or grinned. Walter told me that he and a couple of our cousins were engaged in a mock war using what is now called slingshots, using rocks as ammo. He said he looked out from behind a tree just in time to get hit in his mouth by a rock propelled by one of his cousins. The rock broke part of his took off..

When World War II broke out in December, 1941, Walter Silas was probably almost 20 years of age. He did not want to go into the army, so he enlisted in the U. S. Navy. Doing so changed his whole life.

Apparently, when he was given an aptitude test by the Navy, they figured him for a radioman's job. He was sent to some schools where he studied two-way radio transmissions, including using the Morse Code. At one school in the State of Idaho, he tried out skiing and broke an arm.

When he completed his training he was shipped out to the South Pacific. He was assigned to a squadron of dive bombers. His position was radioman and rear gunner. If he ever was involved in an actual bombing, I do not remember him speaking of it.

When the war ended, he was discharged and came back home to Jena, Louisiana.

He also drew a stipend from the tax-payers, but that soon ended. He was joint owner of the 1939 yellow Oldsmobile I mentioned in Leslie Henry's story. By the way, I just remembered. Walter and Leslie were In Shreveport, Louisiana looking for work when the yellow Oldsmobile got hit by a railroad switch engine. Luckily, they were not in the car. Other cars had them blocked and they were on the tracks. The engine hit the car quite smartly and made a big dent in the side of it. Walter said they bailed out when they saw the engine was going to hit the car. The car was still driveable.

Walter said he was talking the job situation over with Papa one day. Papa went to his old trunk and got a booklet for him to read. The booklet was about a radio school in Tyler, Texas. Walter decided to contact them about enrolling. They accepted him as a student and he successfully completed the studies at this school.

While Walter Silas was looking for work around Pineville, Louisiana and Alexandria he was staying (I think) with our brother Alphonse who was in the radio repair business. It was during this time Walter met his future wife, Ezalea Wilson. Ezalea was a registered nurse, working at the Baptist Hospital in Alexandria.

I do not have the information of when they got married, nor where they got married.

Walter Silas and Ezalea had four children: Anita, Dianne, Duane and Gary.

In our older years, I guess I was closer to Walter than to my other brothers. We seemed to have more in common and I visited with him often.

My brother Walter Silas passed away on November 28, 2008 in Tyler, Texas. He is buried at Whitehouse, Texas, alongside his loving wife Ezalea who predeceased him.

I miss my brother Walter a lot. When we were not visiting in person, we were talking on the telephone.

# WILLIAM HERBERT SMITH

The year of 1928 was a presidential election year. It was also the year of my birth, either the 11th of November or the 12th of November, depending on which birth certificate one peruses.

In another segment Titled "You Have Got To Be Kidding Me!" I explain how the FBI found out some things about my birth that I was unaware of.

I was born at or near Harrisonburg, Louisiana, the eighth child and sixth son of Henry and Versa Wright Smith. I have been told that all of the children born to Papa and Mama were delivered at home. I found out that a doctor was in attendance at my birth. This was revealed by the information turned up by the FBI.

If you are wondering why the FBI was investigating me, I was a candidate for the FBI National Academy in 1973.

I tried to start to school the year I turned six, which I believe would have been 1934. The school sent me home, though, because my sixth birthday was still two months away. That meant I did not get to start to school until I was nearly seven years of age. This was the year of 1935.

I actually began my schooling at the elementary school in Harrisonburg, Louisiana. Now, between the times I was born at Harrisonburg and when I started to school there, we probably moved two or three times. The year I started to school we were living on the "Johnson "place, and you guessed it, we were share-cropping.

In 1936 the whole area flooded from a broken levee and the "back-water" rose until it nearly got into our house. Papa kept saying if it rises another inch we will have to move. It didn't, however, and we stayed there. The water eventually receded and everything dried out.

If I am not mistaken, that is the year my brother Joe married Perlie.

In other segments I tell of some experiences I had in the first grade there at Harrisonburg.

I believe we moved from there to a farm between Harrisonburg and Jonesville, Louisiana. It was while we were living there that I received the shock of my life, literally. God was looking out for me, because the electric shock should have killed me.

We lived in a shack which leaked like a sieve. We literally had to put tarps over the beds when it rained. There were no screens over the windows or doors, so the mosquitos were terrible. We slept under mosquito netting and Papa fed us quinine to ward off the malaria fever.

The mosquitos apparently bred in a large pond which was directly in front of our shack. This pond had turtles, snakes and no telling what else. This did not keep me and my brother Pete from wading around in it. Fortunately, we lived there only one year. I think this was the year of 1938 and I went to school at Jonesville, Louisiana. I did not like that school. Two third graders were expelled for getting into a fight with their knives.

My teacher, a woman, wore dark shades all the time and a student could not tell when she was looking in his or her direction. I was terrified of her. I got unjustly paddled by her one day. I think I tell about that in another segment.

From this place we moved back near a community called Manifest. We had lived near there once before, when I got rejected from the first grade.. This second time around at this community was the year that Papa decided to move to town and declared it will be every man for himself.

We moved to Jena, Louisiana and I believe I started there in the fourth grade. I have told of some experiences I had while living in or near Jena. I basically lived there from about 1939 until I went into the U. S. Navy in 1950. I graduated from Jena High School in 1949. If you have been keeping up with the dates, and you have figured out my age, you are right. The year I graduated from high school I was 21 years of age. I quit school twice and I got caught up in a change-over by the school system from 11 grades to 12 grades. Anyway, I made it be the skin of my teeth, the first off-spring of Papa and Mama to graduate from high school.

I was not the only who got caught up in this change-over. There were only 14 in my graduating class and the others were in the same fix I was.

In 1950 I was about to be drafted into the U. S. Army because of something called the Korean War. I did not know where Korea was! It was not the army for me! I joined the U. S. Navy in September of 1950 and immediately traveled all the way to San Diego, California.

Needless to say I have "been around the block" a few times.

# MY LIFE IN THE FIRST GRADE

Since my birthday was in the month of November, I did not get to start to school until I was nearly seven years old.

At that time we were living at the "Johnson" place near Harrisonburg, Louisiana.

I remember a few things about my first year in school.

My teacher was a Miss Boothe. She had long wavy hair and I was her favorite student. I knew this because she would call me up to her desk, place me in her lap and tell the class stories. One story was about her little brother who had died from blood poisoning. It was possible that I reminded her of her little brother.

Schools in those days (1935) had recesses, one in the morning and one in the afternoon. We also got out for an hour at noon to eat our lunch.

During these times, on the school grounds, a lot of the boys played games with marbles. There was not much grass on the school ground so there was a lot of bare ground. This made it easy to "shoot marbles".

At first I just watched the other boys play the marble games. A circle would be drawn in the dirt about three or four feet in diameter. To determine who got to shoot first, all who wanted to play would shoot or lag towards a line and whoever got closest to the line without going over it would be the first player.

All who wanted to play had to put some marbles in the ring. The shooters would kneel down and shoot from the circle toward a specific marble, usually a pretty one, if it was positioned to give the shooter a clear shot. The object was to knock the targeted marble out of the ring. If that happened, the marble was his to keep. If he hit the marble squarely, his "taw" would "stick" and he would get another shot, only this time from much closer. If he did not knock his target out of the ring, he would have to wait his turn and shoot again from the circle.

A good shooter with a good "taw" could clear the ring of all the marbles, which was rare, but did happen.

The game looked fairly simple and I knew that I could shoot a marble. So the next day I brought me some marbles, along with my "taw." Now, there was a boy who showed up to play who was not there the day before. The other boys called him "Oodie" (spelling uncertain). I later learned his last name was Boothe, whether he was related to my teacher, I do not know.

I made my contribution to the bunch of marbles. Oodie lagged and got first shot. I saw right away I was in trouble. Mr. Boothe proceeded to clear the circle of all the marbles, which he pocketed and left. The game was over and I had no more marbles. Well, I was not going to stand for that. No, I did not jump him to get my marbles back. I had two older brothers going to school there. I found one of my brothers and told him my sad story. Said brother found Mr. Oodie Boothe and got my marbles back. I do not know if I got the same marbles back that I lost, or if I got the same number. At any rate I was happy to get my marbles back and did not enter anymore marble games. Looking back on this, I probably had my first experience with what is known as a "ringer." Thank you, brother Henry.

There was another game with marbles which was played on the school grounds. This involved shooting marbles into a series of holes dug into the dirt. The holes were dug with a trusty pocket knife. (Yes, young boys in those days carried their pocket knives at all times.) The holes were about two inches deep and about 1 and ½ inch in diameter.

The first shooter would shoot from a starting line to the first hole. If he hit the hole he could continue on to the next hole. If he missed the hole, however, he had to leave his marble where it stopped. The next shooter could then shoot. If he hit the hole, he could then attempt to knock the stationary marble into the hole. If he was successful, he kept the marble and the loser had to start over again. The shooter would then continue on to the next hole, risking a miss and risking the loss of his marble.

It was not all that easy to hit those holes because the ground was rough and uneven

Another popular game that was played was "chase" or "fox and hound." By lot a participant was chosen to be "it" or the "fox." He would take off running and the other boys would chase him until he got "tagged. It was then someone else's turn. We boys learned to run fast, dodge, twist and turn to avoid being "tagged."

When I watch young boys now playing football, I can spot the ones who grew up playing chase.

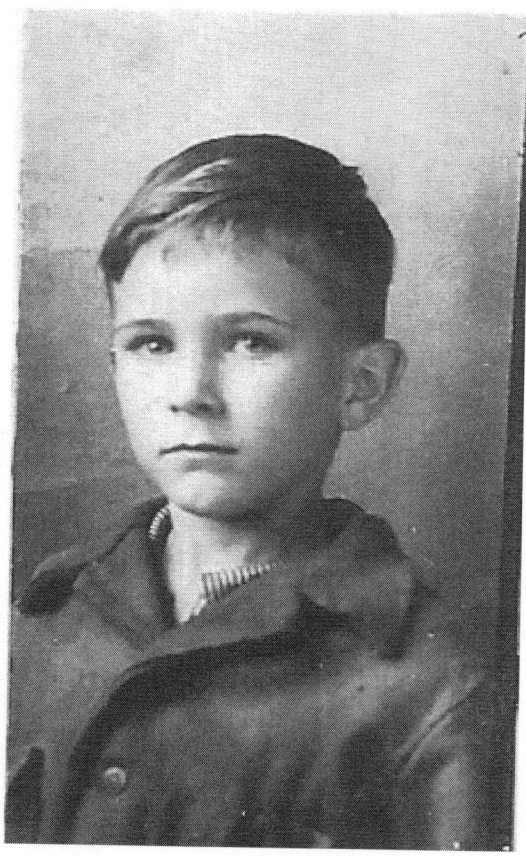

*Herbert in First Grade Photo*

# JENA HIGH SCHOOL

I reviewed my list of articles which I have written in this effort, and I am sure somewhere in there I told of some sorry decisions I made about staying in school.

The rest of the story is I finally got back in high school in the fall of 1947. I successfully completed what was my Junior Year and moved on to the 12th grade. That was the year the state changed over from 11 grades to 12 grades. Now I was a senior, but I still needed five credits to graduate.

The school had a whole new curriculum, with a bunch of new courses available.

In order to graduate I had to take Spanish, Shorthand, Typing, English and Geometry. Believe it or not, I managed to pass all of these courses.

During this school year, the school decided to publish a High School Annual. I was fortunate enough to be selected as a staff member for this, the high school's first High School Annual. It was named 'The Giant Tribe.'

Also this year, the school decided to publish a school newspaper. We named the paper 'The Campus Cruiser' and I was on the staff of this also.

In addition to all that, I was voted Vice President of my senior class.

I also wrote the sports column for the school newspaper. I would write the article and submit it to Miss Juanita Kendrick, my English teacher. She would check it, show me my errors, and give me a grade on it. It would then be published in the school newspaper. I would then take it to the Jena Times, the town newspaper, and they would publish it, paying me a small fee, based on the column-inches.

I graduated from Jena High School in 1949. I finished in the top 25 percent of my class and earned scholastic scholarship.

I was able to enroll at Northwestern State College in Natchitoches on three scholarships, but none was an athletic scholarship.

In another segment I tell about my semester at Northwestern.

I want to add I was the first one in my family to graduate from high school. There were seven siblings older than me. Some never got past the fifth grade. It probably was not their fault. Education was not a priority in the Smith Family. Field work was.

I am very thankful that I was able to graduate from high school. It opened up a whole new world for me.

*Herbert Smith Graduate Photo*

# QUITMAN THOMAS SMITH

Papa and Mama's last child was born at Harrisonburg, Louisiana on November 15, 1930, almost exactly two years after I was born. I have joked about Pete's name Quitman when telling people about my family. I would tell them Mama finally told Papa to "quit, man." Actually, Mama named him after one of her relatives who was named Quitman. I don't really know where the name Thomas came from.

Walter told me they began to call him "Pete" because he was always playing around an old mule we had that was named "Pete."

I was different from all the rest of my family because of my height. Pete was different from the rest of us because of his ruddy complexion and almost red hair. He also had what was called a "cow-lick" on the front of his hair. None of the rest of us had that particular hair formation.

Pete also was saddled with pretty quick temper. Besides being two years older than him, I was bigger than him. That did not stop Pete from flying into me when he lost his temper. Our fighting was usual just wrestling matches. I could out-wrestle him easily enough and pin him down on the ground. I would make him promise to leave me alone and he would agree. As soon as I let him up, he would come at me again and it starts all over again. When I had him down, he would start hollering and Mama would yell at me to leave Pete alone. That did not set well with me because it was the other way around. Usually, I would just run from him, because I could out-run him. That would make him furious and he would start screaming, that is when Mama would get involved

When we reached the teenage years and got to be pretty big fellows, the wrestling matches got pretty serious, and I always got the blame. Sometimes when this happened, I would walk into town, hitch a ride into

Pineville and stay with my older brothers for a while. When they got tired feeding me, they would send me back home.

When Pete was in the sixth grade he got injured in a school yard accident. He and some more boys were playing "chase" and one boy stepped on his foot while he was running and it pulled Pete's hip out of socket. Papa took him to a doctor in Jena, but he couldn't help him and referred him to the Baptist Hospital in Alexandria. Of course Papa and Mama were handling all of this. They got someone to take him to Alexandria and I stayed home. I learned later that the people at the hospital let him lay on a gurney all night in a hallway. Why no doctor saw him, I do not know. If I were to make a guess, the hospital people recognized Papa and Mama as someone who did not have any money. It was the next day before a doctor saw Pete. The doctor was able to get his hip back in place.

Later on, we began to notice Pete walking crooked. Papa took him back to the doctor and was told his hip was out of its socket again. I am not real sure the doctor at the hospital properly took care of Pete. It was a special situation after Pete lay on a gurney all night. The doctor should have put him in a cast to hold the joint in place while it healed.

The hospital in Alexandria could not help Pete this time and referred Papa and Mama to the Shriners Children's Hospital in Shreveport, Louisiana. The doctors there gave Papa and Mama two options. Number one was to replace the hip. At that time plastic joints were being used to replace hips. Option number two was to stiffen the hip where it could not be flexed. Papa and Mama chose number two. Pete came home with a body cast extending from his chest to the ankle on his right leg. He stayed in the cast for eight weeks. This was during the summertime. We had no air-conditioning, not even a fan. I know Pete suffered. Once a day we had to turn him over on his stomach. Even doing that, he developed a large bed sore on his back near the end of his spine. He carried that scar the rest of his life.

Unfortunately, Pete grew up very bitter about the whole situation.

Pete graduated from Jena High School in 1951, the second of Papa and Mama's children to graduate from high school, two out of nine children.

The irony of his graduation was the quotation someone placed with his graduation picture in the Jena High Yearbook read, "I took to my heels as fast as I could." Pete was disabled, with a stiffened hip, walked with a limp and could not run.

Pete eventually came to Pasadena, Texas to find work. He met the love of his life, Elizabeth Blackshear. I think they were married in 1956. They had one child, a girl, named Nancy.

My kid brother Pete passed away from a heart attack on April 7, 2006 at the age of 76. He is buried in a church cemetery near Mansfield, Louisiana. Me and Pete did not visit much and talk like me and my brother Walter, but I miss him just the same.

I have run out of family members to talk to.

*Group Photo of Papa and his seven sons*

# NETTIE GRACE COLEMAN SMITH

The love of my life was born at home, near the small community of Prospect, Louisiana, on January 10, 1935. Her father's name was Leroy Coleman and he was the only male in his family. Nettie's mother's name was Edith Lovell Coleman, who had no brothers.

Nettie was the second daughter of Leroy and Edith. Altogether, they had five daughters, and no sons.

Nettie's father was a carpenter and her mother never worked outside the home.

The Coleman family had moved into Pineville, Louisiana where Leroy could find work.

I had two brothers living near them in Pineville. While visiting my brothers, I met the Coleman family for the first time.

In the late 1940's I got a job with a new company called Dairy Queen. Dairy Queen had two places, one in Pineville and one in Alexandria, Louisiana, just across Red River. I worked at both places.

The Pineville location was right across the street from the Coleman residence, so I got to visit with them quite a bit. Coming from a family of mostly boys, I was surprised and pleased to visit a family with a bunch of girls.

Nettie graduated from Bolton High School in Alexandria, Louisiana. She was a straight-A student.

I joined the U. S. Navy in 1950 and was stationed at San Diego, California. The Navy encouraged us to write home. I wrote to my parents, but they were not too good at answering my letters. So, I decided to write to Nettie. This was in 1951 and she was sixteen years of age. I was pleasantly surprised when she answered my letter. She had beautiful penmanship and I enjoyed reading her letters.

When I went home on leave, I visited her and her family. She had grown up!

I began to court her and things got serious between us. In 1952 I was sent to a school at Newport, R. I. I requested and received permission for a delay in reporting. I stopped off at Pineville. While there on leave, I proposed to Nettie, and after we talked to her Dad, she accepted.

Time was short. After applying for a marriage license, I had to get a blood test and we had to wait 3 days. We were married on April 25, 1952, and I left shortly thereafter for Newport. Nettie had her seventeenth birthday in January. I had turned 23 the previous November.

I did not see her again until, I think it was July of 1952, after I had traveled back to San Diego, California.

A year and one month later, our oldest son Timothy was born.

Praise God, He sent me a fine, beautiful, Christian girl as my wife and the mother of our four children.

*Nettie Grace Coleman Smith Photo*

*Wedding Photo Herbert and Nettie Smith*

# SMITH FAMILY LIVING ARRANGEMENTS

As I have probably mentioned elsewhere, Papa and Mama married in 1907 and their first was born two years later in 1909. They then had children pretty regular until 1930 when Mama had her last.

I was born in 1928 and memories of my very young first years are practically non-existent.

I do know that the whole family of eleven people lived in the same houses (?) until about 1935 when my sister Mildred got married and moved out.

The places where we lived would now days are called shacks. Before 1935, when all the kids were at home, the probable sleeping arrangements were something like this: the youngest, Pete, slept with Papa and Mama; the two girls, Claudia and Mildred slept together. That was two beds. This left six brothers to sleep in two remaining beds, three to a bed, summer and winter. It wasn't too bad in the winter, but in the summer, three to a bed got kind of close.

Papa and the oldest boys all worked in the fields, coming in sweaty and dirty. We had no running water. As a matter fact, we often had only rainwater to use for cooking, cleaning up, drinking and so forth. The barrel we used to catch the rain water was also the breeding place for mosquitos. Of course we did not know this at the time. All we knew, the barrel always had what we called wiggle-tails in it. Now we know those were mosquitos in the making.

There were times when we lived in areas where there were lots of mosquitos. They were not a problem in the wintertime, but in the summertime they were terrible.

When they were bad, we had sleep under mosquito nettings. On hot nights, when not a breath of air was stirring, three to a bed, sleeping under mosquito netting, you can guess what kind of conditions existed. I know one place where we lived between Harrisonburg and Jonesville; the building had only shutters over the windows, no window panes. Because of the heat, these windows had to be left open. We had no electricity, therefore, no fans and definitely no air-conditioning. We just sweltered and longed for daylight where at least we could get outside.

During these times is when Papa fed us quinine to ward off malaria. We could avoid the mosquitos at night with the mosquito netting, but once outside we were at their mercy.

The beds were double beds. Each had at least one mattress. These were so-called "tick" mattresses. They had no springs and could be rolled up. The bed springs were separate. They folded lengthways and were hinged.

This kind of arrangement made it easier when we had to move, which was nearly every year.

Do people live like this now? Some probably do. Sometimes when I am talking to friends about politics, and the friend vouches for Democrats because they are for "pore people, I ask if they know any "pore" people. And they generally say "Yes, I am pore." Then I ask if they own any property and they say "Yes." And I ask if they own a vehicle and they say "Yes." And then I tell them they are not "pore."

I tell them I can take them to Louisiana, Mississippi, and Alabama and even East Texas and show them some truly "poor" people. These pore folks do not own any real estate. They rent, any vehicle they have is probably an old clunker many years old which requires lots of work done on it.

These people have been waiting decades for the Democrats to do something for them. Their lives have not improved, yet they keep electing them, because "This time our Democratic Congress is going to improve your life."

There I go, getting on my soapbox, but that is the way I feel.

I will point out here that my parents were die-hard Democrats, and at one time even I was a Democrat, but I saw the error of my ways and changed.

# SERVING MY TIME AT THE NAVAL AIR STATION LEGAL OFFICE

After I got settled in at my duty station on North Island, I began to enjoy my work. The job was not too hard. I spent a lot of my time typing legal papers for the Legal Officer.

When I was first assigned to the NAS Legal Office, there was just one Legal Officer, a Lieutenant Commander. Later a lieutenant was assigned there. One of the most interesting individuals I worked with there was one Henry Wein. Henry came into the Navy as a Seaman Apprentice, an enlisted position. Henry had a law degree from a very prestigious university in California, from which he had graduated top in his class.

Henry could have entered the Navy as an officer. He did not, however, want to obligate himself to the six years the Navy wanted for him to be an officer. Therefore, he came in under the Navy Reserve system as an enlisted man, served his two years and went home. What was remarkable, he had a personal office assigned to him and he operated as a "legal" officer just like the ranking officers there. Henry and I got along famously. At that time I was the leading Petty Officer, supervising the other enlisted personnel in the office. In the group photos following this article, Henry is in the bottom photo, the short fellow, standing in front of the flag. Henry was probably only about five-foot two inches or so. He was a very intelligent young man.

Another person I met while stationed there was Gene Littler, a golf-pro. He had to come in the Navy also kind of like Henry Wein. I do not know how long Gene was in. He was assigned to the Special Services. He was on hand daily at the golf driving range instructing dopes like me on the fundamentals of the game of golf. I am afraid little of it stuck.

The Navy had replaced all the manual typewriters with electric typewriters. Of course, I was accustomed to using the manual machine, and it took me and all the rest of the crew quite some time to get used to using those IBM electric typewriters

To make matters really bad, the Legal Officer demanded typing which was without errors. That meant no strike-overs, perfect margins, no misspelled words, and etc. That was hard to do when we were not accustomed to those new typewriters.

The enlisted personnel were encouraged to keep in contact with our families back home. The Commanding Officer of the base really hated to get letters from some mother lamenting that she had not heard from her darling boy or girl who was in some far off place, serving his country.

I did write to my folks. Mama did write me a few times, but Papa never did.

Before I joined the Navy, I had worked at the Dairy Queen on Main Street in Pineville, Louisiana. I had two brothers living close by and usually stayed with one or the other while I was working.

Living near my brothers was a family with which my brothers visited a lot. This was the Leroy Coleman family, and they had five daughters.

The oldest daughter was Frankie Lee and she was married. She was separated from her husband and living with her parents. I think she was sixteen at the time.

The next younger daughter was Nettie Grace and she was a year or so younger than Frankie Lee. My brother Pete had dated her a few times.

Nettie had three younger sisters, Nell, Irene and Patricia.

My younger brother Quitman (Pete) visited often with our two older brothers and we both got acquainted with the Coleman family. At that time Pete was still in high school.

I needed someone to write to, so I asked Nettie if I could write to her and she agreed.

I began to write to Nettie and she sent me a couple of photos of herself. Nettie's penmanship was beautiful and I discovered we had a lot of things in common to talk about. I began to realize I was starting to really like this young lady. Above all, I discovered she was a Christian.

I had to serve in the Navy about a year before I could request military "leave." When I did get to go home, I went to the Coleman's to see

Nettie. While I was there we dated a few times, but I soon had to return to my duty station in San Diego, California.

We continued to write to one another and I realized I was falling in love with this young lady.

The Department of Defense did away with the old Articles of War, and this was replaced with The Uniform Code of Military Justice, USMJ.

I was sent to a UCMJ school in Newport, Rhode Island to learn all about these new rules and regulations.

I requested permission for a delay in reporting to this school so I could stop in Pineville and visit Nettie. My request was granted. I was smitten!!

Shortly after I arrived at the Coleman residence, I asked Nettie to marry me and she conditionally accepted, depending upon what her father said. She told me I would have to ask her father for her hand in marriage. On this night, her father was already in bed, but he was still awake, reading a book. I just barged right in and stated my purpose. Her father asked me if I was going to support his daughter as my wife and I told him with an emphatic "Yes, Sir!" He then gave us his permission and we immediately began to plan our marriage. After all, I had only a week or so to do this.

In Louisiana at that time, prospective husbands had to get a blood test, which I did the next day. Nettie's mother had to sign for her when we applied for a marriage license, because she was only seventeen. The bad part, though, we had to wait three days before we could be married.

The wonderful day finally arrived. We were married at her house. My brother Alphonse was my best man and he had to loan me five dollars to pay the preacher. I wonder if I ever paid him back. Nettie's boss at the cleaners where she worked after school stood up with Nettie at the ceremony. Her name was Mrs. Allison.

The date was April 25, 1952 and it was a glorious day. We borrowed Mr. Coleman's car and left. We went to the Baptist Hospital in Alexandria, Louisiana to visit Nettie's aunt, who was confined with sickness. After everyone left the Coleman's we returned and spent our Honeymoon Night at her house.

I had to leave the next day to report to that school in Newport, Rhode Island. Naturally, I did not want to go, but I had to.

I successfully completed the school and travelled back to California to my duty station at the Naval Air Station, North Island, San Diego, California.

I did not see my young bride again until about July, when she travelled alone to California to join me.

As of this writing, Nettie and I have been married over 60 years.

*NAS Legal Office Photo*

# MY NAVY DUTY STATION

After completing my basic training at the U. S. Naval Training Center in San Diego, California, I received my orders to report to the Administration Offices at the U. S. Naval Air Station, North Island San Diego, California.

I reported in to the Officer of The Day and was told where I was to bunk and to whom I was to report to for duty.

I found out the next day I was to be assigned to the Legal Office in the Administration Building. My rating in the Navy would be Yeoman. A yeoman does office work, typing, filing and other duties as may be assigned by the Legal Officer.

The Legal Officer is available for personnel to talk to about legal problems. He is also responsible for administering courts martial to certain offenders. When a sailor is brought up on charges, the Legal Officer is in charge of seeing that the proper papers are drawn up to be presented at the court martial.

Our office had two civilian employees whose job it was to take testimony in shorthand at the court martial. They transcribed this testimony for the court record.

The yeomen in the office were responsible for typing up the actual charges which were signed by the legal officer. The first Legal Officer I worked under was a Lieutenant Commander. He was later replaced by a full commander.

The Legal Officer was also responsible for the paper work involved in what was referred to as "Captain's Mast."

These offenses were minor in nature and punishment was meted out by the Commanding Officer of the base.

When I got promoted to Lead Petty Officer in the Legal Office, I had certain duties which I was responsible for.

One thing I had to do every six months was to change the combination of the office safe. This was not a simple job. It required taking the back panel of the safe door off to expose the inner workings of the combination. We kept a lot of sensitive material in the safe and Navy rules required that the combination be changed every six months.

Once a month, there was a dress inspection of all military personnel on the base. Leaving only critical personnel on duty at all duty stations, all other men and women had to stand inspection by the base Commanding Officer.

It was my duty to accompany the Commanding Officer on this inspection tour. There would be several high ranking Navy officers in the inspection group, but right behind the Commanding Officer was yours truly.

He would walk along inspecting the men and women, looking at their uniforms, shoes and etc. When he found something amiss and approached the person about it, it was my responsibility to get the name and duty station of the offender.

When I returned to the Legal Office, I had to pull that person's file, type up the charges and have all the paperwork ready for "Captain's Mast" the next day. Needless to say, I was not very popular amongst my fellow sailors.

*Herbert Smith Navy*

# STARTING A FAMILY

After completing the school at Newport, R. I., I was sent back to my duty station at NAS, North Island at San Diego, California. I sent for Nettie Grace right away.

She traveled by train alone and made it to San Diego sometime in July. We had been married since April 25, 1952. I was surely glad to see her and thankful she had made it safely.

The first place we stayed was in a hotel in San Diego. I think we were there about a week or so. I was able to find an apartment and we moved there. The apartment was a small affair. The bed was in the living room and when it was not in use, it folded up into the wall. The apartment had a small kitchenette and a small bathroom.

We were living in the apartment when Nettie announced she was pregnant. We got her set up to visit a Navy doctor on a regular basis. I had never been around a pregnant woman before. Nettie began to get large. I was too dumb to realize what kind of stress she must have been under. She was seventeen years old, pregnant, a long ways from her folks and living with a husband she did not know very well.

We did not have a car, so we had to travel by bus or taxicab. I had to go work every day and sometimes I had to pull duty on the weekend. Nettie spent a lot of time alone.

One night Nettie woke me up complaining her back was hurting. I began to rub her back until we both went back to sleep. She woke me up again. Her back was still hurting. I was very sleepy. I would rub her back and go back to sleep. After several times, it dawned on me we had better start timing those pains. We did and they were five minutes apart! We had to get her to the hospital. It was in the middle of the night. We had no telephone. I woke the landlady up and used her phone to call a taxi. Nettie got her things together and when the taxi arrived we were ready to go. We started for the Navy Hospital and now the pains were really hitting her. The driver took off. The driver kept yelling for her not to have that baby in his cab.

We made it to the hospital and checked her in. They sat me down in a waiting room and told me it would probably be awhile before the baby would be born. The nurse suggested I go somewhere and get a sandwich. I found a place nearby and ate a sandwich. I returned to the waiting room. A nurse came to me and asked if my name was Smith and I acknowledged that I was indeed Herbert Smith. Then she announced that I was the father of a fine baby boy. I had not been gone very long and it seemed to me that was pretty fast. Nettie told me later the doctor and nurses were amazed about how easy and fast the baby came, especially for a woman as young as she was and it being her first.

We named the baby boy Timothy Blane Smith. Timothy was Nettie's granddad on her mother's side, Timothy Lovell. Tim was the first grandbaby in the Coleman Family.

Tim was not only the first grand baby of the Coleman Family, he was the first male baby in the whole extended Coleman and Lovell families. Nettie's dad was an only son and we believe that Nettie's granddad Timothy was an only son. Timothy Lovell had two daughters. Her aunt had two daughters, and Nettie's mother had five daughters.

Frankie Lee Coleman O'Neal had a baby not long after Tim was born and it was a girl.

We checked Nettie out of the hospital and paid her bill. It was seven dollars and fifty cents. That was for the meals she ate.

We were eligible for Navy Housing and signed up for a place to live. We got a duplex and moved from the apartment and got set up in it. It was on the edge of San Diego, up on the side of the mountain. Thank goodness it was furnished, because we did not have any furniture.

Later that year I requested, and got, permission to take leave to return to Louisiana to visit. We travelled by Trailways Buses.

We decided to stop over in Pasadena, Texas and visit Nettie's sister Frankie and her husband, Nolan O'Neal. We visited a couple of days and proceeded on to Alexandria, Louisiana, where Nettie's daddy picked us up. They were still living in the house where we were married, on Jeansonne Street, Pineville, Louisiana.

We were very popular while we were visiting Nettie's folks. All the women relatives came to visit to examine that new baby boy and maybe get a chance to change his diaper.

My parents were also real proud of another grandchild. Of course, with all their kids, they already had a passel of grandkids.

We spent a couple of weeks there and our time was up. We boarded a Trailways bus and headed back to San Diego.

# WORKING AND RAISING A FAMILY

Nettie, Timothy and I started out as a family in Pasadena, Texas in 1954. Nettie and I had been married in April of 1952. Timothy was born in May of 1953.

We rented a house in what was called Pasadena Gardens on East Park Lane.

In the meantime, I was inquiring around about buying a house. Nettie's brother-in-law, Nolan P. O'Neal, told us we could buy a house under the G. I. Bill for a small down payment. A lot of new houses were being built in an area called Red Bluff Terrace, so we went for a look. By that time we were cruising around town in a 1946 Chrysler Windsor. The best, and only, car we had ever owned.

We looked at a bunch of new houses and would have liked one on a corner. They, however, were five dollars more per month and we could not afford one.

We decided on one in the middle of the block of Huntington Drive. The address was 2506 and it was to be our home for the next thirty years. We made a twenty-five dollar down payment and closed the deal. We began to move in, but we had very little furniture. We did have one of those new-fangled things called a television. We had bought it in California while I was in the Navy. We also had a baby bed which Nettie's father made and which we still have. I think we moved in to the new house in February of 1955.

We went to Finger's Furniture and bought some furniture; a gas stove, a refrigerator, a dinette set with six chairs, a couch, a side chair, two end tables, a coffee table, a floor lamp, two table lamps, a bed frame with head board, a mattress and box spring, and a double dresser with a mirror. We got all this for a little over eight hundred dollars. Remember, I was making only about three hundred dollars a month. Nettie was not working.

We began to make monthly payments to Finger's Furniture. Later on I was pleased that I had a hand in apprehending an armed robber who robbed the furniture store. Then someone broke out the front glass of the store and Fingers hired me to night watch until they could get it fixed.

In about September of 1955, Nettie revealed she was pregnant again, so in May of 1956 Michael Lee Smith was born. Now we were a family of four.

In about November of 1956, Nettie revealed she was pregnant again. In July of 1957 Jeffrey Dean Smith was born. Now we were five. Three grandsons now for the Coleman family that had no other grandsons. Only two other males, which were Nettie's dad and her mother's dad.

Things rocked on and I was promoted to Sergeant in 1959 and got a small pay raise.

In about June of 1960, Nettie revealed she was pregnant again. She became depressed. She had never been around young boys very much, only a baby sister. Nettie was convinced she would have another boy. As a matter of fact, our family doctor confirmed that he was 90% certain it was going to be another boy. Well, they were both wrong. In March of 1961 Nettie gave birth to a beautiful baby girl. Nettie was ecstatic! The doctor (Dr. George Alexander) told me later, privately, that he was reasonably sure the baby was a girl. However, because he wasn't 100% sure, and knowing Nettie's feelings, he kept it to himself. He figured if he told her it was a girl, and he was wrong, she would be devastated.

We named the little doll Amy Lou.

During this time I began to pick up some off-duty jobs to work to make some extra money. One of the places I worked quite a bit was at the First Pasadena State Bank. The bank had so much business they needed two officers to work traffic around the ten drives-in windows. I usually worked on Friday when the rush was the greatest. Funny thing, the officer who offered the job to me was none other than now Captain Douglas T. Warren, the man who tried to set me up to get me fired back in 1955.

Captain Warren began to have marital problems and actually managed to shoot himself in the arm one day. He eventually resigned from the Police Department and I got his off-duty job at the bank.

He was also the Captain who resigned and left the vacancy at the captain's level. I was promoted to fill that vacancy.

My association with First Pasadena State Bank became a long term affair. I started out with them when the bank was at Munger and Shaw. The bank built Pasadena's first skyscraper on the corner of Southmore and Tatar. This building is empty now and will eventually be demolished.

I spent many an hour working there at the bank. I had my own master key to the bank and kept a locker in the basement where I could change from street clothes to my uniform. I got to know a lot of people in the banking business, one of whom was Mr. S. R. "Buddy" Jones, the bank president. Mr. Jones was instrumental in helping me get our son Michael Lee an appointment to the United States Air Force Academy. Mr. Jones has passed on now, but we will be eternally grateful for his help.

# FROM SWABBY TO COPPER

I served four years in the United States Navy, from September 1950 to July 1954. In July of 1954 I was notified that I was going to be discharged two months early.

The Personnel Officer encouraged me to reenlist. When he was asked what my chances were of going to sea if I reenlisted, he said about one hundred percent.

I had served my whole four years at The U. S. Naval Air Station on North Island in the bay of San Diego, California.

Nettie Grace and I had been married in 1952 while I was stationed there. Our oldest son, Timothy B. Smith was born at Naval Hospital in San Diego in 1953.

When the Personnel Officer told me I would be shipped out to sea, I thanked him, went to where all the discharge forms were, gathered up what I needed, and proceeded to type up all my discharge papers, including my official Discharge Certificate.

I got the Personnel Officer to sign off on all the necessary papers and a short time later, I was out of there.

I would be traveling by myself, because I had already sent Nettie and Tim home to Louisiana. With my enlistment nearly up, I figured I would be either sent home, or shipped out if I reenlisted.

When I arrived in Louisiana I was going to have to decide what I was going to have to do for the rest of my life.

I was eligible to go to school under the GI Bill. I kind of liked the idea of becoming an accountant, so I enrolled in a business college in Alexandria. Unfortunately, the school was owned and operated by this elderly lady whose goal was to save all the girls in the class from dirty men. On every break she talked to the girls about this subject.

I decided to change my course of study. Louisiana College in Pineville was about to crank up for the fall semester, so I moved my course of study there. My goal now was to become a basketball coach and go back to Jena and coach basketball.

One of the courses the counselor signed me up in was journalism. The first assignment the professor gave us was to write a short story. He wanted to see what he was dealing with, I guess.

I wrote a short story and submitted to the professor. At our next class he began to talk about writing. He held up a sheaf of papers and said he expected everyone to write stories like the one he was about to read to them. To my surprise, he began to read my short story to the class. I am including a copy of that short story in these writings. It is titled "The Phantom Intruder."

Nettie's sister Frankie had married a man who had become a police officer in Pasadena, Texas. They came to Louisiana to visit us and the rest of Nettie's folks. Nettie and I were struggling financially. We did not have a car. We had to bum rides and/or ride the buses. Frankie and her husband, Nolan, became aware of this. Nolan told me that the Pasadena Police Department was going to hire some more police officers, in case I was interested in being a police officer.

At that time, he was the only police officer I was personally acquainted with. To be frank about it, when I considered becoming a police officer, I figured that if Nolan could be a police officer, then surely I could. I talked it over with Nettie and she was agreeable. I asked Nolan to send me an application for employment, which he did. I filled out the application and mailed it back to the City of Pasadena. Not long afterward, I received a letter from the Civil Service Director asking me to travel to Pasadena to take a Civil Service Test.

After spending the night at Frankie and Nolan's, I went to City Hall and showed up for the test. The man in charge, dressed immaculately in a fine three piece suit, administered the test. From the way he acted and appeared I presumed he was the mayor of Pasadena.

After we finished the test another man walked in. He was dressed in work clothes, and wearing rubber boots. He was introduced to us as the mayor of Pasadena! I discovered the man administering the test was Marvin Jackson, the City Secretary and Civil Service Director.

*In My Lifetime*

After the test was over, I caught a bus back to Louisiana and was back in the classroom the next day. A few days later I received another letter from the Mr. Jackson telling me that I had passed the Civil Service Test with a score of 100. The letter advised me to return to Pasadena for an oral interview with the police department.

A copy of test scores and a copy of Appointment list are included herewith.

Now was the big decision. Again Nettie and I talked it over and we decided to make the move. I withdrew from Louisiana College, we packed up what few things we had, borrowed a trailer and with the help of my brother, we moved to Pasadena.

The first few days we stayed with the Frankie and Nolan, but then we rented a house in Pasadena Gardens on Parklane Street.

Nolan told me we could buy a new house for $25.00 down. It would be financed under the G. I. Bill

I found out what day I was supposed to report for the interview and went to the Pasadena Police Department at 112 N. Walters. I went to the front door of the station. I had never been there before. I opened the door and the lobby was just about full of men standing around. When I entered, everyone looked at me and I heard someone say, "That's him."

All the men there were waiting for that interview. Then it was my turn. I was shown into a small room where two men were waiting. The man behind the desk told me to sit down, which I did. He began to ask me a lot questions, none of which I remember. He introduced himself as Vareece Berry, the Chief of Police. The other man was Ralph Davis, the Fire and Police Commissioner.

Finally, the chief looked at me and said, "You're a no-good ------ -- -- -- ------------!" I started to get to my feet and he laughed. He told me that when I became a police officer, a lot of people would call me that. He wanted to know if I could handle it and I told him I could.

I believe it was at this point all those on the Appointment list were fingerprinted, which was October 25, 1954. A copy of my fingerprint card is included herewith.

I suppose they liked me and I was hired. The rest is history. I was twenty-six years of age.

*Police Officer Herbert Smith Photo*

# TIMOTHY BLANE SMITH

Our first-born, a son, was delivered into this world on May 21, 1953, at the Balboa Naval Hospital, San Diego, California. His first name, Timothy, came from Nettie's maternal grandfather, Timothy Lovell. We chose the middle name, Blane, because we liked the sound of it. Nettie Grace had just turned eighteen in January of that year. We had been married about a year and a month.

We were renting a small apartment in San Diego. Neither of us knew anything about becoming parents. Nettie was under the care of a U. S. Navy doctor and progressed satisfactorily through her pregnancy. He had told us she needed to walk a lot, so we did walk nearly every day, up and down the side of the mountain where we lived.

One night, as the date of her delivery neared, she woke me up complaining with her back hurting. Old sleepy head me, I would rub her back until I went back to sleep. She would wake me again to rub her back. After about three times, suddenly it dawned on us to time the pains. They were coming regularly, about five minutes apart. We got up and got dressed. We had no telephone. I went to the landlady, woke her up, and used her telephone to call a taxicab.

Once in the taxicab, I told the driver to hurry, because my wife was having a baby. He began to really move on, while yelling, "Don't you have that baby in my cab!"

We made it to the hospital and we hurried on in. The nurses put Nettie on a gurney to take her to the delivery room. The receptionist told me I might as well go somewhere and get some coffee, because I would have a while to wait. I found the mess hall in the hospital, got myself a hamburger and a cup of coffee, and then went back upstairs. A nurse came in asked me if I was Smith. I answered yes and she told me I was the father of a fine baby boy. Well, that did not take long. We found out later the nurses and the doctor was amazed that the delivery went so fast. They figured that since it was Nettie's first baby, it would take a while.

Nettie spent three days in the hospital. Our bill was something like $7.50 and that was for her meals. Well, I did have to pay for my hamburger and coffee that night.

Now that we were parents, big changes had to take place. We would have to move, for one thing. I applied for government housing and got relocated in a duplex further up on the side of that mountain. We had very little in the way of things to set up housekeeping. It was a good thing the duplex was furnished. We did decide to buy one of those new things called a television.

Nettie recovered quickly and Timothy began to grow. He was sure a fine healthy boy and had beautiful blue eyes.

I had gone through boot-camp there at the U. S. Naval Training Center. Adjoining USNTC was the United States Marine Training Center, and we always watched those Marines going through their basics.

Well, we ended up in Pasadena, Texas and I was working for the Pasadena Police Department. Timothy went through the school system and graduated from Pasadena High School. During his senior year he joined the Marine Corps ROTC. He sure looked great in his ROTC uniform.

After he graduated he came in one day and told us he had joined the marines. That was a surprise to us, because we had planned on him going to college. Nettie asked me if he could do that and answered her yes, because he was eighteen years of age.

He shipped out for San Diego, California and went through boot camp right there where I used to watch the marines train.

Tim stayed in the U. S. Marines twenty years and retired as a Gunnery Sergeant. We are certainly proud of his achievements.

He met and married the love of his life, Linda Joyce Harris, a registered nurse. He met her while stationed at the USMC Air Station in Yuma, Arizona.

On December 8, 1983, Tim's wife Joyce gave birth to our only grandson, Joshua Blane Smith. He weighed in at over ten pounds and hasn't stopped growing since. No, I am kidding. He eventually attained the size of 6 foot and 250 pounds, a very large and strong young man.

After Tim retired from the Marines he obtained a Teacher's Certificate and began teaching school in Yuma. He became successful in teaching children with learning disabilities.

Timothy now takes care of their several rental properties in Yuma and visits Joshua regularly where he is imprisoned at an Arizona prison facility. Needless to say, mine and Nettie's hearts are just broken over that sad state of affairs.

Joyce is now suffering from Parkinson's disease, but continues to work

Joshua is serving the last part of a fifteen year sentence for possession of pornographic materials.

Nettie and I will take this opportunity to warn you parents to keep a close watch on what your children are using the internet for.

*Timothy Blane Smith Photo*

# MICHAEL LEE SMITH

Our second son, Michael Lee Smith, was born in Pasadena, Texas on May 26, 1956.

Michael grew up here in Pasadena, Texas and graduated from Pasadena High School in 1974.

Mike, as we later learned to call him, instead of Mickey, which he never liked, was mostly a straight A student. In high school, being a straight A student, he was eligible for free tickets to the Houston Astros baseball games. He was able to take me to the ball games a number of times, a very proud dad.

At an early age, in what was then called Junior High School, Mike set his goal at becoming an airline pilot. The very thought of him flying an airplane scared me, but I kept my mouth shut.

We knew that he could get a very good college education and be taught to fly if he attended the United States Air force Academy. We contacted the appropriate people with the Air Force and learned what was necessary to get an appointment. Appointments to the military academies are political.

Having been on the police department for a number of years, I had become acquainted with quite a few influential people. Mike knew what he had to do and that was to keep his grades up and stay physically fit. At the time, he was working at the San Jacinto Inn at the San Jacinto Battleground. He was working after school. When the owner of the place, a Mr. Bobo, learned of Mike's effort to get an appointment, he told Mike he played poker quite frequently with Congressman Bob Casey. He told Mike he would recommend him to Mr. Casey.

By this time Mike was a senior in High School. The Air Force liaison got in touch with Mike and advised him he had received a "primary" appointment to the United States Air Force Academy. This meant he would not have to compete with other candidates. In the meantime, I had been in touch with several local politicians and one very prominent businessman, S. R. "Buddy" Jones of the First Pasadena State Bank, where I worked off-duty.

The appointment came through and our son Michael Lee Smith was off to the United States Air Force Academy, a very prestigious institution.

He graduated from the U. S. Air force Academy in 1978 with the rank of lieutenant in the U. S. Air Force, and a degree in engineering. Nettie and I were there to see him graduate, an awesome ceremony.

Mike went on to graduate from flying school, where he got an award for being one of the best formation fliers. His commanding officer remarked that "This officer knows how to fly an airplane."

He was later promoted to captain and flew various aircraft for the Air Force. After he had been in the Air Force about nine years, he decided to resign his commission and get a job flying with one of the airlines. He was hired by Pan Am and flew with them until the company went bankrupt.

Mike is now flying the awesome 747 with Delta-Northwest ranked as Captain, making international flights to the Orient.

He and his lovely wife Diane live in Monroe, Michigan in the summertime, and live in Port St. Lucie, Florida in the wintertime.

Nettie and I are very proud of them.

*Captain Michael Lee Smith Delta-Northwest Airlines*

# JEFFREY DEAN SMITH

Son number three, Jeffrey Dean Smith, was born in Pasadena, Texas on July 7, 1957, some fourteen months after Michael.

Jeffrey and Michael in their infant years were nearly the same size. As they grew older, Jeffrey became the taller of the two. Jeffrey attended Pasadena High School, but never graduated.

He got out on his own at an early age. He met and married Amanda Weinstein. They later divorced and Jeffrey never remarried. They had no children

Jeffrey is a great computer guy. With no formal training or education, he is able to assemble a computer from scratch, just furnish him the parts. For a number of years he did computer-aided drafting, making real good money.

Jeffrey injured his back and had to have an operation, which sidelined him from the drafting job.

He is now working as a courier, delivering payroll checks to various businesses, mainly in the Fort Bend County area.

Jeff finally got his GED and is doing fine, living alone in Houston, Texas.

Nettie and I are very proud of our largest son, the gentle giant.

*Jeffrey Dean Smith Photo*

# AMY LOU SMITH BEATY

Our only daughter, Amy Lou, was born in Pasadena, Texas on March 24, 1961. She graduated from Pasadena High School in 1979.

Amy's friends in high school called her "wonder-woman" because she looked like the actress Linda Carter who played the part of "Wonder Woman." in the movie. Amy was tall and slender with black hair, long dark eye lashes and beautiful blue eyes.

After Amy graduated from high school and enrolled at San Jacinto College, she met her first husband. They were married about eight and 1/2 years and finally divorced, with no children involved.

After her divorce, she met the true love of her life, Larry Joe Beaty. They were married on September 19, 1992 in Pasadena, Texas.

Amy started taking computer courses at the college and it wasn't long until she started working part-time in the Computer Department at the college. Then the college offered her a full-time job in that department, which she took. She continued her computer courses.

She stayed on at the college and retired in 2011 with 31 years at that institution. She was 50 years of age when she retired.

On July 6, 1999, our favorite granddaughter, Makayla Danielle Beaty, was born. She was born in Pasadena, Texas. She is presently enrolled at the First Baptist Christian Academy in Pasadena, where she is in the seventh grade, already. As of this writing, Makayla is approaching 5 feet and 8 inches in height. She will be thirteen years of age in July.

After Amy's retirement she had the opportunity to go to work for DeVry University, Chicago, Illinois as a programmer. They allow her to do most of her work at home on her computer, with only a monthly trip to Chicago. She works on a contract basis and the pay is very good. This is in addition to her very good retirement income. We are so proud of her.

Amy, Larry and Makayla live in Houston, not too far from us.

*Amy Lou Smith Beaty Photo*

# PAPA AND MAMA'S FIRST PIECE OF PROPERTY

Papa and Mama bought their first piece of property in either 1939 or 1940. It was located on the road going from Jena, Louisiana to Aimwell, Louisiana, about three miles from Jena. Papa was 55 years of age and Mama was 51. They had been married 33 years.

The road at that time was gravel. Papa had no vehicle, so he walked to Jena to work. Sometimes he would get a lift, but most of the time he walked. He would have to leave before daylight in order to get to his job by work-time. Once at Jena he would meet the man he worked for and they would travel to the work site.

He would work all day and most of the time, he would walk all the way home. Since the road was gravel, it was very dusty from vehicles traveling by.

Papa was not a very big man. I would guess his height at about five-nine and he probably never weighed more than around 160 pounds. When he walked he had a steady pace he kept up. When I walked to town with him, he would caution me to set a steady pace and stay with it, do not hurry, but do not drag along. I was taller than him and could walk faster, but I would slow down and walk along with him.

It was especially bad in the heat of the summer with vehicles speeding by stirring up the dust, no wind blowing, the dust just hanging in the air.

On one trip to town, on a Saturday, I think, Papa carried a garden hoe with him. He said it needed to be fixed. On the way to town we would walk by a black-smith shop. He left the hoe with the smith and told him we would pick it up later.

On the way back we stopped to pick up that hoe. Papa got the hoe and checked out and apparently he was agreeable with the work done on it. He asked the man what he charged for fixing the hoe and the man said, "Oh, about a nickel." Papa paid him the nickel. In this day and time I cannot fathom an instance where a job would be done for a nickel. I do not know what the man did to the hoe, but it must have been a minor thing.

The place that Papa and Mama bought had a well from which we had to draw water. I do not know how deep the well was, but the water was always nice and cold. The well had a board casing which was about eight inches square. It was just large enough to let the well bucket down to the water. I think the board casing was made of cypress.

One time the water got to smelling bad and Papa said something had fallen into the well. He never ventured a guess about what it was, but me and Pete figured it was a rat. Anyway, we had to "pump" the well out to get the bad water out. One does that by drawing up many buckets full of water until all the bad water was out.

In the other places we lived, we drank spring water, creek water or rainwater. The rainwater was caught in barrels. These were always full of what we called wiggle-tails. They would be near the top of the water, so if we wanted to dip some water out, we had to bump the side of the barrel. When the barrel was bumped, these things would go to the bottom of the barrel and we could get us a dipper of water. Later in life I learned these varmints were mosquito larvae.

When we first moved out to this place, we had neither electricity nor any telephone. That was not unusual, because we had never had these before. I remember we had one old coal-oil lamp to light up the inside of the house. When going from room to room, one had to take this lamp along to light the way. Papa used the lamp most of the time, because he liked to read. As far as our homework, we tried to get through with it before dark.

When the REA finally ran electric lines along the road, we were able to get some electricity in the house. Papa was also able to have an electric water pump put in the well. For a good while we still didn't have water in the house. There was a hydrant at the pump and we carried water from there into the house.

In the back corner of the yard there was an out-building. It appeared to be about 20 feet by 20 feet. Half of it we used for storage because it had a floor in it. The other side had no floor, just dirt. We did finally get a water hose to go on that hydrant. Pete and I would run that hose into that off side where there was no floor. We draped the hose over a joist and let hang down. We got us some boards to stand on and we would take a cold shower. That water was coming up from pretty deep in the ground and it was very cold, even in the summertime. We felt good afterward, though.

We had maybe a couple of acres of land with the house. Papa and I and Pete put up a fence around the property. This we did in the late evenings, Saturdays and Sundays.

We also had a pretty good garden. Mama knew how to grow a garden. Of course Pete and I did all the hard labor, mostly with shovels, hoes and rakes. Weeds and bermuda grass were a constant problem.

Once we got running water in the house and put in a bathroom, we had to dig a place for a septic tank and then dig a field line for the run-off. Before we got running water in the house we had to use an outdoor toilet. We were surely glad when we got that commode in the bathroom.

I can't say for sure, but I think the original house had a flat roof on it. Anyway, Papa decided to do some remodeling. He wanted a peaked roof, so he had to cut rafters and put on decking. It was good that he decided to go ahead with that, because Pete and I were growing up and I guess Papa figured before long we would be gone. All the other sons had already left; through marriage and the military service.

While we were in the process of getting a different roof over our heads, a severe thunderstorm came through. We had put the roof decking on and had covered it with tar-paper. That storm hit and began to blow that tar-paper off. Me, Pete and Papa had to get up on that roof and go to tacking that tar-paper back down. The rain was pouring and thunder and lightning was rolling. We all got soaking wet, but we managed to get the job done. I was about fifteen at the time and Pete was thirteen.

I know that Papa and Mama were proud of that piece of property and they had a right to be. As far as I know they had never owned any real estate before. We had always worked someone else's real estate (farm) on a share-cropping arrangement.

# THE SMITH BROTHERS STRING BAND

During the thirties and early forties, my five older brothers formed a band, of sorts. The all could play guitars, mandolins, and banjos. However, only my brother Homer could play the fiddle.

Papa could play the harmonica and the fiddle. I guess that was how my brothers learned to play as they did.

Alphonse could play the guitar pretty good even though his right arm and hand were disabled from polio.

As far as I know Papa never played with them at any of their performances.

The band played for dances, store openings and the like. I have been asked if the band had a name. If they had a name, I never heard it. Me and my younger brother Pete knew very little about their activities. They never let us go with them to any of their performances and we never learned to play any of the instruments.

While we were living at Jena, Louisiana, after we moved off the farm, I remember Homer sitting in the local café (Nick's Café) waiting for someone to play his favorite tune so he could copy the words down. If he didn't get all the words the first time he would have to wait until someone else played the tune again. I do not think he ever played the tune himself, probably because he did not have enough money to spend in the juke box.

By listening to the music, he learned the melody and could then sing the song and play it on his instruments.

World War II broke up the band. Homer met and married Eric Maxine Wright (no relation to Mama's people) Joe was already married with at least one child. Leslie Henry was drafted into the U. S. Army and Walter enlisted in the U. S. Navy. Later Joe was drafted into the Army, even though he was married and had three kids. He did not stay in very long.

Homer's wife came from a family of Church of Christ believers who did not believe in using musical instruments in their worship service. Homer quit playing and eventually became an ordained minister in the Church Of Christ.

Joe ended up with Papa's fiddle. I think he learned to play it some. Sometimes in the fifties his house burned to the ground and the fiddle was lost.

Who knows if the war had not started, we might have been hearing and seeing the Smith Brothers String Band on the Grand Ol' Opry.

*The Smith Brothers String Band Photo*

# COURTSHIP AND MARRIAGE

After I got settled in at my duty station there on North Island, I began to enjoy my work. The job was not hard. I spent a lot of time typing legal papers for the Legal Officer.

The Navy had replaced all the manual typewriters with electric typewriters. Of course, I was accustomed to using the manuals, and it took me a long time to get used to using those IBM electric typewriters.

To make matters really bad, the Legal Officer demanded typing which was without error. No strike-overs, perfect margins, no misspelled words and etc. That was hard to do when we were not accustomed to these new typewriters.

We were encouraged to keep in contact with our loved ones back home. The Commanding Officer really hated to get letters from some mother lamenting that she had not heard from her darling boy or girl.

I did write to my folks. Mama did write me a few times, but Papa never did.

Before I joined the Navy, I had worked for a while at a Dairy Queen on Main Street in Pineville, Louisiana. I had two brothers living close by there and usually stayed with one or the other of them while I was working.

Also living near my brothers was a family with which my brothers visited a lot. Their name was Coleman. They had five daughters.

The oldest daughter was Frankie. She had been married, but was separated from her husband. I think she was about sixteen years of age. I was told that her and her husband fought all the time.

The next youngest daughter was Nettie Grace and she was a year younger than Frankie. My brother Pete dated her a few times. I had met the whole family of course.

Needing someone to write to who would answer my letters, I decided to write Nettie Grace.

I began to write to Nettie and she sent me a couple of pictures of herself. Her penmanship was beautiful. Our letters became longer and longer and I began to realize that I was falling in love with this young girl.

I was in the Navy for about a year and a half before I could get any military leave. When I did get to go home, I went to the Coleman's to see Nettie. While I was there we dated several times. I soon had to go back to San Diego.

The Navy did away with the old "Articles of War." These were replaced by the Uniform Code of Military Justice. I was sent to a school in Newport, Rhode Island to learn all about this USMJ. I requested permission for a delay in reporting to that school so I could stop in Pineville and visit Nettie. I was smitten. My request was granted.

Shortly after I arrived at the Coleman residence, I proposed to Nettie and she conditionally accepted, depending on what her father said. She told me I would have to ask her father for her hand in marriage. On this night, her dad was already in bed, but he was awake, reading a book. I just barged right in and stated my purpose. He asked me if I was going to support his daughter as my wife and I told him "Yes, Sir." He gave his permission and Nettie and I immediately began to plan our marriage.

In Louisiana at that time, prospective husbands had to get a blood test, which I did the next day. Nettie's mother had to sign for her when we applied for a marriage license, because she was only seventeen. The bad part, though, we had to wait three days before we could be married.

The wonderful day finally arrived. We were married there at her house. My brother Al was my best man and he had to loan me five dollars to pay the Church of Christ preacher to perform the wedding. Nettie's boss at the cleaners where she worked after school stood up with Nettie. Her name was Mrs. Allison.

The date was April 25, 1952 and it was a glorious day. We borrowed Mr. Coleman's car and left. We only went to the Baptist Hospital in Alexandria to visit Nettie's aunt. She was confined with sickness. After everyone left the Coleman's, we returned.

I had to leave the next day to report to that school in Newport, Rhode Island.

I successfully completed the school and had to report back to my duty station at NAS, San Diego, California. I did not see my young bride again until about July when she traveled alone out to California to meet me.

# "I AM GONNA SHOOT THEM CATS"

We moved away from the Jonesville, Louisiana area and relocated back near Manifest, Louisiana. We had lived in this area before. I believe this recent move was about 1938. I was ten year old.

The small house we lived in was perched on the side of a hill, not too far off the black-top highway. This highway ran roughly from a community called Whitehall to Harrisonburg, Louisiana. The highway followed the edge of the hills where the land drops off toward the lowlands.

I do not remember exactly how many rooms the house had, but we were crowded. My two older sisters and one older brother had married and moved away, leaving Papa, Mama, Alphonse, Homer, Leslie Henry, Walter, me and Pete.

We probably lived there a year and a half. As usual Papa was sharecropping. The land which we farmed was on the opposite side of the highway. It was kind of flat and easy to farm.

About the house, the kitchen was at the very back. Of course, the back door was in the kitchen. Near the back door was a standard paned window. Normally, the windows were kept closed because they had no screens. This window, however, had one of the glass panes missing.

We had this big ol' pet cat that kind of strolled around like it pleased. I do not know whether it was male or female. It was tolerated because it kept the mice and rats under control..

There was a small back porch on the house. One night after everything was settled down and we had finished supper, Papa was sitting in the front room reading by our coal-oil lamp. His chair was near one of the two windows in the front room.

On this particular night, our cat was outside doing whatever cats do after dark. Hopefully it was hunting rats. Unknown to us, our cat had attracted the attention of another cat. No one lived near us, so we did not know where this cat came from.

All of sudden our cat yowled like a banshee and came through that opening where the pane of glass was missing. Right behind our cat was this strange cat. Through the kitchen, up through the house into the front room where Papa was sitting near that window streaked those cats, both screaming bloody murder.

Our cat leaped for that window near Papa, but alas, it was closed. Both cats bounced off that window, tore across Papa's legs, which were extended, and back through the house. They both exited back out through that opening in the back window. It was all over in less than half a minute.

Papa sat there for a few seconds and got up. He said, "Get me my shotgun."

Mama asked, "What are you going to do?"

Papa said, "I am gonna shoot them cats."

Now, cats are pretty smart and I think they can sense when they are in danger, like when something or someone is after them.

Papa got his shotgun, went outside and searched the place over for them cats. He had no kind of light to take outside with him. We never heard him shoot, so we figured he did not find the cats. They were probably up in a tree watching him.

Well, the cat got pardoned and went about doing its duty of controlling the vermin.

In spite of Papa's anger, the cat kept its job.

# "RECAPPED" TIRES DURING WWII

During World War II we were living out of the town of Jena, Louisiana on the "Aimwell Highway," which was, at that time, a gravel road.

One of my older brothers, it might have been Alphonse, bought an old 1931 model Chevrolet. Still at home at that time were Papa, Mama, Alphonse, me and Quitman. Homer had gotten married and Henry and Walter had gone into the service of their country.

Papa and Al were the only ones working. Papa was working as a laborer for a brick mason and Al was repairing radios for the Western Auto Store..

Now, remember, Papa and Mama never confided anything to us kids. In other words, if they knew that Al had bought the old car, they never mentioned it to me or Pete.

One evening it was getting late. Mama, me and Pete were at home and we were waiting for Papa and Al to come home. They usually walked home from town, about three miles. Mama was grumbling about "them being late getting home." I guess she meant Papa and Al.

I mentioned that the road we lived on was graveled and during the war there was not much traffic on it.

On this particular evening, it was well after dark and we were sitting on the front porch, just waiting and watching the road toward town. We began to hear a growling noise coming up the road from towards town. Mama said "That's them."

Now I did not know anything about cars. If Papa ever owned one it was before I was old enough to remember. In this case I knew it was a car coming and it was running on at least one rim. It was making that growling noise on the gravel road. Sure enough, it was Papa and Al and they were in this old 1931 model Chevrolet. Mama always expected the worst, so she knew it was Papa and Al.

We eventually replaced the ruined rim and got a set of used tires for it. There was nothing wrong with the engine. It was the standard six-cylinder Chevrolet job of which Chevrolet made millions (of engines).

In retrospect, I figure that Papa and Al decided to buy this car because they got tired walking a total of six or more miles per day going to and from work

My sister-in-law, Eric Maxine, Homer's wife, taught me to drive. They would come for a visit and here we would go in that old Chevy.

Pete also learned to drive, maybe from watching me. Me and Pete began to drive that thing up and down the road. We would take Papa to work and then pick him up in town when he got off from work.

Al moved to Pineville, Louisiana and went to work for Montgomery Ward in Alexandria, Louisiana. He repaired radios for them.

Anyway, those used tires on that Chevy got real worn. In those years automobile tires had rubber tubes in them. The treads on those were worn down to the thread. The sidewalls, however, were good. I will add that the tires were made of rubber also.

Pete and I knew we had a problem because when that thread wore through; the tire would blow, ruining the tube.

We managed to get some old used tires that had bad sidewalls, but had good treads; we decided to use those old tires to cover the ones on the car. In order to do that we had to cut the "beads" off the tires were going to put over the others. So, with our trusty pocket knives we went to work, cutting the "beads" off.

The old tires on the car were pretty flexible, so we would take them off, let the air out of them, remove them from the rims, and removing the rubber tube. Once we got the tire off we would wrestle and fold into the tire from which we had cut the "bead." Low and behold, once we got that tire inside the other one, we had a homemade recap. Of course we did not know then what to call it. Back then I am not sure there were any such things as recaps for automobile tires.

Well, we managed to do all four tires like that. As you might expect, we were pretty dirty and sweaty after all that. So, we took off, driving the car. However, we discovered that when we took off, the rear tires spun inside our homemade recaps. We had to do something about that.

The problem: the inner tire was spinning inside the outer tire. Solution: fix the tire so it would not spin inside the outer tire.

The obvious thing to do was to bolt the tires together so the inner one would not spin in the outer.

Putting together a few bucks, we went to town and bought a bunch of round-headed stove bolts and a lot of washers.

I believed we put a total of eight bolts on each tire, four on the inside and four on the outside.

Taking the tires off the car again, we deflated them, one at a time and removed the tubes. By the way, the air pump we used was hand operated.

We punched holes through both tires, the inner tire and the outer tire. We pushed the stove bolts through from the inside, placing a washer under the head of the stove bolt. We needed the rounded headed bolts to keep from puncturing the inner tube.

We tightened those bolts up nice and snug and we had us some "recapped tires. Looking back, I guess we should have doubled the number of bolts we put in those tires, but we probably didn't have enough money to buy more.

As long as we drove slowly, there was no problem. When we picked up speed those recapped tires would really begin to flap. At least the inner tire quit spinning inside the outer tire.

During the war we just had to make do. We would drive that old Chevy to school. We had to park it across the street from the school near "Slay's Service Station." The reason we did this was because nearly every day when we got out of school, a tire would be flat. We would have to jack the car up with an old "screw-type" jack, take the tire and rim off the car, remove the tire from the rim, using tire tools, pull the rubber inner tube out so we could pump it up to find where it was leaking. There was a large container of water nearby at the service station which was used for that very thing. We had to submerge the tube under the water to see where it was leaking air. Once we found the leak we had to dry it off, mark the spot (usually with a pencil) and prepare to patch it. These old rubber inner tubes had developed many leaks so each was covered with numerous patches. These old patches were called cold patches. A person could buy a tire repair kit which contained rubber patches and a tube of special glue. The lid of the can was made where one could scratch the surface of the inner tube before applying he glue. The patch had a backing on it which was pulled off before applying it to the area where the glue was applied. When done properly, these patches worked very good.

After patching the tube, we would pump it up, check it in the water to make sure it was not leaking, let the air out, place it back in the tire, put the tire back on the rim and pump air back in it. Then we replaced it back on the car. We were then prepared to crank her up and head for home, ready to do our chores once we got there Later we had to get our homework.

# COUNTRY LIFE

Before we moved to Jena, Louisiana, we lived between two small communities, Rhinehart and Manifest.

Our house was pretty close to the blacktop highway. In that part of the state a lot of the houses were built on the side of a hill. In our case, the hill sloped up away from the highway behind our house. On the other side of the highway the hill sloped away toward the lowlands. Actually the highway was built along the edge of hills, up away from the lowlands

Our house was probably one which came to be known as a "shotgun" house. All the rooms were built in a line from front to back. In our case just about every room had a bed or beds in it.

The back of the house was close to the ground, while the front was way up off the ground. Because it was built this way, there were a number of steps up to the front porch.

I will add here that the family farmed an area of land across the highway from the house.

Still living at home at the time was Alphonse, the oldest, Homer, Leslie, Walter, Quitman (Pete), and myself. With Papa and Mama, that made eight people living thee.

Back in those days, doctors made house calls, because most folks did not have the means to travel to town to see the doctor.

One night someone got sick. I do not know who it was. It might have been Mama. Anyway, Papa told Homer to run to town to get the doctor. The town was five or six miles away, as I remember. Homer ran out the front door into the darkness. There were no electric lights at our house, only a "coal-oil" lamp.

We heard a commotion, a thud, grunts and exclamations and so forth. Homer came limping back in. Papa asked him what happened and Homer said he missed the steps. Papa looked around and picked another son, Henry, I think, and dispatched him with the admonition to take the steps this time.

I was only eleven years old at the time and Pete as nine. We were not awake if and when the doctor came. We were probably told to go to bed, which we always did forthwith. Never did know for sure what was wrong and what the doctor did to remedy the situation'

Papa and Mama never talked about family affairs in front of us kids.

At this particular place where we lived we used spring water. There was a small creek that ran down out of the hills which were behind our house. Papa found a place near the house, at edge of the creek, where water was bubbling up out of the sandy bottom. He took some cypress boards and built a square box, open at the top and bottom. It seems to me it was about 24 inches square and about the same in depth. He dug out a place around where the water was bubbling up. He took he box and worked it down into the water over where the water was coming out. He left about 6 inches up above the level of the water. With his pocket knife he had cut a small notch on the downward side of the box, on the creek side. The water settled down and cleared up. The box filled up and began to pour out through the notch he had cut. In a day or two the water had cleared up and was good to drink and cook with. The water was cool, even in hot weather. We kept a gourd dipper handy to use to get us a cool drink of water.

Mama kept jugs of milk in the water to keep the milk from spoiling.

It was while we were living at this place that Papa had an incident with a half-grown bull yearling. We had a milk cow which usually Papa milked. One evening he went out to milk the cow and in a little while he came back in, out of breath and had a lot of dirt on his clothes. He sat down and rested. Mama asked him what had happened. He said that little bull yearling got after him when he was trying to milk the cow. He said he had to bull-dog the little bull three times before he could make it to the fence.

At that time Papa was about 53 years old, about five feet, eight inches tall and probably weighed in at about 160 pounds.

Well, Papa got his handsaw and went back out to the barnyard. He roped that little bull yearling, snugged him up to a post and sawed his horns off. From then on all the animal could do was butt.

After that, Papa finished milking the cow.

# THE MOVE TO JENA, LOUISIANA

Our family moved to Jena, Louisiana in 1939. The house Papa found for us to live in was a lot bigger than any we had ever lived in. It was located in what was then called Old Jena and it was near the railroad tracks, I would say about 75 yards.

When I started to school that year, I was in the fourth grade. The school yard was just on the opposite side of the railroad tracks and across the street from us. For the first time Pete and I was able to walk to school.

The school building was of brick and, I think, was three stories tall. There were no elevators, only stairs. I did not know any of my fellow students. Of course that was not unusual, because previously we had moved nearly every year to a different location, depending on where Papa found a place to work as a share-cropper.

A couple of things I remember about going to school there. One, I was introduced to grapefruit juice. The school was given a large supply of canned grapefruit juice, a can for every student. Some of the students did not like the juice and would not drink it. I drank mine, even though it was unsweetened. When the teacher discovered I drank my juice readily, she began to bring me more cans. She had to open the cans by punching holes in the lid. I finally got my fill of grapefruit juice. The other thing I remember, the school house burned to the ground. I do not know how many grades were in that building, but to make emergency classrooms for the students, they had to partition off the basketball gymnasium.

The school had to have more classrooms, so they built a number of temporary buildings, covered with tarpaper. The First Baptist Church also made available space for classes.

I learned later the basketball team had to practice and play games on dirt courts, when they were dry, of course.

We were not in Old Jena very long, but long enough to sustain a serious cut on my foot. I stepped on a broken glass bottle, lacerating my foot pretty good. I was taken to the doctor for stitches, a new thing for me. Even though I now lived in town, I still went barefooted.

Papa and Mama found a place for sale some three miles out on the Aimwell Highway, actually a gravel road. The house had a living room, dining room, a kitchen, and two bedrooms. There again, we had never lived in a house that large. It did not have a bathroom.

I never learned how Papa and Mama managed to buy this place. I believe the house was on about three acres. Mama's people were shop owners and bankers. Mama's maiden name was Wright. A large hotel in Jena was named The Wright Hotel. Her brother owned and operated a shoe repair shop. Some of her nephews were bankers. Obviously, Mama's people were people of property. Up until Papa and Mama purchased that place on the Aimwell Road, I did not know of any of Papa's people who owned real estate.

In retrospect, I think Mama was able to get a loan from one of the banks where my cousins worked. With that Papa and Mama purchased their first piece of property. They had been married some forty-one years

Papa got a job as a laborer, working for a man who was a brick mason and concrete contractor. It was very hard work. Papa had to walk to town, about three miles, work all day and walk home that evening. Sometimes he got rides, but most of the time he walked.

When I got old and big enough to work for the same man, I also walked as Papa did. The road was gravel and very dusty. Walking in gravel was also very tiring. The land was not level; there were hills we had to walk up. When I started working for this contractor, he paid me a dollar an hour. When I got paid, I had more money in my pocket than I had ever had in my life. We usually worked five, ten hour days, and sometimes half a day on Saturday.

When we moved from the farm to Jena, there were still six sons at home. There was Al, Homer, Leslie, Walter, Quitman (Pete) and me. My brother Joe had gotten married when he was about seventeen and moved away from home.

At one time I think five of the six boys and Papa worked for this contractor. This contractor got the job of building the first movie theater in Jena. I did not help on that job. My brother Homer fell off a scaffold with a wheelbarrow load of brick mortar and broke his hip. When the theater was being built, I was too young to work.

Years later, after the War started I became old enough to work. Homer had got married and left. Leslie and Walter went into the military service. Al stayed at home while he worked at Western Auto.

Now it was only Papa, Mama, me and Pete at home.

My sister Mildred, who divorced her husband L. V. Scarborough, moved back home, had a young son named Lynn.

My sister Mildred developed leukemia and after a long hard battle, died in 1947 at the age of thirty-four. Papa and Mama took over raising their grandson, Lynn Scarborough and he became like a brother to me and Pete.

By this time, Al had moved to Pineville, Louisiana. He got a job with Montgomery Ward, repairing radios.

Time passed and the War ended. My brothers, Leslie and Walter, returned home, along with millions of other G.I.'s, all looking for work. My brothers were paid an allotment after they were discharged, for about a year, I think. They needed transportation, so they bought a 1939 yellow Oldsmobile.

With that car and a little money in their pockets, they began to run the roads, looking for eligible girls. They were having so much fun, Pete and I began to go with them, I kind of put going to school on the back burner.

When my brothers ran out of money, they had to leave home and look for work. That grounded me and Pete.

When school started, I went back. I discovered that I liked to play basketball. Basketball was a big deal at Jena High School. It usually fielded championship teams.

When practice started, I showed up. The coach let me know right away I was not eligible because I had quit the previous year.

Well, I showed him a thing or two. If I could not play basketball, I could see no reason why I should go to school. I quit again.

Mama stayed on me all the time about going back. When I went into town and Miss Kendrick, my English teacher, saw me, she was onto me about going back to school.

Finally, when school started up again in the fall of 1948, I went back to school. I guess I finally figured out there was something at school besides playing basketball.

The first thing I found out, now there were twelve grades in school. I also discovered, I needed five credits to graduate. When I enrolled I found out that I was a senior, but I needed those five credits to graduate. My senior year I had to take English, Geometry, Spanish, Shorthand and Typing.

Most of my English grades were accomplished by writing. I could not play basketball, but I could observe and take notes. Since I was on the school newspaper staff, I wrote sports articles for it. The Jena Times bought my articles and paid me for them. I always submitted my articles to Miss Kendrick before publishing them. She corrected and graded them.

The Senior Class consisted of fourteen students. We were all "make-up" students that got caught in the changeover from eleven to twelve grades, and/or quitting school for a year or two, like me.

My class, the Class of 1949, was the first class to graduate from the new High School.

I was privileged to be able to take part in the graduation ceremonies.

The year I graduated, I turned twenty-one years of age. Some of the students thought I was a World War Two veteran.

I finished in the top percentile of my class and was eligible for a scholastic scholarship to Northwestern State College at Natchitoches, Louisiana.

That is another story.

# PART 2

# ANNEXATION: PASADENA VS HOUSTON

One of the first things I learned after becoming a Pasadena Police Officer was where the city limits were.

Pasadena was a growing city and the City of Houston tried to put a clamp on the growth of the City of Pasadena. There was quite a lot of unincorporated area south of Pasadena. At some point, the City of Houston annexed a strip of property about 100 feet wide north of Spencer Highway. This strip extended east to the city limits of Deer Part. It effectively blocked the City of Pasadena from growing.

I do not recall the dates when this happened, but Pasadena, with the cooperation of the City of Deer Park and the City of LaPorte, was able to circumvent this problem. Meeting in secret (they could do that in those days) The City of Deer Park and the City of LaPorte both deannexed strips of land (probably about a hundred feet wide) along Spencer Highway on the north side. Timing their meetings by the clock (and maybe by telephone) Pasadena annexed these strips shortly after those cities deannexed them. Then Pasadena annexed a very large track of land which extended across the Gulf Freeway and south to include the territory which is now the Space Center.

Naturally this really raised the ire of the City of Houston. They subsequently requested a conference with the City of Pasadena. As a result of a trade-out with Houston, Pasadena lost all the area where the Johnson Space Center is. I do not know for sure what Pasadena ended up with, but I am sure it came nowhere near the taxable area that Houston ended up with.

I think Comer Whitaker was the mayor of Pasadena during this period of time. I think our mayor let Houston get the best of Pasadena.

# DEERS-A-WALKIN'

For a number of years after we moved to Texas, I hunted in Louisiana. Mostly we hunted the white-tailed deer. Of course there were other things in this area available for us to hunt in addition to deer. We could also fish because Cocodrie Bayou and Wallace Bayou merged right at our campsite.

Our campsite was about a hundred yards from the bayous on a ridge, so we never saw the place flooded.

The hunting camp was started many years previously by the Reeves Family. The land and timber actually belonged to a large timber company. Mr. Almarin Reeves lived nearby on his farm. He was the caretaker and manager of the hunting lease. The patriarch of the Reeves family was "Uncle" Erwin Reeves, who lived in Jena, Louisiana. In another segment I tell about Uncle Erwin Reeves.

At some point, long before I started hunting down there, the lease members built a rather primitive camp house. It was made of roughhewn lumber and had a nice fireplace. Later a bunk house was built to accommodate a larger complement of hunters.

The first time I went to the campsite, Gus Austin and I went as guests of an older member. This member drove his pickup. Once we got off the known road and he started through the woods, I had no idea where we were. He remarked that we would travel toward the campsite until we ran off into a drainage ditch and then we would walk the rest of the way.

We did just that. Gus and I had our shotguns and we were dressed comfortably for walking in the woods. I had on a good pair boots.

Our host got out of his pickup and set out walking through the woods. No flashlight. No carbide light. Just moonlight. Gus and I stumbled along following him. Our host was also carrying a shotgun.

In a little while we saw a light through the woods and presently we came upon the campsite. I still did not know where we were.

The hunters were up and getting ready to hit the woods.

Our host told us to follow him and he set out walking again, still with no light.

Soon it began to lighten up as dawn broke. A good ways from the camp, he said one of you stop here. He pointed in a certain direction and said the dogs will be coming from there; keep a sharp lookout for the deer.

I had forgotten that the hunters used deer hounds to flush the deer. Gus dropped off and I kept following our host. A couple of hundred yards further he told me to stop here. He kept walking away from me. He dropped us off in what I figured a straight line. It was still pretty dark.

I found me a tree to stand by and got ready to wait. I loaded my shotgun. It was not wise to stumble through the woods with a loaded shotgun.

Before long I began to hear the dogs baying and I got ready to shoot me a deer. As the dogs got closer, I released the safety of my shotgun.

The dogs came through running and baying. They passed between me and Gus. I did not hear anyone shoot.

After it got good daylight and the dogs quit baying, our host showed up headed back to camp. Apparently he did not see anything either.

At lunchtime we had a bite to eat. After eating it was back to the woods again, this time in a different direction.

I heard the dogs again, but still did not see any deer. We stayed until pretty late and our host was ready to head back to Jena. He enlisted some help and we got his truck out of the drainage ditch. Back to Jena we went. Out host talked very little. We thanked him for taking us to the deer camp and helping with our first deer hunt. Gus and I left the next day and drove back to Pasadena. It was quite an experience.

This deer camp, as I mentioned, was fairly primitive. There was no electricity, no running water, and no bathroom. It was barely a shelter from bad weather.

The water supply which we used came from a large metal tank positioned to catch the rainwater off the roof.

This timber company land was termed "open range" and there were quite a few half-wild cattle and wild hogs in the woods.

Gus and I later went back at the invitation off Almarine Reeves. My brother Pete and James Westbrooks were along this time. We all stayed in the main camp house.

James and I elected to stay in the "attic" which was a half floor about ceiling high. We crawled up there on a crude ladder when it got bedtime.

We woke early next morning when the camp begins to stir. I was in my sleeping bag. I opened my eyes and not too far above my head was a mass of spider webs. They were mere inches from me. Every nook and cranny was a spider hole. James and I carefully eased back down to the ground floor. We never got back up there.

The camp itself was some three miles through the woods. The property close to the main highway, belong to a farmer. There were gates to go through and we had to get permission to pass through his property.

The only other way to the camp was up Cocodrie Bayou and that was about three miles by flat-bottomed boat.

One year as we were making plans to go there for hunting season, we were told the camp house and bunk house had been burned.

This meant that a new camp house would have to be built. Fortunately, one of the Jena members was a brick mason. Everyone pitched in and bought the necessary materials. The mason laid the cinder blocks and a carpenter did the woodwork. The old fireplace survived. The new building was built to fit against the fireplace.

The chimney of the fireplace was made of what was called "mud-cats." Mud-cats were made of clay and moss. A framework of hickory saplings would be built, tied together with vines, haywire or whatever was available. The mud-cats would be shaped in balls about half the size of a football. They were firm, but pretty soft. They were layered in and around the wood framework.

The work was slow, because the mud-cats had to be left to dry some before others were put on top of them. Once they got hard, though, they were fairly substantial. Fires built in the fireplace further hardened the mud-cats.

We had a concrete floor, a fairly large living area and an area for a kitchen. There was room in the living area for four double beds, none too close to the fireplace

Since the woods were open range, there were quite a few cattle around. During the off season, these cattle would gather around the campsite. The campsite had been cleared of bushes and trees. Grass was plentiful around the camp. We had to install a fence around the camp building to keep the cattle and hogs away from the building. There were two gates.

The cattle would generally leave a mess around the camp with their droppings. That is one reason we did not want them in the yard.

There was one member of the lease who was a doctor in Jena. There was also a crippled man from Jena who occasionally came to the camp with a member. The man had been crippled from birth. He was also the town drunk. He could walk fairly well when he was sober, but not at all when he was drunk. When he was drinking, he crawled on all fours.

The good doctor showed up one day while we were there and he had the crippled man with him. Yes, he was drunk. The doctor was driving a four-wheel drive vehicle with no doors. There were no seat belts in those days. With no doors, one held on for dear life.

When the doctor pulled into camp and stopped, the drunken fellow fell out onto the ground.

It was in the afternoon and we had been discussing who was going to cook supper. This man caught the topic of the conversation and said he would do the cooking. He began to crawl toward one of the gates going into the yard. There was, however, between him and the gate, a fresh pile of cow manure. One of his hands landed squarely in the fresh dropping. He paused momentarily, wiped his hand somewhat on his coveralls and continued on his way to the camp building, still avowing he was going to cook supper.

Immediately we had six willing volunteers for the job of cooking supper.

I don't know where the man slept that night. He did not sleep in the camp house. I think the doctor took him back to Jena, thank goodness.

I had bought a pretty nice used double bedstead with mattress and box springs. My age gave me seniority somewhat, so I picked a spot close to the fireplace. We needed plenty of sleeping room, because I had three sons, Gus had one and James had one. Pete had only a daughter.

At this point, there were no windows in the openings. We had plans of putting in glass windows later, or shutters.

At night, with all the young boys sitting around in front of the big fire in the fireplace, we would tell stories, suitable for young ears.

Someone mentioned that there were probably bear in those woods around the camp. There might have been some black bear in these woods, but I had never seen one. If there were, they would avoid people.

What we did have there were some very large packrats. They were as big as squirrels. These rats were always prowling around in the kitchen area. At night sometime I could hear them rattling things.

I had a very good police-type flashlight which I kept near my bed. I also kept my service revolver close at hand. My oldest son usually slept with me and the other two slept in a bed between us and the kitchen.

One night, after everything got quiet, I heard some noise in the kitchen. The fire in the fireplace had died down to a soft glow. I rose up quietly and shined my flashlight toward the kitchen. There he was, sitting in the window of the kitchen, a large packrat. I quietly cocked my weapon, keeping my flashlight centered on that varmint. When I had a good target opportunity, I dropped the hammer. The rat disappeared.

Loud confusion erupted in the cabin. Everyone was awake, wanting to know what happened. Returning to the comfort of my sleeping bag, I told everyone to relax, it was just that old bear at the window and think I scared him off.

The next morning I found the dead rat. I had hit dead center and demolished him.

We never realized it at the time, but apparently there were some locals who did not like us Texans hunting down there. Almarine Reeves loved to hunt with us, because we were always ready to hit the woods. A lot of the other members wanted to just hang around the camp. This was strange, their feelings toward us, though, because we were all natives of Louisiana.

After we rebuilt the cabin and started going back down there, we discovered that someone was using the cabin. We never locked it, because we thought maybe someone might need it for shelter in bad weather.

On one trip there, I noticed that the headboard of my bed, right about where my head would be when I was asleep, had been penetrated with about a dozen .22 caliber bullet holes. A pretty good pattern, too!

I got the message. I realized it was the beginning of the end for our deer hunting in Louisiana.

Before we went back there the next year, our new cabin was burned. Gus's bed was closest to the fireplace. Right in the middle of the remains of his bed was a shovel. Apparently whoever burned it, just threw shovel and coals upon Gus's bed and left.

Before we could start rebuilding it, they came and knocked the cinderblock walls down.

That was the end of our Louisiana hunting lease.

By this time Almarine Reeves was dead. He did not have to endure what had happened to his fine hunting camp. He was killed in an automobile accident near his place on the main highway. It was never the same without him, anyway.

After he got killed his son-in-law, Austin Ray Snow took over the running of the camp. In another segment I tell about Austin Ray Snow.

One night we were all sitting outside the cabin around a nice campfire. Snow had his two sons, my three sons were there and so were Gus's and James's.

We were talking and listening to the night sounds. The night was clear, a big moon and bright stars. Across the Cocodrie Bayou was an area we called the "island." It wasn't really an island. The bayou made a giant loop. Across a low and narrow area of this peninsular, probably where the bayou had flowed at one time, the back waters from time to time would flood the area, making a kind of island, until the flood waters receded. The locals called it the "island."

Sitting out there at night, occasionally we could hear a great horned owl hooting. The sound would be coming from across the bayou, the area known as the island.

When the old owl started hooting, Austin Ray Snow would say, "Deers a-walkin'."

We inquired what he meant by that. He said the old owl did not like the deer to be walking through his hunting territory. It interfered with the owl's hunting, so he would hoot at the deer, hoping the deer would move on somewhere else.

## Deers-a-Walkin'
### By Herbert Smith

Flames of the campfire flickered,
Night sounds echoed in the stillness.
Paw Paw! What are those sounds?
Night creatures, Honey.
Why are they making those noises, Paw Paw?
They are talkin' to one another of their own kind.
Bugs talk to one another,
Frogs talk to one another,
and night birds talk to one another.
What was that, Paw Paw
Deers-a-walkin' Honey.
That was a big ol' hoot owl.
Who was he talking to?
He was talking to some deer he saw in the dark.
Why?
The ol' owl is huntin' for food;
The deer are disturbin' things.
The owl can't hear what he is listenin' for,
The ol' owl hoots at them—
Maybe they will move on, and he can hear better.
They watched the fire and listened to the night sounds.
The owl hooted again.
The old hunter placed some more sticks on the fire.
With love in his old eyes, he looked at his granddaughter,
Paw Paw! Deers-a-walkin'!

# THE HUNTER AND THE GAME WARDEN

The Hunter lived in Concordia Parish, Louisiana. He was married to the daughter of the man who managed our Louisiana deer lease. That is where I got acquainted with him. He was an accomplished hunter. He had served eight years in the military and was a pretty tough individual.

He could survive in the woods with no problem. He drank water from puddles formed when it rained. He slept in hollow logs. He could field-dress a deer in just a few minutes, and pack the carcass out of the woods on his shoulders. He could start a campfire without matches, which he often did.

Of the Hunter's weaknesses, he had a couple which kept him in trouble. One was hunting out of season; the other was hunting at night with a spotlight. Both of these actions were very illegal. He, however, had been doing this all of his life.

He had been permanently injured in an oil rig accident, the injury being to his left arm. He got a cash settlement from the oil company because of the injury. In Louisiana at that time the maximum benefit for the loss of an arm was $10,000. He took his money and bought a Chevrolet, four-wheel drive Blazer.

At some time after this, while he was at home and an old buddy was visiting him, they decided to do a little spot-lighting.

The game warden lived nearby, about a mile or two away.

The Hunter and his buddy took the Blazer and headed for the woods. He had rigged up an old automobile headlight as a spotlight. This meant they had to wire it directly to the battery. Once they reached the area where they wanted to hunt, they hooked the light up.

If you know how a Chevrolet Blazer is built, the fenders are smooth and not much of a place to sit on and nothing to hold on to. I am not real sure if he even could rest his feet on the front bumper.

The Hunter got up on the fender, holding the light in one hand and his shotgun in the other. I do not know how he managed this, because he had very little use of his left hand and arm. His buddy was driving.

They found an old logging road to ease along on and the Hunter was shining his improvised spotlight around through the woods, watching for shining deer eyes.

Everything was going according to their plan, but they had seen no deer.

As they approached a large oak tree by which the old logging road ran, a dreaded figure stepped out from behind the tree, into the headlights of the Blazer. As soon as his buddy saw the man, who was the Game Warden, he slammed on his brakes. The Blazer stopped, Snow did not.

The Hunter landed at the feet of the Game Warden, shotgun, spotting light and all. The Game Warden said, "I've got you this time."

The Hunter got to his feet, ignoring the Game Warden, turned and they both listened as his buddy drove the Blazer backward through the woods. He had managed to turn the vehicle around and kept driving away from the scene of the crime. They listened until the noise stopped, noise of crashing saplings, small trees, treetops and etc.

The Hunter told the Game Warden, "That was my Blazer."

The Game Warden said, "I know. Let's go."

The Hunter was carried into town and booked. After a couple of days, he made bail and went looking for his Blazer. The trail was pretty easy to follow. He found where his buddy had run it off into a large drainage ditch.

He could not find his buddy. He learned later that his buddy had walked out of the woods, hitch-hiked a ride to the coast and caught a ride in a copter out to the oil rig where he worked. I know the Hunter would not reveal who had been with him, so his buddy did not get arrested.

He managed to get his Blazer back to his house. I do not know how much damage was done to it, but I feel it was extensive.

The Hunter and the Game Warden had an on-going contest and I am sure this episode did not cure him from hunting out of season, or spotlighting. He was just hard to catch.

In another story I tell of how the Hunter died. He was what I call a "oner" which means, one of a kind.

# A MUG SHOT IN THE MAYOR'S RACE

A campaign for the mayor's office in the City of Pasadena has always been interesting, to say the least.

Apparently, there has been, and maybe still is, two political factions in Pasadena. These factions have battled it out over the years for the job of mayor.

I always tried to stay clear of these fights, because I did not need any more enemies.

There was a very popular political person in our city who was very successful in his political campaigns.

At one time he was on the City Council. This man had a teaching degree, had been a police officer and finally got his law degree. Needless to say, he managed to make some political enemies.

At one time, I believe he was in between terms serving the city, it was alleged that he hit a woman and she filed on him for aggravated assault. He was duly arrested, booked, fingerprinted and his picture taken. I do not know what happened to the charges against him. I truly believe that this incident was a set-up to get him mugged and printed as having a police record

At a later date, he decided to run for the office of the mayor. It was a dirty campaign. All interested parties knew it was going to be a tight race. I do not remember who the other candidate was.

During this campaign, I was Superintendent of Identification and Records. I received a call from a certain ranking officer asking for copies of the "rap" sheet and mug shot of the above described candidate, who had been arrested. I made the copies as had been requested, duly noting on the rap sheet to whom the copies were being delivered.

A day or so later I was surprised to learn that copies of these items had been distributed all over Pasadena.

Now, I do not know who actually distributed those items. All I knew at the time was the officer to whom I gave them.

The candidate who had the items distributed against him won the election.

I believe to this day that he thought I was the person who distributed them. Later, when I had the opportunity to talk to him, I told him it was not me who was responsible. I gave him the name of the officer to whom I had given the items.

This man was a good friend of mine. He has passed on, now, and the City of Pasadena has lost a fine citizen.

# A REMARKABLE COINCIDENCE

About 1947 or 1948 after our two older brothers left for greener pastures, my younger brother Pete and I had to fend for ourselves. I was working here and there to make a little money, but Pete was unemployed. Pete had been injured in a schoolyard accident and was permanently disabled.

We had "inherited" our brothers" yellow 1939 Oldsmobile, which the two of them bought when they returned home from the War.

The fact that we had a car and a little gas money meant there was always a few guys hanging around ready to go with us. It really did not matter to them where we were going, they just wanted to go along.;

One day we were busy standing on the street corner at the main intersection in Jena, said intersection controlled by Jena's only traffic light. I do not remember who all was helping us stand around. We got ready to head on toward home for the day, figuring we had done all we could on that street corner.

As we moved toward our vehicle, we were joined by one of the group, a boy named Doyle Wright, who asked if he could go with us. We told him we were going home, but that did not deter him. He requested permission to spend the night with us. We could think of no reason why he could not, so the three of us boarded the yellow streak and headed for home in a cloud of dust. (The main road to our home was graveled.)

I had worked for a time for the taxi company there in Jena and had acquired an old revolver, which I carried with me on my taxi trips. At the time, I was about nineteen years of age.

When our friend found out I had that gun he suggested we go rabbit hunting. After supper, we went into the woods behind our house in search of a rabbit to slaughter. I managed to shoot at a couple, but missed.

The friend and Pete tried their luck, but without results. I believe we fired a total of six shots, which were all the cartridges I had.

Returning to the house we sat around awhile talking until it got bedtime, and we all went to bed. I do not remember what, if anything, Papa and Mama said about us bringing this stranger home with us. He was about our age and I guess they figured, "why not?"

The next day we drove back into Jena and went our separate ways. This individual left us and we resumed our spots at the favorite corner. There was a drug store on the corner with a soda fountain in it, when we had some money to use. We stood around with some others of the same vocation, watching people and traffic.

Whenever we saw a sheriff's unit, we rarely observed who was in it. We really did not want to attract the attention of the deputy driving it, so we usually studiously ignored it.

A sheriff's unit pulled up to the traffic light and stopped to wait for the green light. Then we saw someone in the rear seat waving at us. We looked closely and lo-and-behold our overnight guest was the person waving at us from the sheriff's unit.

We stared at him and then we stared at one another in disbelief. Now what in tarnation was he doing riding around in the back seat with a deputy sheriff?

We never saw him again. However, we did find out he was being hunted by the sheriff's office while he was spending the night with us. That foxy devil!

He was a border-line juvenile, I suppose. I had no idea how old he was at the time. Anyway, the sheriff had been looking for him high and low.

It seems that he had been living somewhere in Texas with his sister. He decided to travel home to Jena. I guess he was not inclined to hitch-hike like Pete and I did a lot. He stole a car and headed back to Louisiana. It is possible he did not want to hitch-hike because he might have been wanted by the Texas authorities.

Somewhere along the way toward Louisiana, he ran into a gas pump at a service station, broke the pump off and started a fire.

Where he left the stolen car was never revealed, or how the police determined he was the one who stole it.

Fast forward, to the early 1970's.

We were living in Red Bluff Terrace at the time and I had been on the police department since 1954. I had attained the rank of captain.

A new family had moved in kind of across the street from us.

At this point I want to mention some advice the older police officers gave us new guys when we were hired. They told us it was not a good idea to become too friendly with our neighbors, because we might be called upon to arrest them.

So, when this family moved in, I did not rush across the street with open arms to welcome them to the neighborhood.

I did subsequently learn their last name. There was the parents and three children; a teenage girl, a teenage boy and a young boy about six or seven.

The teenage boy was about the same age as our youngest son, Jeffrey. I thought nothing about it when I observed them hanging around together.

Most of the time during this period, I wore my police uniform to work.

I began to notice whenever I came home, the teenage boy would disappear. If he and Jeff were out front when I drove up, they would go to the back yard. When I went out back, they would go back to the front. Now, I did not fall off the turnip truck recently, as the saying goes. This activity aroused my curiosity. I knew that Jeff was not avoiding me. It was the other lad. I finally got Jeff to tell me his first name. At my first opportunity, I inquired of this lad at the juvenile division. When I told them the young fellow's name, they knew him well. I wanted to know for what. They said, auto theft, burglary, thefts, you name it. I was also told he had been to Gatesville several times. Gatesville at the time was where serious juvenile offenders were sent by the Juvenile Court.

The juvenile officer wanted to know why I asked and I told him the guy was hanging around with my son Jeff.

Break that up right away, he said. This guy is bad medicine and Jeff should not be associating with him.

We found out that was easier said than done. Jeff, by then was better than six feet tall, hardheaded and stubborn.

One Labor Day weekend, Nettie and I decided to take a short trip to San Antonio. Jeff had a job and requested permission to stay home and work. So, Nettie, Michael, Amy and I went to San Antonio without him.

I gave Jeff strict instructions about letting anyone in our house while we were gone. He promised he would let no one in the house. We told him it was okay to entertain his friends on the front porch, but not, under any circumstances were they to go into the house and he agreed.

We enjoyed our trip and returned Monday evening. The first thing I noticed was one of my handguns was missing. I never locked my weapons up. Our sons were trained to keep their hands off them unless they had my permission. The missing weapon was a little .25 caliber semi-automatic which had been on the shelf in our bedroom closet.

Jeff insisted that no one had been in the house. What probably transpired, the boy's sister kept Jeff distracted while he entered the house.

I made a report to the police department and listed this young man as a suspect.

I talked the Juvenile Officer again and was told they were already looking for him on an auto theft charge.

A day or so later, the Juvenile Officer called me to advise he had recovered my gun.

They had arrested the suspect in the stolen car. When the officer got the car theft cleared up, he asked the suspect, "Where is Mr. Smith's gun?"

The answer, "My old man has it."

Question, "What is he doing with it?"

Answer, "He took it away from me."

Question, "Why did he take it away from you?"

Answer, "I was trying to shoot him with it."

I discovered I was also missing a compact tape recorder that Nettie had given me for Christmas. It was recovered from the suspect's sister's bedroom. I had a pretty important tape in the recorder, but it was never recovered.

Nettie and I got our business straight with our son Jeffrey.

The boy was sent back to Gatesville. That left the teenage girl there. She was four or five years older than Jeff and she took her brother's place hanging around with Jeff.

I decided to have a talk with the girl's father about this situation with Jeff and his daughter. This girl did not go to school and would call Jeff at all hours of the day and night. I could not leave our phone off the hook, because I was on call. Talking to Jeff did no good. I tried to talk to the girl when she called, but she was usually drunk or pilled up and would not listen to me.

During the course of my conversation with the girl's father, he asked where we were from and I told him I was from Jena, Louisiana and Nettie was from Pineville, Louisiana. He said his wife was from Jena! I asked for her maiden name and he told me it was Wright. He said the family lived about halfway between Jena and Midway, Louisiana, which was not far. When I realized where these people lived, it dawned on me who they were. I asked if his wife had a brother named Doyle and he said yes!!

What a remarkable coincidence!

Then I realized that the young man at Gatesville had a good teacher, his uncle.

I remembered we never removed the keys from that yellow Oldsmobile. Unknowingly, we had invited a car thief into our home. We were fortunate he did not sneak out during the night, steal the Oldsmobile and light out for parts unknown, to avoid being arrested by the LaSalle Parish Sheriff's Department.

# YOUR LOCAL SUPERMARKET
## FOOD AND DRUGS

We had our favorite supermarket where we shopped regularly for our food. I will not name the supermarket specifically, because there are other supermarkets that were guilty of the same thing.

There is in our society a concerted effort to keep children off drugs. You have, "Just say no to drugs;" the DARE program and others.

One day, as we drove up to our favorite supermarket, for the first time I really saw their sign for the first time, which read, Your Local Supermarket, Food and Drugs.

I thought, now that is something. I could visualize young Johnny with his mother and father driving up to the store and Johnny asking them, "If drugs are illegal, then why is this store selling them?"

Once inside I located the manager and identified myself as a retired police officer. I brought up the subject of the supermarket chain's sign, as indicated above. He listened politely and thanked me for bringing this to his attention.

I thought no more about it until one day I drove by the supermarket and noticed the big sign on the front of the store had been changed to, Your Local Supermarket, Food and Pharmacy.

I do not know if my input resulted in this change of policy by this big supermarket chain, but I like to think it was. Maybe they had other complaints about it. At any rate they made the right decision and changed the signs on all their stores.

# THE "DRAFT" OR THE U. S. NAVY

One day in September 1950, I went into Nick's Café in Jena, Louisiana to get something to drink. Sitting at the counter was Duane Hooter. I had gone to school with him.

We passed the time of day, as the saying goes, and I learned he was about to leave town. I asked him where he was going and told me he was going in the U. S, Army. I wanted to know why he joined the Army and he said he did not join, he was drafted!

Drafted!! I did not know men were still being drafted into the Army. After all, World War II had been over for some five years. Wait a second, now. I asked him how old he was and learned he was the same age as me.

I sat there musing, losing interest in the cold drink I had bought. Maybe I was about to be drafted. He said you better find out. I walked to the Court House and contacted the Selective Service Clerk. My inquiry was answered with a yes; my notice was in the outgoing basket to be mailed that very day.

I asked the lady to hold the notice for a day, because I was going to Alexandria, Louisiana to enlist in the U. S. Navy. She agreed, but for only one day.

The next day I caught a ride to Alexandria and enlisted in the U. S. Navy. I learned later that my draft notice arrived at my parent's home the next day. Papa took the notice and returned it to the clerk, telling her I had enlisted in the Navy.

Following my enlistment in the Navy, I was shipped to New Orleans, Louisiana for processing. During this time I learned there was a war going on in a place named Korea.

I, and several other men, were there about a week. We were sworn in and all the paper work completed. We were told we were going to San Diego, California for boot camp training. The Navy man in charge gave me the package of orders and told me I was in charge of that group and I was to deliver them and myself to the U. S, Naval Training Center in San Diego, California.

I had never been in charge of anything in my life. What was I to do with this bunch of strangers. Some were from Louisiana and some were from Mississippi

For some three days and nights we traveled by rail towards California. We stopped for a little while at Kinder, Louisiana. I was tired out and was asleep. I found out later that my brother Pete had driven Papa and Mama to Kinder to see me before I traveled on to California. I knew nothing about it. They did not try to find me on the train and I missed telling them goodbye.

Those men I was in charge of ate, drank, partied and chased women all the way to California. Fortunately we all got there safely

I arrived at the U. S. Naval Training Center in San Diego, California, where I completed boot camp training. That was quite an experience for me.

I will tell of one embarrassing incident while was in training.

Jet engines for aircraft had been developed and some of those aircraft were stationed across the bay from the Training Center. Occasionally those aircraft would fly right over our training area.

We were on the parade ground listening to the company commander, Chief Petty Officer, lecture us about Navy rules and regulations. We were at Parade Rest. While in this position, with eyes straight ahead, we were not to move a muscle.

I was one of the tallest in my company. One of those jet aircraft zoomed right over our heads with a powerful lot of noise. I could not resist. I quickly looked up to get a glimpse of the airplane. That Chief Petty Officer apparently was looking right at me when I moved my head.

He screamed at the top of his voice, "YOU! Yes YOU!" I knew he was yelling at me and I kept looking straight ahead. Off that podium he came. He stopped directly in front of me, still yelling at the top of his voice. He berated me up and down and allowed as how if I wanted to look at the airplanes, he would help me. He brought me to attention and marched me out of the group and ordered me to lie down on my back.

Now, he said you can look at all the planes. He proceeded to march the company around and around me while I lay there, mortified out of my mind.

After he got tired of that he ordered me back into the ranks and we continued about our business of learning about the U. S. Navy.

I successfully completed boot training in the latter part of November 1950. All the other swabs got their orders and were gone. Mine were not immediately forthcoming. I cooled my heels at the USNTC through December. I missed going home for Christmas. After the first of the year, 1951, I finally received my orders. I was assigned to the Legal Office at the U. S. Naval Air Station at North Island, there in San Diego Bay.

# THE PASADENA POLICE ACADEMY

My date of employment with the Pasadena Police Department was November 17, 1954.

We were told we would be going through a school. They called it the Pasadena Police Academy. It was a school designed for training new police officers, and man, was I knew.

The City of Pasadena furnished me two suits of khaki outfits, a matching brown jacket, a police cap, a sam-browne outfit, which was a wide belt, holster for my pistol, and a shoulder strap. We were also furnished a set of handcuffs, a "slapper" (in lieu of a billy club) and a cartridge holder for our extra ammunition.

We were told we would have to buy our own weapon. Revolvers were the required weapon at the time. I did not have a weapon and I did not have the money to purchase one. Not to worry, they said. I could borrow the money from the City Credit Union. I did not know what a credit union was, but if I could borrow some money from it to buy my weapon, I would do so. I had to join the Credit Union first. That cost five dollars. I think the five dollars was included in the loan for the weapon. The weapon I needed was a .38 caliber revolver and it cost some $47.00, if I remember right. After negotiating the loan from the credit union, I went to the local Oshman's Store and bought a .38 caliber Smith and Wesson revolver, brand new and a box of ammo.

The academy started and there were a total of nine men in the school. Besides myself, there was Donald J. Blake, William C. Calvert, Jr., Roy L. Evans, Jr., Garland H. Hilborn, Jr., John F. Burdwood, Jr., Elvis D. Richardson, Donald L. Turner, and Cecil C. Burkhalter.

Burkhalter had been hired earlier and was already working, but the Chief of Police decided to include him in the Police Academy.

Of course we had all taken the City of Pasadena Civil Service Test. The City Council authorized eight additional men for the police department.

The Civil Service Test Scores were as follows:

| | |
|---|---|
| William Herbert Smith | 100% |
| Donald J. Blake | 93% |
| William C. Calvert, Jr. | 92% |
| Roy L. Evans, Jr. | 89% |
| Garland G. Hilborn, Jr. | 89% |
| John F. Burdwood, Jr. | 88% |
| Elvis D. Richardson | 83% |
| Donald L. Turner | 82% |

We were all appointed to the position of Probationary Patrolman in the Pasadena Police Department.

The academy was ready to start. All the instructors were already working for the Police Department or the City, except for an FBI agent, L. W. "Woody" Dishongh.

The FBI agent was our Range Officer. He taught us the basics of shooting a revolver, and he was very good. We spent a full week on the pistol range, learning how to shoot. I had shot a pistol a few times, some in the U. S. Navy. In the Navy we had to shoot a .45 caliber semi-automatic and I did not do very well with it.

The other three weeks were all classroom work. We were taught how to write reports, even how to hold our flashlight and clipboard while writing tickets. We were shown how to direct traffic in an intersection and/or around the scene of a collision. We were taught how to take notes. We were taught a lot about traffic laws, city ordinances and so forth. I do not remember being instructed on how to conduct ourselves while testifying in a court of law.

We did not have any physical training, no martial arts training or anything like that.

After four weeks of training, we graduated and were ready for the streets.

I found out that "Woody" had been keeping score on the pistol shooting and Roy L. Evans came in first with a score of 92 and I was second with a score of 90.

Vareece Berry announced there would be a shoot-off between me and Roy Evans to determine who was "Top Gun". I do not remember how many shots we fired, but we were being timed. I beat Roy out and became the top marksman of the police department.

# City of PASADENA

**THE INDUSTRIAL CITY OF THE SOUTHWEST**

CITY HALL • PASADENA, TEXAS • TELEPHONE GRand 2-4341

CERTIFICATION                    November 15, 1954

    Mayor Clyde T. Gary
    City of Pasadena, Texas
    Dear Sir:

        In response to the requisition from the Police Department for eight Probationary Patrolmen, the names of the following applicants are hereby certified to you for appointment to the position of Probationary Patrolmen.

| Name | Score |
|---|---|
| William Herbert Smith | 100 % |
| Donald Joseph Blake | 93 |
| William Chester Calvert Jr | 92 |
| Roy L. Evans Jr | 89 |
| Garland H. Hilborn Jr | 89 |
| John F. Burdwood Jr | 88 |
| Elvis David Richardson | 83 |
| Arthur D. Zachary | 83 |
| Donald L. Turner | 82 |
| Byron D. Horn | 81 |

                              Yours Truly,

                              Firemens and Policemens
                              Civil Service Commission
                              M. F. Jackson
                              Director

*City of Pasadena Certification List*

# City of PASADENA

### THE INDUSTRIAL CITY OF THE SOUTHWEST

CITY HALL • PASADENA, TEXAS • TELEPHONE GRand 2-4341

CLYDE T. GARY
MAYOR
PASADENA, TEXAS

APPOINTMENT

November 16, 1954

Firemen's and Policemen's Civil Service Commission
Pasadena, Texas

Gentlemen:

In response to the certification, the following persons are appointed, as probationary patrolmen, effective Nov. 19, 1954.

(17)

William Herbert Smith
Donald Joseph Blake
William Chester Calvert Jr
Roy L. Evans Jr
Garland H. Hilborn Jr
John F. Burwood Jr
Elvis David Ricardson
Donald L. Turner

yours very truly
Clyde T. Gary, Mayor

# "UNCLE" ERWIN

When I was just a young tad, after we moved from the country into Jena, Louisiana, I would see this elderly fellow standing on a street corner preaching. Now that was an unusual sight to me. Our family rarely went to church as I was growing up. As a matter of fact, I do not remember there being a church near where we lived, and we lived at a number of places.

I learned this old fellow's name was Erwin Reeves and Papa said he lived on the western edge of town. One day Papa pointed his house out to me. There was a rock wall along the front of his house. I would often see a large black and white spotted dog lying on that wall.

Time passed, and I got married, started a family, got a job in Pasadena, Texas and moved there. I was followed over to Texas by my brother Pete, Gus Austin and James Westbrooks.

After we all got located in Texas, we started going back to Louisiana to hunt deer. We got on a deer lease on Cocodrie Bayou south of Jonesville, Louisiana. The man who ran the lease was Al Reeves. I did not know it at the time, but Al's father was Erwin Reeves, the street corner preacher.

The first time Al brought his father down to the deer camp, and introduced him, I remembered who he was. By this time Mr. Reeves was in his eighties and we all began to call him Uncle Erwin.

Al Reeves said that his father had started this lease many years earlier. When Al and his father first started going to that location, to hunt, they had to build a rough lean-to for shelter. This lean-to was made of tree limbs. They would rake up big piles of leaves and gather moss to lie on at night. They would build a small fire right in front of the lean-to keep warm and roast meat over.

They always wore rubber hip-boots when they were hunting because most of the time the woods were very wet. When they decided to turn in to sleep, they would just pull those hip boots off and sleep in their clothes with their feet toward the fire. They would use a small tarpaulin for cover.

Al said one cold night they had gone to bed and a lost man wandered into their camp. He had seen their camp-fire through the woods. He had become lost while hunting. Al said that was an easy thing to do in that area because lots of hunters had gotten lost in there while hunting. Being a native of that area, it was usually up to him to find the lost hunters.

Anyway, Uncle Erwin invited the man to eat some roasted deer meat and bed down with them until morning. According to Al, the man crawled into their lean-to between him and his father. The man promptly went to sleep. He did not, however, remove his cold, rubber hip boots. It was a cold, rainy and wet night.

The next morning after eating, they sent the man on his way with directions on how to get out of the swamp.

Al was kind of irritated because the man had not removed those cold rubber hip boots before going to bed. He let his father know how he felt. Neither of the men was of the type to use profane language. However, Al did suggest to his father, whom he respected very much, quote "The next time you invite some scissor-bill to sleep with us, make him pull off those cold rubber boots.

One fall, Al and his father were down at the lease hunting. There were just the two of them. Uncle Erwin had his favorite place to sit while waiting for a glimpse of a deer. It was a section of an old cypress log. Apparently it was near a deer run, because he had shot a number of deer from this vantage point over the years.

In those days and in that area, deer hunting dogs were permitted. Al had several good deer hounds. Al usually rode a horse as he followed the dogs when they "jumped" a deer. The dogs would "bay" when they hit a hot scent of a deer. They would start trailing the deer, all the time "baying" continually.

On this day the hounds abruptly quit "baying" and started howling. Al wondered about that, because this was very unusual for the deer hounds.

He immediately went to the dogs and found them around his father, who was lying on the ground behind his cypress log. He had fallen off the log backward. He was dead.

Uncle Erwin was eighty-eight years of age and died of a heart attack, doing what he loved to do; hunting deer from his favorite stand there near Cocodrie Bayou.

The deer hounds found him and started howling to lead Al to his father.

# RAY WIGGINS

I do not remember where or when I first met Ray Wiggins. Ray lived near Enterprise, Louisiana. The road on which we lived was called the Aimwell Road. The Wiggins family lived somewhere out past us on what I presumed to be the Aimwell Road. I know that they traveled this road on their way to Jena, Louisiana. Regretfully, I never visited him at his home.

Ray did not go to school with me. He went to Enterprise High School.

Ray was big fellow, probably a couple of inches taller than me. I know he was much heavier than me. He was red-headed and very strong. He would have made a very good football player.

There were times when he would stop off at our house to visit me and my brother Pete.

I think Ray was the same age as me. Ray loved to wrestle. He always wanted to wrestle me. I was no fool, and I told him so. It would be no contest. One day when he challenged me and I refused, he offered to wrestle me and Pete both. It was still no contest. Pete and I both could not put him on the ground. He was just a big country-fed farm boy.

I found out later that he loved to fist-fight, also. The story around Jena was that one of the Jena toughs challenged him to a fight. No contest there either. They said he hit the guy one time and the first thing to hit the ground was the back of the guy's head.

While we were growing up, my brother Pete was involved in a school yard accident. He was in a game of chase and another boy tripped him, dislocating his left hip joint. The incident caused Pete to become permanently disabled.

When Ray found out that the boy had intentionally tripped Pete he wanted to whip the boy. I would not allow it. I am glad I did, because Ray would have really hurt the fellow. Sometimes I thought Ray did not know his own strength.

I kind of lost touch with Ray until one day I saw him in Jena and he was in an Army uniform. He had a car, so went cruising, looking for girls. I was always shy around girls, but Ray wasn't. It usually did not take him long to round up a couple of country girls for dates.

With him being in the Army, I really got out of touch with him. The Korean War started in 1950. Since Ray was already in the Army when the war started, I suppose he enlisted. I think I got to see him one time while we were both in the service.

I did not see Ray again until Nettie and I moved to Pasadena and I went to work for the Pasadena Police Department. He found out somehow where I was working and came to visit me. He was married, also, and was working for an insurance company out of Beaumont, Texas. He told me he was having marital problems and did not know how to resolve them.

While we were visiting, he told me a little about his tour of duty in Korea. He was on the front line during the worst part of this war. His platoon would often be out in the field searching for the enemy and they often clashed. He said there were times when they would take prisoners. They would question the prisoners and get valuable information from them. Being far in advance of their headquarters, they were in difficult situation with these prisoners. They did not have the manpower to send them back to headquarters, they could not retain them, and they could not release them. There was only one thing to do and that was to get rid of them. He said most of them they hung, some from bridges they came across.

I have talked with other veterans and learned that the enemy did the same thing with our guys they captured.

Ray got a battlefield commission to lieutenant. That meant that his lieutenant was killed in action. Ray was fortunate that he made it back to the states safely. A long time after I wrote this article I read in a recent issue of the Jena Times that Ray had been awarded the Bronze Star while he was fighting in Korea. He had never mentioned this to me.

I do not think Ray ever got over his experiences in Korea. I know that the war had affected him very much. After WWII when the soldiers came home and had problems coping, it was called "battle fatigue". There is another name for it now it is call Post Traumatic Stress syndrome (PTSD). That is probably what affected my friend Ray.

One day I got a call from a mutual acquaintance about Ray. I was told that Ray had committed suicide. I just could not believe it. It must have been a combination of his war experience and his marital problems.

I really like Ray Wiggins and I miss him a great deal.

# MY FRIEND, JOE MATHEWS

In the line of duty I became acquainted with a young man named Joe Mathews.

Joe got into some minor difficulties with the law, mostly traffic offenses'.

At some point in his early life he bought himself a motorcycle.

Joe was either kin to or acquainted with a family down the street from where we lived on Huntington Drive.

At our house at that time, Nettie and I used the front bedroom. One night after we had gone to bed a motorcycle rider came by the house and I mean to tell you he rattled the windows. As I listened to him as he proceeded on toward the East and the Deepwater Subdivision. He would wind it up every time he shifted gears and I had no trouble hearing him, even though he was probably a half a mile or more from where we were in the bedroom.

The next day Nettie and I were out in the front yard doing some yard work. I heard that motorcycle coming and it was still a good ways off. He was doing the same thing and I knew he was headed for Huntington Drive.

I asked Nettie to go in the house and get my police identification, which she did. Sure enough, I did not have long to wait. Here the rider came down Huntington Drive.

I walked out into the street and waited on him. He came to a stop and what do you know. It was Joe Mathews. Helmets were not required in those days. Joe was always very polite and always called me Mr. Smith.

I walked up to him, not needing to show him my ID because he recognized me right off, speaking to me and saying "Hello, Mr. Smith."

I said "Joe, when you came by here last night, you probably woke up the whole neighborhood." He did not deny it was him. He apologized by saying he was sorry and would not do it again. After talking a few minutes, I told him to be on his way.

A few years later, we bought a tandem wheel camping trailer and we needed a place to park it. I decided to put in an extra driveway on the opposite side of the house. One morning I was out there with a shovel digging up the yard, preparing for that driveway. Using a shovel is a lot of work. I knew because I became acquainted with one when I was a teenager.

This driveway had to be about thirty feet long and about eight feet wide and four inches deep. I had a long ways to go, using that shovel.

While I was working a pickup truck pulled up to the curb and Joe Mathews got out. When he found out what I was doing, he told me to sit down and rest and he would return in a little while.

Before long he came back pulling a trailer on which was a backhoe. He got that piece of equipment off the trailer and proceeded to dig out a nice strip to pour my new driveway. It took him only about thirty minutes. It would have taken me weeks and many blisters to do that, one shovel full at a time.

I thanked Joe profusely. He loaded his equipment and drove off.

I do not think I have seen Joe since that day and I do not know even if he is still alive.

If Joe is still alive, and I hope he is, I want everyone to know that I consider Joe Mathews my friend.

# HERMAN THE GERMAN

On my hunting trips to Louisiana I had occasion to meet a fellow by the name of Herman.

If I ever learned his last name, I have forgotten it. Herman was a German by birth, so we called him "Herman the German." He did not seem to mind.

Herman first came to the United States as a German prisoner of war. He was captured by U. S. soldiers in Europe, exact location and under what circumstances we did not know.

Herman liked it in the U. S. while he was here as a prisoner. He was subsequently sent back to Germany after the war ended. He then immigrated back to the U. S.

After coming back to the U. S., he met and married a local woman. I believe she was the daughter of "Uncle Erwin Reeves" mentioned in other parts of my memoirs.

He settled in that area of Louisiana where we went to deer-hunt.

The man who managed our deer lease owned a tract of land bordering on the highway. This was near a small community named Monterrey, Louisiana, Concordia Parish.

After his wife died, the owner of the property was killed in an automobile collision.

This tract was divided up between his children and/or other relatives. Herman's wife inherited a piece of the property, bordering on the highway.

Herman and his wife bought a nice mobile home to place on their property. The home was located some 75 yards from the highway. Not many people in those days, in that area, could afford concrete driveways.

They usually just drove off the highway, across a culvert and through the front yard to their home.

Herman and his wife had no concrete driveway so they had a bunch of muddy ruts in their front yard. Now, Herman did not like that, because he was always getting his truck stick, especially in the rainy season.

One year when we went to that area to hunt, their mobile home was pointed out to me. Herman had surfaced his driveway with tree saplings! All the way from the highway to his mobile home he had covered his driveway with small saplings. He had cut these, trimmed them and placed them neatly to form a reasonably hard surface to drive on. All the saplings were of uniform length and size. He must have put out a great deal of physical effort obtain these saplings from the nearby woods. Someone told me all he used was a hatchet.

Herman was innovative in his hunting, also. One time he was directed about where to locate in preparation for the hunting drive. He raked up a large pile of leaves, crawled under them to conceal himself and waited for a shot at a deer. I think he got one, too.

Herman was an interesting fellow. We could always depend upon him to pitch in and help out around the hunting camp.

# PART 3

# HOW I BECAME A POLICE IDENTIFICATION OFFICER

After graduating from the first Pasadena Police Academy, we all got our assignments. I was assigned to the Evening Shift, from 2:00 PM to 10:00 PM. The Shift Sergeant was one T. H. "Sonny" Grimmet. All of us Probationary Patrolmen were on six month's probation.

Right off the sergeant discovered I was a good typist. He kept assigning me typing jobs, like taking statements and affidavits. I told him that one of the other new officers was as good at typing as I was, but he was having none of it. He let me know right off that I was the person he wanted to do this type of work. I had no choice in the matter because I was on that six months' probation.

The department liked to have someone who typed be the radio dispatcher. I did not like the job of dispatching. The dispatcher had to keep track of all the patrol cars, dispatch them to various calls and log them in on a radio log sheet. He also was responsible for dispatching the fire department equipment. When a call came in about a fire, the dispatcher had to sound the sirens to call in the volunteer firemen. One siren was right near the police building and the other was near the City Maintenance Garage. There were different numbers for the different types of fires. For instance, for a grass fire the dispatcher sounded the siren twice, for a residence fire, it was three times and for a business fire it was four times.

The sirens were activated by using the police radio mike. There was a switch on the wall that had to be turned on to make the connection for the police mike. So, when a call came in and the fire sirens had to be activated, the switch was flipped and the button on the radio mike was pressed to sound the sirens. Right away the fire department trucks would begin checking in. If you forgot to turn the switch on the wall off, then you sounded the sirens every time you cleared a piece of equipment. It was very important that you remembered to turn that switch off. Now you had two radio logs to keep up with, because sometimes police units became involved when a fire occurred.

So much for dispatching. One day I was talking to the officer who was working in the Identification Division. His name was Joe Howerton. He began to tell me about identification work. It sounded fascinating. He told me if I was interested in that kind of work, I could enroll in a correspondence school to learn. I got the information from him and wrote the company to get their packet so I could see what it was all about. The company, The Institute of Applied Science in Chicago, Illinois, sent me the information.

I think the school cost a total of $120.00. I was told I could pay it out at $10.00 per month. It was a big decision for Nettie and me. I was making about $300.00 per month. I was already paying out that pistol, and we had a house payment and we needed a car.

This was before the era of Off-Duty Jobs for police officers. I went ahead and enrolled in the correspondence course. They sent me the first lesson. The program was, you studied the information they sent and then you took the test they included. If you are thinking an open book test in fingerprinting was easy, think again. After taking the test, I would mail it back in an envelope provided. Then I would get another lesson, and so on.

I did not tell anyone at the police department about this course in Identification I was taking.

There were some promotions within the Police Department. I heard later Joe Howerton was expecting a promotion and he did not get it and he resigned from the department. The chief transferred another officer to the Identification Division. He was Allen O. Laster.

One day while I was dispatching Officer Laster was conversing with me. He mentioned he was going away to a school called the FBI National Academy in Virginia. This academy was at least a couple of months long and another officer would be needed to take over the job of Identification Officer.

I figured that would be the time to reveal my studies in the Identification Field. I told Officer Laster that I was enrolled in The Institute Of Applied Science, studying police identification.

About two days later I was transferred to the Identification Division. I do not remember the date I was transferred. I did find out I was the Identification Division. I was to be the only officer in the division.

Allen Laster and I had about two weeks for him to show me all the ropes of doing this job. During that time I had to learn to process prisoners, take photographs of crime scenes, develop the photograph negatives and make photographic prints from these negatives. I had already learned to classify fingerprints from the lessons I had been taking.

The new job required a lot typing. I rolled three sets of fingerprints of each prisoner, one for our file, which I filled out at the processing, one for the Texas DPS and one for the FBI.

When I returned to my desk, I had to fill out the other two cards and prepare them for mailing. I also had to classify the departmental set of prints, and type a file card for it.

I was basically working seven days a week, with no overtime and no compensatory time. But I was glad to get away from that dispatching job. I was on call for crime scene work, which could mean anything from taking pictures, to taking a plaster mold of a shoe print or a tire print. I dusted a lot of crime scenes for latent fingerprints. Sometimes I was called out two different times in one night.

By this time Nettie and I had bought a used car for our use. On callouts I had to use my personal car to make the scenes. This meant I had to go to the station, get my equipment, drive to the scene, process the scene, drive back to the station and leave my equipment and then drive back home. I could not leave the camera in the car because of the possibility of it being stolen.

So, I was then a bona-fide Identification Officer and I learned a lot of new things.

*Herbert Smith in Identification Division at 112 N Walters Photo*

# PASADENA POLICE DEPARTMENT'S FIRST IDENTIFICATION VAN

Early on, having chosen identification as my field of endeavor, being transferred back to the Identification Division was always welcome.

I had been transferred out of and back in the Identification Division more than once.

In the early 1970's I found myself back in the Identification Division. By that time there was more than one officer there. There was a time in the 1950's when yours truly was the only identification officer. At the risk of repeating myself, I was required to process all the prisoners, which meant checking our files to ascertain prior records, if any, photographing their mug shots, rolling their fingerprints, typing of all the associated paper work, classifying the fingerprints, filing the fingerprint cards by the FPC number, developing the film of the mug shots, being on call for on-scene identification work, which included processing the scene for latent fingerprints, lifting any latent fingerprints and preserving them for evidence, photographing the scene if necessary, and any other crime scene work which might be needed. If a suspect was identified and we could get his or her fingerprints, I would compare the latents against the known prints. If a match was made I had to prepare the fingerprint evidence for presentation in court.

Since the Identification Division had no police unit assigned to it, I had to use my personal vehicle to make crime scenes. (I mentioned this to my insurance agent one day and he said "I did not hear that and do not repeat it in my hearing.")

*Herbert Smith*

I had been requesting a vehicle for the Identification Division for some time. My choice for a vehicle was a van. You can imagine my surprise when, in 1970, my request was granted. We were able to purchase a nice van for an identification vehicle. There were some other things which I requested which came through, also. We were able to buy a small gasoline powered generator, some flood lights, a vacuum cleaner, some traffic cones, and a nice crime-scene identification kit. We had shelves and cubicles installed in the van. We had a platform put on the roof and a ladder for access. This platform was for the Identification Officer to stand on to photograph the crime scene when that view-point was necessary. Of course the generator was for the flood lights in areas where the lighting was inadequate and of course to operate the vacuum cleaner. The vacuum cleaner was used to vacuum up hair, fibers and etc. which were trapped in a special filter designed for that purpose.

The fully equipped van was photographed for one of the Houston newspapers. I have included a copy of that photograph, the quality of which is not too good.

I am proud to say that this was accomplished on my watch as Superintendent of Identification and Records.

Nov 15, 1970

PASADENA POLICE'S FIRST I.D. VAN 11-15-70
EQUIPPED WITH:
A GENERATOR
VACUUM CLEANER WITH TRACE EVIDENCE FILTER
TRAFFIC CONE
CRIME SCENE PROCESSING KIT
CAMERA
ROOF PLATFORM FOR POLICE PHOTOGRAPHER
FLOOD LIGHTS FOR NIGHT WORK
EVIDENCE BAGS + LABELS
EQUIPMENT NECESSARY FOR TAKING
 PLASTER CASTS OF TIRE AND/OR FOOT-
 PRINTS

*Pasadena Police Departments First Identification Van Photo*

# PASADENA POLICE DEPARTMENT'S FIRST IDENTIFICATION "RAP" SHEET

I do not know exactly when I designed the "rap" sheet for the Identification Division. It had been my frustrated experience to try to keep a record of who all requested and received information from our identification files. In police work it is vital for the investigating officers to know who all else is requesting copies of arrest reports, mug shots and etc. Up until I decided to implement the rap sheet, it was a confused mess.

Fortunately, I was able to design the "rap" sheet and then was able to get the form added to the Police Departments long list of printed forms.

In another segment I told the story of how a copy of a mug shot got distributed around town during a mayor's race. The mug shot was of one of the candidates in the race. On the Rap Sheet a notation was made of the officer who requested the mug shot.

By the way the candidate of whom the mug shot was made won the mayor's race.

I am thankful for the fact the Rap Sheet was available for the notation to be made of who received the mug shot which was distributed around town during the election.

# EFFICIENCY RATINGS AND PROMOTIONS

In the early years at the Pasadena Police Department, promotions were regulated under a state civil service law, and I suppose they still are.

When promotional exams were given, three factors were considered: (1) Seniority; (2) Efficiency Rating and (3) the actual civil service test score. These factors were used to determine which person scored the highest. If the Chief of Police decided to by-pass the number one person, and the person by-passed decided to appeal, the chief had make his case before the Civil Service Board. The person still had the right to appeal his case even higher if he chose to do so.

I do not recall the numerical values considered in determining the final score. There was a maximum number for seniority. In other words, an officer could not score more than 100 total on a promotional civil service test.

Officers were rated every six months by their superiors for their efficiency.

Captains rated lieutenants, lieutenants rated sergeants and sergeants rated patrolmen.

It was not a good system. I worked under one ranking officer who gave every officer under his command an "Excellent." This was before the numerical system. I think the categories were "Poor, Fair, Good and Excellent." This supervisor's reasoning was that if an officer was less than excellent, he had no business being a police officer. I personally believe he just did not want to accept the responsibility of calling a spade a spade.

Needless to say, there were times when these efficiency ratings were challenged by the officer receiving a sub-standard score.

Every few years the efficiency rating system was revised or simply changed outright. The Civil Service Director usually did the changing. Believe me, none of the officers liked this system.

One year he designed a system in which scores in the various categories required using decimal figures. In other words, a score for an officer's appearance might be 75.075 or 76.99, etc.

I had one lieutenant whom I graded under this system. I believe this lieutenant lusted for the Chief of Police's position. He thought his efficiency rating meant a lot toward this goal.

On one rating period his score ended up one tenth of a point less than his previous one. I do not remember what, in particular, was the reason I graded him down in that one category. He became very irate and appealed his case to my superior, who backed me up.

Regrettably, the lieutenant never spoke to me again.

He should have known that appointments to the job of chief were mostly politics and his efficiency rating had very little bearing on the mayor's choice for Chief of Police.

I believe after I retired the efficiency rating system was completely did away with. These types of ratings grew to be more of a favoritism venue. A ranking officer could always give his favorite subordinate a high score.

# LISTENING TO DEPARTMENTAL 24 HOUR TAPES

Before the days of the Internal Affairs, complaints against certain police officers were investigated by the ranking officers in the division where they worked. This often required hours of listening to tape recordings.

When the police department moved from 112 N. Walters to the new location on Davis Street; a system of recordings were installed. There was an open microphone at the front desk, one in the city jail (booking desk) and the telephone lines to those places were wired to the 24 hour recorder.

I am not aware of any other microphones or any other lines being recorded. The telephone lines being recorded had a signal beeping device which warned the parties talking that the conversations were being recorded.

When a complaint was made which involved those locations, we had to determine as close as possible when the incident occurred. I do not recall how many recording channels there were on these tapes, but there were at least eight.

While I was Patrol Commander I had to help investigate a number of complaints involving these venues. The tape recorder was on a 24-hour basis. At or near midnight, every night, the night shift supervisor had to remove the old tape and install a fresh one. He then labeled the old one and stored it in the property vault. These tapes were kept for a certain length of time, the existing information on them was erased and the tape made ready to be used again.

There were times when a complaint was lodged on something that had been erased.

The playback device had a visual monitor which we could watch to try to pin-point the exact time and which channel the recording was on. It was a slow, time consuming task.

Many times I asked Lt. C. R. Holt to assist me in finding a specific recording on the tape. We knew which channel was which from experience. So, if the complaint came from the Booking Office we knew immediately which channel to monitor. The only thing, we could not tell, most of the time, exactly what time the incident occurred. This required us to listen to long periods of recordings of routine police business.

Sometimes we heard things recorded that we did not want to hear, things that would be grounds for a complaint. When we heard one of these things, I would look at Lt. Holt and he would look at me and we both would say, "I did not hear that."

Later, if a complaint came in involving one of those things we overheard, we would then have to go back and find it. We would verify these findings and make reports of the incidents. If the incident was serious and would involve further investigations, we would seal the tape and hold it.

Most of the time the complaints were minor and the situations would be disposed of routinely without further action.

Such was the burden on a poor old Patrol Captain's shoulders.

# ASSISTANT CHIEF OF POLICE
# CHARLES R. HOLT

Charles R. Holt was a graduate of the 7th Pasadena Police Academy in 1961.

Charlie is a native of Louisiana, having grown up around Leesville, Louisiana, where he graduated from high school.

He served in the United States Army and while in the Army he married the love of his life, Catherine.

Charlie and his family came to the Pasadena area after he was discharged from the U. S. Army. He worked initially with Houston Power and Light.

He learned that Pasadena was hiring police officers and he applied, graduated from the Academy and became a Pasadena Police Patrolman.

Charlie and I worked together many years at the Pasadena Police Department. Since we both hailed from Louisiana, we became good friends. We hunted deer together and later we did a lot of traveling together.

I learned Charlie is a very talented individual. He is a very good cook, he can play the guitar, the mandolin and the harmonica. He is now teaching himself to play the fiddle.

Charlie and I were on the Pasadena Police Combat Pistol Team and enjoyed competing in numerous pistol matches around the country.

Charlie told me he had four years of "shop" schooling while he was in high school. I think all of this schooling was in woodwork.

It is to be noted here that yours truly did not have one hour of "shop" classes in high school. I wish now that I had taken at least one class on woodwork.

Charlie is a very good finish carpenter. He did practically the entire pecan paneling in our new Monument Baptist Church. He did a fantastic job.

One of his hobbies was working on guns. He did two woodworking jobs for me. One was a fine set of mesquite pistol grips for my Model 19 duty weapon.

Another job he did for me was a walnut stock for my .243 caliber hunting rifle. He got all the parts of the rifle and built the rifle for me. He did an excellent job on that rifle stock, including the checkering. I still use that rifle and have taken many a deer with it. It is a beautiful piece of work!

Charlie was also very good at gun-smithing, which in this case was slicking up the action of pistols to make them easier to shoot.

Charlie had some unusual experiences at the Pasadena Police Department, just as I did and he could probably write some interesting stories from his career there.

One story I heard him tell was about an arrest he made one night. There was this woman who most of the officers were familiar with, because she was an alcoholic. She was not very big. I never arrested her, but I did have occasion to observe her at the police station. She was probably about four-foot ten or eleven and weighed no more than about 80 pounds. She was a very pretty woman, just very small.

Apparently, she was very popular at the various "watering holes" along Spencer Highway. She really had the appearance of a small, young girl, and sometimes she dressed as such.

On one such occasion, she became very drunk and ended up with a man who rented a small cabin near a hardware store on Shaver Street. There were several of these cabins which the owner rented out to single men, men who were also addicted to alcohol. In the case I am referring to, she spent the night with this one individual. He then passed her on to another of his friends. She ended up being passed back and forth for a week or more among these men. All they had to do was keep her drunk.

Fortunately, she was rescued by the landlord and he finally got her out of there.

Charlie arrested her one night. This woman had a vehicle and could drive. Charlie came upon this automobile which had run up against a fence. A quick check revealed the driver was behind the wheel, the motor was running and the driver was passed out.

The driver was this diminutive lady and she was completely nude. In those days the department had no female officers. Charlie cut the engine of the vehicle off, got the lady out of the car and placed her in his patrol unit. He proceeded to the Police Station with her. One Sergeant R. E. Rhodes was Shift Supervisor. This occurred at the Old Police Station at 112 North Walters.

Charlie got the lady out of the patrol unit, and, carrying her under one arm, he entered the lobby of the station. Sergeant Rhodes was standing in the lobby when Charlie walked in with this lady under his arm, with her posterior forward. Charlie said later he thought Sergeant Rhodes was going to faint. The sergeant did run for a blanket to cover the lady before they deposited her in the female jail cell.

Charlie retired in 1993, ten years after I did. We belong to the same church, we are both on the church kitchen committee and we do enjoy sitting around telling these many stories from our years with the Pasadena Police Department.

Charlie's last duty station at the Pasadena Police Department was in the position of Assistant Chief of Police, a position from which he retired in 1993.

# OFFICER SAM

Sometime in the 1960's the City of Pasadena started hiring civilian police dispatchers. Actually they were hired as prospective probationary patrolman. The idea was to get them on the payroll so they would not go somewhere else for employment. They were put through the routine background checks and would be ready when the next police academy started.

During this time a man by the name of Sam was hired and started out as a civilian dispatcher.

The Evening Shift Supervisor at that time was Captain D. T. Warren. I was the Evening Shift Sergeant. The captain and I often worked together in one unit.

The city was divided up into three patrol districts, one, two and three. The city covered a large area and had lots of streets. The city was also expanding rapidly and there were new streets being added all the time.

Sam had moved to Pasadena from up north and was not too familiar with the streets in Pasadena. It became apparent that he was having trouble dispatching units to addresses in their districts. Naturally, this confused the officers involved and resulted in Sam being warned by Captain Warren and myself about the problem.

Finally, we called Sam in to our office and told him he had a week to learn the streets so he could correctly assign the units. If he was not able to do that, he would be terminated.

In the Dispatcher's Office there was a wall map of the City of Pasadena. Sam got busy and determined what street was in each district. He then assigned a unit number alongside that street. When he obtained the address where a unit was needed, a glance at the map showed him what unit to assign. He could then correctly dispatch a unit to that location.

Sam was able to save his job by this very innovative method. When the next Police Academy started, Sam was ready. He went through the 10th Pasadena Police Academy in 1964.

Later on when I began to shoot competitively at pistol matches, I learned that Sam was a very good pistol shooter. He joined our Pasadena Police Pistol Team and became a regular competitor. He helped our team win several trophies.

While at his home one evening he started suffering chest pains. He drove himself to the emergency room, but they could not save him.

I liked Sam and enjoyed shooting with him on the team. Sam was a good Police Officer.

# THE MISSPELLED WORD

I learned right away after I went to work at the Pasadena Police Department that police officers are not the world's best spellers, nor do they have the best of penmanship.

I do not hold myself up as a champion speller, but I can usually spot misspelled common words.

Police officers have to write lots of reports. Some of these reports are read and transcribed by the Records Clerks, preparing the report for submission to the District Attorney's office for possible trial.

I assure you, some of the handwritten reports submitted were almost unreadable. The clerks were constantly requesting help in deciphering what the police officer was trying to say in his report.

Back then, when I had to check reports as the Shift Supervisor, I was amazed at the sorry penmanship and spelling used by the officers. These officers had at least a G. E. D. or a high school education. Later, toward the end of my career, we had some college graduates as patrol officers, and, believe me, some were not much better.

In the 1950's all the reports were collected at the front/dispatcher's desk, held together with a clamp. When the head Records Clerk came in she would pick up all the reports and take them to the Records Division for later typing, indexing and etc.

I will mention here that there was usually one officer who always arrived early, before the head Records Clerk and he would go through these reports. There were times when it would be revealed that he would pull a report to take directly to the Chief of Police. I don't know if he just wanted to be the first to tell the chief about an incident, or what. Maybe he was just a tattle-tale.

Getting back to my story about the misspelled word, apparently, the head clerk became upset by some of the spelling in the police reports. I personally knew that a lot of words were misspelled, but I generally ignored most of them if the report made sense.

The clerk took it upon herself to draft up a memo from the chief's office regarding misspelled words. The memo was the standard "From" and "To," but without the chief's signature.

She posted the memo on the bulletin board in the lobby of the police station where all the officers could read it. Like a good police patrolman, I, too, read the memo. Well, guess what? In the memo a word was misspelled. To make matters worse, the word she misspelled was the word "misspelled." She spelled it with only one "s." She spelled it "mispelled." This is not a difficult word, but a common word, but one that is easily spelled wrong.

All things being equal, I figured that if a person was going to issue a memo about spelling, then all the words in the memo should be spelled right.

I could not help myself. I had to do something! I obtained a pencil with red lead and when no one was watching, I drew a circle around this word that was spelled wrong.

Well, things got exciting, the very idea of some wise guy doing something like that to the chief's memo. Quite a large investigation ensued but the culprit was never found. They never found out who drew the red circle around that misspelled word in the chief's memo.

# THE CONFESSION

While I was assigned to the Detective Division we received a complaint from the parents of a young girl that a man had molested her.

The girl was about twelve or thirteen years old. She had stayed home from school that day. Both of her parents worked and the girl was alone in the house.

The house was a new one and the family had not lived there long. As is the case with many new houses, the new owners find various things that need fixing. The builder advised them to make a list of the things and he would have his repairman take care of them.

I got in touch with the builder and got him to identify the man who had gone to the house that day.

I located the man and carried him to the police station for questioning. He was an older man.

When I told him what he was accused of, and he vehemently denied the accusations.

I kept talking to him, trying to gain his trust. I described exactly what the young girl had put in her statement, including the accusation that he had performed oral sex on her.

He immediately became irate and loudly denied doing that. His words were to this effect, "Yeah, I put my hand on her just like she said, but I did not put my mouth on her." I asked him if he would give me a statement to that effect and he agreed. I put him under oath, warned him statutorily, and took his statement where he confessed that he did indeed put his hand on the girl's private parts. He did, however, deny the oral sex charge.

All I needed was his confession that he had put his hand on her private parts. I really did not need the other allegation to make the case.

He was filed on for sexual molestation of a minor female.

I do not recall the final outcome of the case. I was never subpoenaed to testify in the case, so I presume he pleaded guilty.

I had a solid case on him.

# THE SLEEPING DEFENDANT

I was minding my own business at home one Saturday evening when the infernal telephone rang,

I was on call and was right in the middle of barbequing some steaks.

The nature of the call was a shooting at a residence. I drove to the station, gathered up my equipment, obtained the address and drove to the crime scene.

It was a nice neighborhood, with brick homes and so forth. (Nettie and I still lived in a frame house, in a lower middle class neighborhood)

The detectives were already there and were waiting on me. I was joined at the scene by one of my identification officers. He, also, was off duty. He had heard the broadcast on his scanner and decided to lend me a hand, and I was glad to see him.

It so happened that we both knew the shooter. He was a local attorney. The man he shot was his brother-in-law.

The attorney and his wife, along with his brother-in-law and his wife were partying. The suspect was drunk. He stated to the detectives that he and his brother-in-law got into a heated argument, over what, was never clear. He went to his bedroom, got his pistol and shot his brother-in-law, killing him. He readily admitted the deed.

The detectives arrested him and carted him off to jail where he gave them a full confession (I guess). Anyway, they filed murder charges on him. My assistant and I completed our job at the crime scene, by taking pictures, marking and bagging evidence and so forth.

Months later I received a subpoena to testify in this case.

That was about forty years ago, so I guess the story can now be told.

A couple of things happened while I was testifying which deserve mentioning.

As a prosecution witness it was my duty to identify all the physical evidence in the case that my assistant and I had processed.

I had no problem with any of the items until the prosecutor handed me the spent hull from the murder weapon. I took the item and looked it over and for the life of me I could not remember marking and tagging that hull. The jury, the judge, the prosecutor, the defense attorney and courtroom full of spectators were all waiting and watching me. I finally looked inside the hull and observed the initial "W" scratched inside the hull. I pointed this out to the prosecutor and the jury and said there is my initial "W" for my first name which is William, which is scratched inside the hull. The defense had no questions and the item was accepted as a piece of evidence. If my memory serves me correctly, my assistant was not subpoenaed to the trial.

I want to point out, it is the prosecutor's duty to get every piece of evidence identified and who is to testify about that piece of evidence before the trial starts. There is an old piece of advice circulated among lawyers, "Never ask a witness a question that you do not know the answer to."

While I was on the stand answering other questions, I became aware of soft noise emanating from the vicinity of the defense's table. I looked around and noticed that the jury, the judge and the prosecutor were all looking at the defendant.

The defendant was slumped down in his chair with his head drooping and he was asleep. It was his snoring that everyone heard. It did not seem to bother his lawyer, who was a former mayor of Pasadena and an old working buddy from their previous place of employment at a well-known local refinery.

Neither did it bother the judge because we proceeded on with the trial and ignored the snoring defendant.

The jury found the defendant guilty and he was sentenced to life in prison. He probably got caught up on his sleep while in prison. I heard later that he had died in prison.

By the time I got home the barbeque was cold, what was left of it.

In those days there was no overtime and no compensatory time off.

I was, however, thankful that I had a steady job so I could take care of my family.

# "OL' LUCKY SMITTY"

This was probably in 1956 or 1957. I know that John Middleton was a rookie police officer, still wearing the rookie uniform which was khakis.

We were working the Night Shift under the supervision of Sergeant G. W. Wornick.

The sergeant was always telling us young cops (I was about 28 or 29 at the time), what to be on the lookout for when we out there on patrol.

The sergeant had a thing about safe burglars stealing safes from business places. As you well know, safes tend to very compact and very heavy. Should one be loaded in the trunk of an automobile, that vehicle is going to be riding very low in the rear.

One night I was partnered with John A. Middleton, a rookie. (Now days, I would be called a "Field Training Officer.)

We were on patrol in District Number 1, which then was the business district of Pasadena. We observed an old Mercury automobile proceeding West on what was then called Sterling Street. The rear end of that vehicle was nearly dragging the pavement. Falling in behind the car, we observed also that the license plate was bent to where it could not be read. We stopped the vehicle.

There were two men in the vehicle. We got them out and obtained their identification. (Yes, in those days, people actually did carry identification) These men were wet up to their knees like they had been wading water somewhere.. When asked about this, they stated they had been wading through some tall grass and weeds.

We checked the vehicle further and discovered they had removed the rear seat cushions of the car. In that open space they had loaded several large coils of copper wire.

We took them to the Police Station, about three blocks away, and turned them over to Sergeant Wornick. This was before the era of Detective Divisions at our department.

The wiring had the name of a large electric company in LaPorte, Texas.

Under questioning, the men revealed they had stolen the wire from this electric company, and this was their second load. They had parked their old Mercury on a street behind the company, waded through the high grass and weeds, climbed the fence and managed to get this wiring over the fence and out to their car, thus the wet trousers.

The company and the LaPorte authorities were routinely notified and took the wire and the suspects off our hands.

We were following the advice from Sergeant Wornick by being on the lookout for vehicles like this.

Sergeant Wornick's comment was "Ol' Lucky Smitty."

# THE ANONYMOUS NEIGHBOR

A man and his wife arrived at the police station one day and reported that the wife had been getting numerous anonymous, and suggestive, telephone calls.

The caller was very persistent in his desire to meet the lady.

The detective (not me) took all the information for his report. The lady called later and said the man was continuing to call. The calls were always while the husband was not at home.

The detective decided to set a trap for this individual.

He told the lady to change her tactics and enter into a dialogue with the guy.

Once they got into their conversation, she was to lead him on and make him think he was making headway.

The lady was keeping the detective updated on the progress of the situation.

She called one day and told the detective she was ready to make a date with the guy.

The detective told her he would call her back with specific instructions.

The detective found a place for the meeting where he could hide nearby without being seen.

The next time the guy called the lady set up the meeting, following the instructions of the detective.

The following information was derived from the detective's report. The detective stationed himself at the appointed place and time, concealed from where the meeting was to be. He reported that shortly the lady arrived in her car and stopped on the side of the road. It was in an isolated area with little or no traffic. In a few minutes another car pulled up near the lady's car. A man got out and approached her vehicle. He began a conversation with the lady. The detective stated, to his surprise, the trunk lid of the lady's car opened up and her husband got out. The detective had not planned on this. As soon as the suspect saw the husband he made a dash for his car and the fight was on. The suspect finally got halfway back into his car and the husband slammed the car door on the guy's leg. The detective said he ambled on over to where the activity was occurring, taking his time. In the meantime the husband was taking care of business.

The detective arrested the bruised and battered suspect for making anonymous telephone calls and harassing the lady.

He did not file on the husband for assault on the suspect.

Surprise ending! The suspect was their next door neighbor.

I think the neighbor moved away rather suddenly.

# THE FROZEN CHICKEN

I was not involved in this case, but because it was very unusual, I decided to tell about it.

In the 1000 block of East Shaw in what was then known as the Corrigan Shopping Center, there was a supermarket. This was a very busy shopping center during this time (in the 1950's).

One of our police patrol units was proceeding west on East Shaw Street, actually headed toward the old police station. Traveling ahead of them was another vehicle. At about that location there is a bridge over Little Vince Bayou. When that car passed over the bridge the driver was seen to throw something over his car into the bayou.

The patrol unit was occupied by a senior officer and a probationary patrolman.

The officers decided to stop the car and find out what he threw into the bayou.

They stopped the car and questioned the driver. He was asked what the object he threw into the bayou was. He told them it was a frozen chicken. Why did he throw away a frozen chicken? He said he had just bought and decided he did not want it, so he threw it away. That did not sound right to the officers so they got him out of the car and obtained his identification.

The officers told him to open the trunk of his car. There they found treasure –trove of evidence.

They arrested him and took him to the police station. He was littering.

In the trunk of his car they found boxes of blank social security cards, boxes of blank driver's licenses from various states, boxes of blank checks from various companies and banks, a check stamping machine, a typewriter, and quite a bit of money.

During the next several days with further questioning, it was revealed that he was wanted in nearly every state in the union. In the police world he was called "The Traveler."

He told the officers he had bought the frozen chicken at a supermarket. It was his method of operation to make a small purchase and present a forged check as payment, receiving the change in cash. He had necessary identification to get his forged payroll check cashed; all of his identification was fake also. Once he got his cash, he did not need the frozen chicken, so he tossed it in the bayou, not knowing there was a police unit right behind him.

There were "holds" placed on him by literally dozens of law enforcement agencies across the country. The FBI got involved because he had been crossing state lines to do his crooked business.

I do not know where he ended up in prison, or how much time he got. I heard later that he had died in prison.

I wonder if he stayed awake at night wondering why he decided to buy that frozen chicken.

# THE "CANDYMAN"

When the Pasadena Kiwanis Club chartered a new club, I became a charter member. The new club was named The Pasadena 'Good Morning' Kiwanis Club and it met at 7:00 AM for breakfast.

The Kiwanis Clubs are civic organizations made up of local business people whose goal is to raise funds for charitable purposes.

When we elected officers of the club, a new member was elected treasurer.

I did not know this man prior to his association with the Kiwanis Club.

To raise money our club voted to sell Washington Delicious apples. It was a wise choice. We really sold a lot of Washington apples.

Being around this man during our meetings and activities, I had him figured as kind of a weird individual. We discovered later that he was embezzling funds from our treasury. He was not reelected to that post.

The club was meeting one day for a rare evening meal at an upscale restaurant in Pasadena. Before we began to eat, this man was asked to bless the food. He stood up and proceeded to pray in a loud voice, which could be heard all over the restaurant. Other patrons were staring at our table. He was an unusual individual.

At this time I was Superintendent of Identification and Records at the Police Department.

Halloween night rolled around and everyone was talking trick or treats. A call came in to the dispatcher that a child had eaten some Halloween candy that had made him sick. He was rushed to the hospital where he died.

Our detectives were at work at once to determine where the little boy had received the candy. Since the boy's little sister had been with him tricking or treating, her bag of candy was seized as a safety precaution.

The detectives learned from the boy's mother that he had eaten some candy called "Pixie Sticks." When the detectives examined the sister's bag of candy, they discovered some "Pixie Sticks." It is my understanding that this candy is a kind of powdered material and a favorite of kids.

A close inspection of the "Pixie Sticks" found in the sister's bag revealed they had been opened and refastened with a stapler. The person doing the re-stapling did not place the new staples in the same holes, so it could be readily determined that the packages had been tampered with.

The examination in a laboratory revealed that the poison cyanide was in the candy which was in the little girl's bag. The little girl was also an intended victim.

The investigation revealed that the fellow who had been a member of our club had obtained some cyanide prior to this incident

My identification officers were involved in the case and were keeping me informed of the progress of their work.

In this working area of the Police Department, the Identification and Records department was adjacent to the Detective Division with a counter separating the two.

A couple of days after Halloween, I had an occasion to view the activity in the Detective Division. Up to this time I had no information about the children and/or their parents. When I looked over in the Detective Division I observed this fellow sitting at a detective's desk. Of course I recognized him right away and I asked my head records clerk if she knew why this individual was being questioned by the detective. She advised me that he was the father of the little boy who had died from poisoned Halloween candy.

I responded, "Well, do not be surprised if it is revealed that he is the one who did it."

About an hour later the clerk came into my office with a strange look on her face and I asked what the matter was. She said "I can't believe what you said about that man. The detectives have just determined that he is the one who poisoned his son." This did not surprise me because I had always had that feeling about him.

This man was subsequently charged with capital murder of his son and attempted capital murder of his little daughter. The motive was insurance money

Apparently his wife had taken the children to a nearby neighborhood to trick or treat. The man knew where they would be doing this. Dressed in a dark costume, he found a vacant house and waited in the shadows for the children to approach. He then placed the poisoned "Pixie Sticks" in their Halloween candy bags.

He was tried for capital murder, found guilty and sentenced to die. He was subsequently executed for the murder of his son.

A note of interest in this case, I learned later that in the church services he gave the Eulogy and sang a solo for his son.

The lead detective in this case was William D. Lanier and he did an outstanding job in closing it.

# THE STEAK RUSTLERS

This case started with a call from the Deer Park, Texas Police Department.

The caller said a man had driven to their department with a dead man in the car.

The dead man had been shot and apparently it had happened in Pasadena.

I was not one of the investigating officers. However, I was called out to type the statements and affidavits of those involved.

I typed the statement of the man who did the shooting. The man had pasture on Red Bluff Road where he kept a small herd of cattle. All of this area was undeveloped back then.

He did not routinely stay on the property. He lived elsewhere. He began to notice some yearlings missing from his herd. He had an old camping trailer which he moved to the property. He planned to stay in it and try to find out what was happening to his cattle.

On the night in question, he had turned the lights out in his trailer and lay down to sleep. His little trailer was not far from the road. Things got quiet and then he heard a car stop out on the road. He got up, put on his trousers and boots. He got his rifle and eased outside. He got outside just in time to hear a small caliber gun go off from near the car. He could see the car sitting on the side of the road facing South. He yelled at whoever it was and ran out to the road. He could see two men and they jumped into the car, made a quick u-turn and headed North on Red Bluff. He quickly kneeled down and fired one shot at the fleeing vehicle. He could not say exactly how far the car was when he fired his rifle. The car did not stop, so he went on back to his trailer and went to sleep. The next morning he found one of his yearlings dead from a gunshot wound.

The investigating officers determined that the dead man was a young white male. There was adequate identification on the body. The body was lying in the back of a five-passenger coupe, from which the rear seat had been removed. The right front passenger seat had also been removed. White "butcher" paper had been placed on the floor of the vehicle.

The driver stated the paper was to keep the blood of the beef off the floorboard. Little did he know that the paper would keep the blood of his partner off the floorboard.

The driver of the car stated this was not the first beef they had taken. The two of them would ease out to the pasture late at night, pick out a yearling they could easily handle, shoot it with their .22 caliber rifle, climb the fence and drag it back to the road. They would load it in the coupe and leave. I do not recall where he said they went to butcher it. They took the animals strictly for food.

Both of the men were in the U. S. Air Force, stationed at Ellington Field near Pasadena.

While I was taking this man's statement about shooting the yearling, butchering it and eating the meat, he literally drooled while talking about it. I got the idea the two had been raised in an environment where there was not much meat to eat.

On this night they were doing the same thing. One of them shot the animal and about that time they heard someone yelled at them. They jumped in the car, the driver made a quick u-turn and they headed away from the scene. He did hear a gunshot as he drove off. Since there was no passenger seat in the vehicle, the other fellow squatted down behind the driver's seat.

He did not know his partner had been hit until he pulled over to check him because he was lying down in the back of the car. He did not know exactly where he was. He started driving around until he came to the Deer Park area. He found the Deer Park Police Station and pulled in there.

The dead man suffered a terrible wound in his back. The projectile, a .306 caliber, had traveled through the metal of the trunk of the car before hitting the victim.

It was really a sad case. I had occasion to take the statement from the shooter. The fact that he had killed a man over a yearling beef nearly drove the man crazy. He said that if the men had asked him he would have given them a yearling to butcher.

As far as I know, the cattleman was no-billed by the Harris County Grand Jury. The air force man was turned over to the military authorities at Ellington Air Force Base.

I did hear later that the shooter had to seek professional counseling over his part in this incident.

# THE TOILET SEAT THIEF

The Pasadena Police Department had some strange cases, kind of like the fishing pole thief.

This one was the case of the toilet seat thief.

During the late 1950's there were many new houses being built in the sub-division known as Red Bluff Terrace. These were plain frame houses suitable for middle income people. They were nice houses. I know, because Nettie and I bought one in 1955. Most were three bedrooms, one bath and one –car garage types of houses.

The builder of these houses was always reporting thefts of building materials from their job sights. These were not pre-fab houses. They were framed up and built from the concrete slab up by carpenters. One type of theft was quite unusual and occurred only from houses where the plumbing was already installed.

The items being stolen were toilet seats.

In those days the toilet seats were made exclusively of wood, in two pieces and were painted white.

Officers were alerted concerning all these thefts, in particular the toilet seats. Not too long hence, the thief was caught. He was in possession of a recently stolen toilet seat which he had taken from a house under construction.

I had no personal part in this case. I became aware of it by reading the arrest report and it was of interest to me because the incident was in the neighborhood where I lived. Also, the perpetrator was one of my neighbors.

The man readily admitted to being the culprit stealing the toilet seats.

He told the officers that he'd had to buy several seats for his toilet because his wife kept breaking them when she sat on them, After they broke they tended to pinch her when she sat on them. This began to get expensive so he resorted to stealing those from the new houses.

The man was gainfully employed and had a good reputation in the neighborhood, up until this incident.

I do not know the disposition of this case. I feel certain he was filed on for theft.

The thefts of toilet seats ceased; just another strange case in the annals of the Pasadena Police Department.

# THE STOLEN PAYROLL CHECK

I probably have mentioned that I worked off duty for the First Pasadena State Bank in Pasadena. This covered about 20 years.

The best problem the bank had was traffic congestion around the ten drive-in windows. On payday Fridays it was a madhouse and I always needed several officers to assist me with the traffic. The bank was doing a lot of business.

During the week the traffic would slack off with just an occasional vehicle using the drive-in windows. At these times my job was more in the line of security, than directing traffic.

One day I was standing near the drive-in windows observing things. I saw this black man come walking up from the East parking lot. The lobby of the bank was closed, but the drive-ins were open. The man proceeded along past the back doors of the bank like he was headed for Tatar Street. Tatar Street ran North and South just West of the bank. He nodded at me as he walked along.

When he got to the end of sidewalk, he cut over and came back along the North side of the drive-in windows. I was standing on the "island" where the drive-in windows were. The man approached me and asked me how to get to the Champion Paper Company. That company was at the very north edge of Pasadena near the Washburn Tunnel. I told him how best to travel to that location and he thanked me.

The next thing he did was to step up to one of the drive-in windows and was taken care of by one of the tellers. It was not often that the tellers had pedestrian customers.

After completing his business, the man walked on back toward the East parking lot. When he got to the edge of the parking lot he threw

## In My Lifetime

both arms into the air as if he had won something. I immediately became suspicious and asked the teller the nature of the man's business. The teller told me he had cashed a payroll check. I asked her what company and she said Champion Paper.

I immediately ran from the teller's booth toward the parking lot. I saw the man get into an old Ford automobile on the passenger side. The car left traveling through the parking lot of the business to the East of the bank. It was too far away for me to get a license number, but I did get a pretty good description of it.

I went back to the teller and told her the check was probably stolen and why I thought so.

A couple of weeks later she told me that I was right; the check had turned out to be stolen from Champion Paper.

The next day I contacted Robert Windle who was working the check detail. I told him what had happened and described he car to him.

Sometime later he called me and told me he had cleared the case up by arresting two men.

With the description of the car, Robert went to the Champion Paper parking lot and found a car fitting that description. He ran a check on the vehicle and got the owner's name. The owner of the car worked for Champion Paper.

He waited at the gate until the man got off work and took him into custody. At the police station he asked the man who was with him at the First Pasadena State Bank on the date in question. He told Robert he had carried a friend there to cash a check.

Robert got this man's name and address and picked him up.

I do not know if Robert charged the driver of the vehicle. I figured the man was in on it because of the signal the check casher sent to the driver that he was successful in cashing the stolen check.

The Champion Paper Company did not have a very good system of getting payroll checks to their employees. The checks were placed in the time-card slots along with the time-cards. Just about anyone could walk along there and slip a payroll check out without being seen

The reason this man walked up to the bank was because the driver did not want the teller to make a note of his vehicle license number.

The suspect made two errors in judgment. He felt he had to approach me to ask about the location of Champion Paper. If he had merely walked back out to the car in the parking lot and left with his cohort, I would never have been suspicious. When he threw up his arms in a victory signal, I knew something was up.

Robert Windle did an excellent job clearing that case up with only a description of the car.

# THE "WANNA-BE" PUBLIC SERVICE DIRECTOR

During my 28 plus years of service at the Pasadena Police Department, I had occasion to become acquainted with only two Civil Service Directors.

The first one was in office when I went to work there and administered the first Civil Service test ever given by the City of Pasadena. I was in that group which took that test.

The second one was the gentleman who administers a number of promotional tests within the police department, of which I took several.

There might have been other directors in the interim, I do not, however, remember them.

I as I said, this gentleman was director during the times when I was taking the Civil Service promotional tests. He was responsible for setting the tests up, hiring a person to create the test questions and listing the study materials from which the questions were to be taken. He also set the study time between sign up time and the actual test. He also had to notify all eligible officers of the pending promotional test and all the particulars thereof.

The Civil Service Director also directs the hiring, training and testing of Probationary Police Officers in accordance with the Texas Commission on Law Enforcement Standards and Education.

This tale has to do with this gentleman's attempt to fraudulently obtain certification from the Pasadena Police Academy as a police officer.

There was a fine young man who was a Pasadena Police Officer for several years. He resigned to go to work for the Texas Commission on

Law Enforcement Standards and Education in Austin, Texas. He was a graduate of one of our local high schools and also a college graduate.

One day this young man called from Austin and talked to the Director of the Pasadena Police Academy. He wanted to verify that a certain individual did indeed complete a course of training in our police academy.. Apparently this person had submitted all the proper paperwork to the Commission in an attempt to be certified as a police officer. In order for a person to be certified as a police officer, he or she has to successfully complete a sixteen week intensive training course.

The person submitting this paperwork was none other than our City of Pasadena Civil Service Director. Of course he had never completed the sixteen week course. He might have visited a class a few times, but that was all.

All this happened after I had retired and I am not sure of the subsequent details. However, I heard the State Commission forwarded all the information to the Harris County District Attorney's Office, along with a formal complaint.

I do not know what happened after that. I did hear that he resigned his job with the city.

This man was in charge of testing high-ranking police officials in our department to determine who would fill certain vacancies.

It was rumored around the police department and city hall that this individual had ideas of lobbying the City Council to create the position of Public Safety Director. This position would put him over both the police department and the fire department. In order for him to be over the police department he had to be certified as a police officer. That is why he tried to become certified illegally. Well, it never worked out for him.

We, two other captains and myself, learned that he and the other directors were ignoring the Civil Service Law on how to grade the promotional tests. That is another story.

# TWO FIREARM MISFIRES IN SUCCESSION

There was an armed robbery at a supermarket at the corner of Strawberry Road and Pasadena Boulevard.

I was not involved in this case, but I did read the reports of the incident.

The suspects fled the scene in an automobile and a witness got a good description and direction of travel. A police unit was real close. He spotted the vehicle and gave chase. The suspects headed into a nearby residential area in an effort to elude the police unit. The driver, for whatever reason, drove between two houses and into the back yard of one of the houses.

The suspects jumped out and fled on foot, followed immediately by the officers, also on foot.

A back-up officer arrived at the scene in the back yard where the suspect's car was abandoned to check it out. After searching the inside, he got the trunk key to unlock the trunk. He unlocked the trunk and raised the trunk lid, whereupon he discovered a third suspect hiding in the trunk. This individual was armed and he aimed his weapon at the officer and pulled the trigger. The gun snapped a misfire. The officer, in the meantime, had drawn his weapon and attempted to fire it at the suspect before he had a chance to try again. Here is where it gets weird. When the officer pulled the trigger on his weapon, his gun also misfired. Not having time to correct the situation, the officer struck the suspect on the head with his weapon and disabled him.

He removed the suspect from the trunk and handcuffed him.

What was this suspect doing in the trunk of the car? When did he get in the trunk? No one knew right then.

Two misfires within seconds from two different weapons? What are the odds of that happening?

The other two suspects were apprehended and the case cleared.

# UNIFORM CAPS, HOLSTERS AND I. D. CARDS

I was always coming up with new ideas. I guess the problem was, I could not keep my mouth shut about them.

A case in point, back in the 1960"s (I think). The Texas State Legislature passed laws concerning training and education of all law enforcement officers in the state of Texas. The state created "The Texas Commission on Law Enforcement Standards and Education."

All Texas Law Enforcement Officers were required to attend certified training schools to attain their certification under the new law. Some officers were "grandfathered" because of their experience and time in service.

This was no problem for me because I was a graduate of the Pasadena Police Training Academy and had certain other training in various law enforcement fields. I was also a graduate of the Institute of Applied Science.

Under the new law, there were three levels of certification: basic, intermediate and advanced.

With my background and training, I qualified for the level of "Advanced."

During my stint as Patrol Commander, I often had to confer with my superior, who had been one of my former patrol officers while I was Sergeant.

One day while we were discussing the Texas Commission on Law Enforcement Standards and Education, I casually mentioned that it would be great if all officers statewide had an identification card to carry with them to show their level of certification. The inspector whole heartedly agreed, stating it was a great idea and nothing else was said about it and I kind of forgot about it.

Several months later I was surprised and exasperated when an announcement was made that all officers would be issued identification cards showing their level of certification, same being promulgated by the Texas Commission on Law Enforcement Standards and Education.

I learned that the inspector was congratulated for coming up with this great idea.

In another session I broached the subject of the uniform holsters the officers were required to wear, including me.

I never liked the type the city issued. It had a long shank which caused the weapon to be carried low with the butt sticking out. This caused the weapon to hit things, scarring the grips and sometimes knocking the rear sight out of line. It also tended to hang under the arm rests of the swivel chairs used in the offices. Some of the older officers, I am sure, liked these because it made them appear to "Quick-draw" specialists.

I obtained and began wearing a "high-rise" holster with my uniform. This type of holster put the butt of the weapon high up and under my elbow. With the old type of holster, in a crowd the officer had to keep his hand on the butt of the weapon to prevent someone from pulling from his holster. With the high rise, the officer just kept his elbow on the butt of the weapon.

It was not long before the department began to phase out the old style holsters and issue the high rise holsters.

Another thing that evolved along that line was the type of weapons the officers carried on duty. There was a lot of publicity about law enforcement officers being "out-gunned" by the crooks. Some crooks were using semi-automatic handguns and they did carry more rounds than the standard six-shot revolver. Some of the semi-autos could hold up to fourteen rounds of ammo.

I never habitually carried a semi-automatic handgun while in uniform. I always relied on my trusty Smith and Wesson model 19, .357 magnum. I had a .45 caliber semi-automatic which I occasionally carried off-duty. My preference, of course, was the model 19 S& W, which I was well acquainted with.

When the department began requiring officers to qualify with the weapon they carried, I qualified with the model 19, the .45 caliber semi, and .38 caliber chief's special. When I qualified, I had to do it once a year. I understand now it is twice a year.

When the department had to start hiring women, a lot of adjustments had to be made in our training academy, which I will not go into here

Someone in the police administration decreed that the women's uniform head cover would be similar to that worn by the school crossing guards. The women police officers hated those hats. They felt like everyone believed they were school crossing guards. I was Patrol Commander when this controversy arose. I came down on the side of the uniformed police women. I went to my Inspector with the recommendation that the women be allowed to wear the same kind of head covering as the men and he agreed. It was done. I got many thanks from the women officers on patrol.

Another thing I tried to get changed was the type of head cover the men had to wear. The old type of hat was heavy, cumbersome and caused the head to sweat profusely. It is a good type of head covering to wear with a class A uniform, but does not do well in everyday patrol work.

For regular patrol I recommended a nice baseball type of cap with a shoulder patch sewed on the front. These would be inexpensive and could be tossed around in the unit without damaging them.

My inspector agreed and said he would think about it.

One day we attended a meeting of the Pasadena Police Officers Association. The president of the association spent a great deal of time bad-mouthing the kind of head covering the officers had to wear.

The bottom line was, this made the inspector mad and after the meeting he told me to forget the baseball cap type of head covering, so much for that idea.

These days a person rarely sees a police officer wearing any kind of head covering. I do not like that. I have seen officers working traffic in the rain with no head covering. If they have some type of rain gear that has no identifying badge or police insignia on it, they could be mistaken for some citizen out in the middle of the intersection trying to direct traffic. It is dangerous!

Of course, these days a lot of the officers pay a lot of attention to how their hair looks. I did not have much hair when I signed on with this outfit, and I have lost a lot since then.

My hair was not very high on my priority list when it came to making a living.

# YOUR BUDGET REQUEST WAS DENIED

As Captain and Superintendent of Identification and Records, it was my responsibility to work up the budget requests for my division.

I would confer with my identification officers and records clerks to get some input from them about the needs of the division. They were always enthusiastic and cooperative in this important endeavor, believing they played a part in the activities of the division, which they did. We would work up a very good and reasonable list of things we felt the division needed. Included in our budget request was the approximate monetary cost of these things.

It was my understanding that every division was doing the same. I also presumed that our individual requests would be incorporated in the overall police department budget. I had this vision of the City Council reviewing my individual budget requests.

How wrong I was! I later found out (after I retired) that the police department submitted its overall budget request (the approximate dollar amount) to the city department working up the city budget.

Upon receipt of the budget request from this city department, the city council would either vote for or against the budget, trimming it sometimes, or adding to it sometimes, as it saw fit. The council never saw individual department requests, unless a department head appeared before the council for a hearing on a special request.

In other words, the police department's budget would become part of the overall city budget. The department would be notified of the specific amount of its approved budget. It was then up to the police department to decide where to spend the money it was granted in the city budget.

In this case it was an Inspector who handled the police department budget requests. It was he who decided who got what. Talk about power!!

After the council set the budget and passed on it, I would give the inspector a week or two, then put in my requests for the things we had asked for in the Identification and Records Division. I would go stand in front of his desk with a look of expectation on my face (I suppose.) He kept the budget paper work in one of his desk drawers, locked up. While I waited, he would carefully unlock that special drawer, and without removing anything from it, leaf through a few pages for a minute or two, lock the drawer and say "Smith, your requests were denied." And that was it

On another occasion, in 1980, I submitted a request for certain things which I felt we needed real bad. After the new budget year went into effect, I submitted some memorandums requesting the items I had asked for in the new budget. Following this article is a facsimile of the answer I received from a Deputy Chief.

When you read the Deputy Chief's memo, remember, he had sole authority on who got what. As to the "third alternative" he never put it into effect.

In his reference to the vehicles, when he referred to shop number 7861, I believe that was the vehicle assigned to me. So, in the event my unit was being used by the call out ID officer, and I was needed on the scene, I would have to drive my personal vehicle to the crime scene. Before the ID division was assigned a unit, I did drive my personal car to many crime scenes. I was told later by my insurance man that my insurance would have probably been cancelled if the company had been aware that I was driving it to crime scenes, especially scenes of major accidents.

Of course it was many years later that I learned that this ranking officer was the sole judge about what division got what at the police department. I remember on one occasion I wanted approval to join up with the Houston Police Department and the Harris County Sheriff's Department on a system to identify suspects without having to call around on the telephone. The system required a CRT, a dedicated line and a keyboard. I requested this system in my budget. When I went to this officer and asked about it he stated that the Mayor had approved only two of the items. What a crock, I learned later. The Mayor had nothing to do with rejecting any part of it. I really felt irritated toward the Mayor about that and I wished later that I had asked him about it.

I really hate to be suspicious about these things, but I can't help but feel that favoritism played a big part in this officer granting request.

By the way, it was popularly known around the police department that this officer always tried to end the budget year with a surplus. He could then go to city hall and brag about saving the city money.

I wonder if he knew that the city comptroller would merely transfer our surplus to some other city department to spend before the end of the budget year.

All things being equal, a surplus at the end of the budget year usually meant a cut in the budget for that department for the following year.

# PASADENA POLICE DEPARTMENT
## INTER-OFFICE CORRESPONDENCE

---

---oOo---

TO: W. H. SMITH, Captain
FROM: Deputy Chief
SUBJECT: Excessive Memorandums

Prior to 10:30 AM this date you delivered to my office four memorandums from you or officers under your command. I have discussed these memorandums with Chief Wornick.

I will address myself first to the two memos reference to ID vehicles.

For your information, we requested replacement of twenty-seven vehicles and eleven additional vehicles in the 1980-81 budget. The amount of funds earmarked for police department vehicles may get us seventeen or eighteen new replacements and no additional. On a priority basis none of the new vehicles will go to the identification division. Furthermore, it is uncertain at this time if any vehicle being replaced will be worth reassigning.

So that you will not have to rely on Sgt. Crawford's memory, the following information on shop unit 7375 was copied from garage repair orders.

February 6, 1980 - Alternator replaced.
March 4, 1980 - Battery charged and electric system checked. (Battery was run down, inside light found left on, radio found left on, voltage regulator wires unplugged.)
March 12, 1980 - Left front vent window frame replaced.
May 13, 1980 - New A/C compressor, dryer accumulator, 4 cans Freon and a belt installed.
May 15, 1980 - New left side door window regulator installed.
May 16, 1980 - Serviced. Brakes, oil, filter, etc.
July 9, 1980 - Two new batteries installed.

With all of this work and new parts having been done to this vehicle, if the A/C is still not working and the window will not roll up and it still leaks, the fault is that of the operator. The vehicle should have been returned to the city garage until the repairs were satisfactorily completed.

I will forward a copy of all the ailments listed in Sgt. Crawford's memo to motor pool personnel and the city garage. You will then have the unit 7375 released to motor pool personnel for transporting to the city garage for repairs. There will be no vehicle available for check out to the ID division. However, shop unit 7861 shall be made available while 7375 is being repaired. When repairs to unit 7375 are completed, we will concentrate on unit 7259.

In reference to your memo request for equipment and remodeling, etc.

We may be able to obtain a file cabinet in the near future. How high the quality will be determined by the limited funds available.

No funds appropriated in the budget for your additional straight chair, but we will attempt to provide you with another chair soon.

Drapes for your office are denied.

No funds were appropriated in the budget for the three small desks, besides there will be room for the large desks when construction is completed.

No funds were appropriated in the budget for any improvements to the building or completing any unfinished portion.

The IBM copiers are on a lease purchase contract. I am checking the possibility and probability of replacing one of the two we have.

I have informed you orally at least two times recently that you will not be assigned another patrol officer in the very near future. The situation has not changed but consideration will be given your request at a later date. Further inquiry will not be necessary.

Your request for "stand by" or "call pay" for ID personnel is again denied. If the personnel affected by our "on call" policy are that displeased or unhappy with it, they have several alternatives.

We will consider their request for a transfer back to patrol division. (I believe all of them requested the ID job.)

They may resign from the classified service and become a civilian. (Civilian city employees are the only city employee authorized to draw stand by pay.)

The third alternative to which I have given considerable thought is as follows:

I will supervise the Records and ID from 7;00 AM to 5:00 PM, you will supervise them from 6:00 PM to 2:00 AM. The two sergeants and four patrolmen will be spread over the three normal shifts, with their days off staggered in order to have one man on duty most of the 24 hours of most of the days. This will not only cut down on reasons for stand by time, but also overtime. You will be notified if this alternative is adopted.

We have no control over the amount of shift differential pay. This is controlled by personnel policy by pay schedule. I have informed you previously that I started working on Bill Storey over a year ago to get an increase in the shift differential pay. I suggested 20 cents for evenings and 40 cents for graveyard shift. But until the increase is adopted through City Hall, the shift differential will remain as it is.

G. W. Wornick
Chief of Police
/s/ Deputy Chief of Police

# THE FBI AGENT

The Pasadena Police Department had a very good working relationship with the Houston Officer of Federal Bureau of Investigation.

Several members of the Pasadena Police Department, including myself, are graduates of the FBI National Academy.

This academy was created by the Director of the FBI, J. Edgar Hoover. Its purpose is to train local ranking officers for administrative positions within their departments.

The fact that we have a good working relationship with that office does not preclude that office from investigating complaints of civil rights violations concerning Pasadena Police Officers.

The particular agent I am writing about shall remain nameless. I am sure by now he has either retired or passed on.

This agent was a strict adherent of the law and was expected to do his job. He was a friendly, yet slightly distant when dealing with the officers of our department. He kind of kept the officer at arm's length, as the saying goes.

When a complaint against one of our officers was received by the FBI that office would notify our chief of police. The officer usually had already presented his version of the incident in his written report. The chief would review the report to decide if there were grounds for sustaining the essence of the complaint. As a rule, the officer would be advised that the FBI would be investigating the incident. The officer would be ordered to cooperate fully with the investigating agent of the FBI, with the caution that the FBI agent could testify to any oral statements made by the officer during the interview.

The case in point did not include me, either as part of the incident or as a supervisor.

I was never investigated by the FBI for violation of any person's civil rights.

I do not know any of the details of this particular case, except it involved a complaint against one of the arresting officers, alleging police brutality.

This was before the days of the so-called Miranda Warnings. When I took a statement from an individual, I gave him the standard warning we used at that time about incriminating himself.

I do not know if the FBI agent warned the officer in this case, but he no doubt did, because the FBI agents were always very thorough.

When an individual made a complaint against an arresting officer, it was because he or she hoped to barter a deal from the district attorney's office for a lighter sentence or an outright dismissal of the case.

In this case the FBI agent questioned the officer extensively about the incident, all the time taking notes in his notebook. He got no admissions during this phase of the questioning. The agent finally folded up his notebook, placed it in his coat pocket. He engaged the officer in "small talk." He got up as if to leave, turned back and asked the officer, "Tell me what really happened out there?" The officer, his guard down, said, "I beat the stuffing out of him."

Bad news, he had forgotten the warning. The questioning was not over. He had just confessed orally to a Special Agent of the FBI. The officer realized too late that the agent could testify to what he had just said.

I do not know what subsequently happened to the officer about this complaint. I do know that from then on, all the Pasadena Police officers were very wary of this agent.

I do not fault the FBI agent. He was doing his job.

# KENNETH WAYNE CRAWFORD

Ken Crawford joined the Pasadena Police Department in 1963. He was a member of Pasadena Police Academy number nine.

I do not know how long Kenneth worked patrol, nor exactly when he was transferred to the Identification Division. His transfer to that division could have happened during one of my tours on patrol.

Kenneth was sent to certain schools to train him in the field of crime scene investigation. Kenneth was a hard worker and learned fast.

However, Kenneth's penmanship and spelling were atrocious.

Kenneth was also a confirmed cigarette smoker. I was sitting my office one day watching him at his desk classifying a set of fingerprints. He was trying to do that while smoking a cigarette. When a person classifies a set of fingerprints, he or she has to bend the head down low over the prints and examine the prints through a magnifying glass. Kenneth was having some trouble trying to do both at once.

I headed to the coffee pot to get me a cup of coffee and walked by his desk. He looked up and I told him, "Sergeant, don't let your job interfere with your smoking." All he did was just glare at me.

I decided to write this because of something a friend told me about Kenneth. I found out he was an "unsung hero."

Somewhere in Pasadena a construction crew was digging a large hole. I do not know if it was a pipeline or what. A construction worker was down in the hole working when a side of the hole caved in covering the man completely. I do not know how Kenneth got notified about the situation, or how come no other worker jumped into the hole to help the man. The friend who told me this said that Kenneth drove up in his patrol unit, exited the unit and ran to the hole. He immediately assessed the situation, pulled his gun belt and gun off, handed it to this friend to hold and jumped into the hole to rescue the trapped worker. He was able to get the man out from under the dirt and out of the hole before more dirt caved in on him.

This was news to me. Kenneth had never mentioned it to me and neither did anyone else. If I had known about it I would have nominated him for an award.

Kenneth, in my eyes, was a genuine hero.

We lost Kenneth later to a massive heart attack. I think he was only 42 years of age.

# YOU HAVE GOT TO BE KIDDING ME, RIGHT?

Prior to going in the U. S. Navy, I was never asked to produce my birth certificate. Since the subject never came up, I was not concerned about it. I do not remember the police department asking me about a birth certificate.

Sometime after I went to work for the police department I decided I had better make an effort to obtain a birth certificate.

Letters to the Louisiana Bureau of Vital Statistics revealed nothing under the name of William Herbert Smith. All my records so far were under that name; my school records and my navy records.

I did need, however, a birth certificate.

An inquiry of the Louisiana people resulted in instructions on how to obtain a Delayed Birth Certificate.

Following their instructions, I did just that. I had to get copies of my school records, my navy records, a copy of an insurance policy issued in my name and an affidavit from my mother.

I forwarded all this to the Louisiana Bureau of Vital Statistics and was given a Delayed Certificate of Birth with the name of William Herbert Smith. Now I was legal.

At some point early in my career I learned of a three month school for police supervisors conducted by the FBI. I knew of at least three Pasadena Police officials who had been to this school, known formally as the Federal Bureau of Investigation National Academy.

After I was promoted to captain, I decided to apply for this academy. I presented my written request to the Chief of Police in office at the time. I got no response. Not a yes, nor did I get a no.

Later, when another Chief of Police was appointed, I repeated my request. Still no response.

Over the next several years I submitted requests each time a new chief of police took office.

In 1972, a new Chief of Police was appointed. I had heard that that the FBI was now paying the expenses. I submitted my request again. This time it was approved!

The FBI sent me the paperwork to fill out. It consisted of a lengthy form requiring a ton of background information on me and my family. I had to list my parent's names, all my brothers and sisters names, addresses and so forth.

I knew a number of the FBI agents that worked out of the Houston Office, including the one assigned to investigate me.

One day this agent called me to update me on the progress of his investigation. The conversation went something like this:

Agent: Captain, your name is William Herbert Smith, right?

Me: Yes, sir, that is correct.

Agent: And your father's name was Henry Smith, right?

Me: That is correct.

Agent: And your mother's name was Versa Smith, right?

Me: That is right.

Agent: And you were the eighth child to be born of Henry and Versa.

Me: That is right.

Agent: Are you sitting down Captain?

Me. Yes, Sir, I am. (I figured this where I get the old rejection)

Agent: Well, Captain, we found the record of your birth, listing Henry and Versa as parents, but the name on the records at the Louisiana Bureau of Vital Statistics is not William Herbert Smith.

Me: Excuse me, Sir, what are you saying?

Agent: What I am saying is, the name of the boy born on November 12, 1928, your listed date of birth, was not named William Herbert Smith.

Agent: Are you sure you are sitting down?

Me: Yes, Sir, I am sitting down.

Agent: The name in the records in Louisiana is Alfred Emmuel Smith!

Me: You have got to be kidding me, right?

Agent: Nope.

Agent: Everything is fine with your application to attend the National Academy. This will present no problem. You are approved to attend the FBI National Academy in 1973. You will be getting official notification of approval and particulars later on.

Me: Thank you, Sir!

My mind was in a whirl! Needless to say, I was dumbfounded. Where did Papa and Mama come up with that name? They already had one Al in the family, as in Alphonse, my oldest brother.

I realized one thing right away. I had to have a copy of that birth certificate to see for myself. I investigated and found out a copy cost $2.00. I sent the Louisiana Bureau of Vital Statistics a money order for that amount and signed the request A. E. Smith.

I got my copy. Sure enough, there it was, just like the FBI agent had told me. Everything on the document was correct, except the name of the baby!

I gave this situation a lot of thought, trying to figure out how this happened. Of course, both of my parents had passed on. Of my older brothers, none could tell me anything. Papa and Mama did not share family secrets with their kids.

The only Albert Emmanuel Smith that I had heard of was the one who had been governor of the State of New York, back in the 1920's. He had been in the news a lot back then because he was the first Catholic to run for President of the United States.

It suddenly dawned on me! I began to remember more of history, Alfred E. Smith v.

Herbert Hoover in the presidential election in the year of 1928, the year of my birth! There had to be a connection.

Of course, I can only surmise. There was no one I can go to for concrete information.

Al Smith was a Catholic, and Louisiana had, and still has, a large population of Catholics. I figured that Al Smith carried Louisiana in the election. Back then there were no telephones or other types of electronic media. I feel that Papa and Mama were sure that Al Smith was going to be president. That included the doctor who delivered me.

Along about that time, I was born. I surmise that the doctor asked Papa what name to put on the birth certificate and Papa probably told him he wanted to name me after the president, who had just been elected. I was born at home, so the doctor waited until later to fill out the necessary papers. He thought Al Smith was going to be president, so he put Alfred Emmanuel Smith on the paperwork.

Well, in December, when Electoral College met, it elected Herbert Hoover president.

I've got kind of a mental picture of this scenario:

Mama: Henry, what did you tell the doctor this baby's name was going to be?

Papa: I told the doctor I wanted him to be named after the president.

Mama: Who is the president?

Papa: Herbert Hoover.

Mama, picking me up off the floor: Come little Herbert, I have to change your diaper.

*Copy of State of Louisiana Certificate of Birth November 11 1928*

# A PMS MURDER?

The call came in from a man who was at work. He told the dispatcher that something was wrong at his home in Pasadena and to get a police unit out there right away. He said he would meet the police there.

The first officer at the scene would report like this. "I rang the doorbell and this lady opened the door, nude except for a sanitary belt. She was covered with blood." The officer ran back to his unit and called for a backup. (There were no walkie-talkies in those days)

I arrived not long after the detectives. I was there to photograph the scene. An ambulance and other officers were there. They had removed the lady to a police unit after putting a robe on her.

There were two children in the house. One was dead from stab wounds and the other badly wounded from the same weapon. Also badly wounded was the family dog.

The husband arrived soon thereafter. The detectives interviewed him, but he could offer no explanation for his wife's behavior.

I went through the home and took quite a few photographs. There was blood everywhere. The hardwood floor was slick with it.

I learned later that the woman was convicted of murder and assault and sent to prison. She must have pleaded guilty, because I never received a subpoena for the trial.

Many years later I learned of a condition some women experience called pre-menstrual syndrome, (PMS). It occurs right before their menstrual period starts. They undergo a serious mental stress situation. Not all women are affected this way, but some are and it is very serious.

I feel reasonably sure that this lady was undergoing this mental stress situation when she just temporarily lost her mind and stabbed her children and the dog.

This occurred before Tampax was invented, thus the sanitary belt, which was used to hold her sanitary pad in place.

# HE HAD THE "DROP" ON ME

This incident took place in 1960. I was the Evening Shift Patrol Sergeant

A gentleman came to the Police Station at 112 N. Walters and filed a report that he had been threatened by a man who had a gun.

The report was taken and he was referred to the Justice of the Peace to file a charge of Serious Threat To Take Life. He had the man's name, location and all the pertinent information.

The man with the gun operated a small independent service station not far from police headquarters. I knew the man. The older officers stated that he was a violent man and had killed a man at a bar during the war.

The victim returned later to the police station with the warrant of arrest for the man on the charge of Serious Threat to Take a Life.

I took the warrant and called a two-man unit in to help serve the warrant.

We went to the gas station looking for him, but it was closed. I knew, however, that the man lived in a small house behind the service station.

I am not sure if the two officers accompanying me were acquainted with this individual.

We walked on back to the small house. The house was built on blocks and had a small front porch. All three of us stepped up on the porch. We were all in full uniforms.

I knocked on the front door a couple of times. Suddenly the door opened and there stood our man, about three feet from me. He had a revolver in his right hand and it was pointed directly at my mid-section. I looked down at the gun and I could see that it was fully loaded. I could see the business ends of the cartridges in the cylinder.

He looked at me with his bleary, blood-shot eyes and asked, "What do you want?" I glanced over my shoulders and discovered I was standing on the porch by myself. What could I say under those circumstances? I said, "I need to talk to you."

I could tell he was drunk. He finally said, "Well, come on in."

There was a bed in the front room and he sat down on the edge of the bed. There was a straight chair directly opposite him and that is where I sat down. I was then I took notice of the fact that my two officers had followed us into the room.

The man laid the revolver down on the bed beside him. I reached over and took the gun, unloaded it, placed it in my belt, and put the cartridges in my pocket. He asked me again what I wanted and reaching in my back pocket I produced the arrest warrant. I told him that he had been filed on for Serious Threat to Take a Life. He began to curse; stating he knew who it was that had filed on him. I told him that he was right, the man he had threatened with the gun had filed on him and he would have to go with us.

The two officers took him into custody and transported him to jail and booked him.

I had occasion to speak with one of the officers many years later and he remembered the incident. He laughingly stated that he and his partner had jumped off the porch to go call for a back-up.

I think about that incident occasionally and realize that when I knocked on that door the man could have thought it was the other guy returning to resume their argument. He could have just fired right through the door.

I never again stood in front of a door when I knocked on it in my official capacity.

In those days I think I had more nerve than I had sense.

I am sure of one thing. The Lord was looking out for me.

# THE VERBATIM POLICE REPORT

When we moved to Pasadena in 1954, I knew next to nothing about election campaigns.

I learned that the city officials were elected and conducted election campaigns. All of this was very new to me.

I also learned that the school district had a school board and they were also elected.

One year during the school board election campaign there was a very hotly contested race for one of the positions on the school board.

At a school board meeting during the campaign, all of the candidates were in attendance. When the meeting adjourned and all returned to their vehicles, one candidate found his vehicle filled with campaign signs…….his. These signs had been posted around the city and someone had removed them and placed them in his vehicle. He denied putting them there himself.

He accused his opponent of this outrage and called the Police Department to lodge a complaint. This was before the advent of school policing.

He also notified the new media to observe these signs in his vehicle. He probably had a lot to say about his opponent, if his opponent was responsible for this deed.

A police officer responded and took the necessary information for his report. He wrote his report and turned it in, thinking that was the end of it.

Wrong!

The next day there was a long article in the local newspaper about the incident.

When the police chief read the officer's report and then read the newspaper's account, the officer's report was returned to him with a note from the chief's office. The note basically said that perhaps the officer could have gotten as much information about the incident as the newspaper reporter.

The officer re-submitted his report. Only this time his report was copied verbatim from the newspaper account, word for word.

Another bad day for that officer, he was summoned to the chief's office for special consultation. I think he had to rewrite his report, and received a tongue lashing.

The officer involved was a good cop. He stayed on for some thirty years and retired honorably.

He has since passed on due to a heart attack.

# YOU HAVE LIVED TOO LONG

In another segment I told of a confrontation I had with an armed man. He was holding a loaded revolver which was pointed directly at my midsection from about three feet away.

This man had a son who was also well known to the police.

I have no personal knowledge of this incident, but a good police officer friend related it to me.

The story goes like this. The man's son and some "friends" were consuming great quantities of adult beverages and were, therefore, drunk.

They were in a mobile home somewhere in Pasadena, exact location unknown. A terrific argument ensued between the young man and one of his "friends." This young man got up, went into another room and returned with a shotgun. He pointed the shotgun at the other fellow and said "You have lived too long," He then shot his "friend" at point-blank range, killing him instantly.

I understand the shooter is now doing life in the Texas State Prison system.

# A FAMILY TRAGEDY

When I went to work at the Pasadena Police Department, there were several men who were allowed to ride with regular officers. They were called auxiliary officers. I do not know what their legal status was as far as making arrests. They rode with the regulars strictly to just help out if needed. They did wear blue uniforms kind of like the regular officers. I do remember they carried sidearms. This was a hold-over from the old days of the department when the department was always short-handed. They usually rode on Friday and/or Saturday nights.

Out of respect for the family involved, I am not going to name the young man in this case. His dad was well-known in the department, because he often rode as an auxiliary officer.

At the time this case evolved, I was working in the Identification Division. As a matter of fact, I was the only identification officer.

I was sent to the scene and found the Chief of Police and the Assistant Chief of Police already there. This auxiliary officer usually rode with the assistant chief and they were good friends.

The home had a detached garage which had no regular floor in it, it was a dirt floor. I was directed to the garage. I had the departmental camera with me and was prepared to photograph the scene. The only type of photography we were using at the time was black and white.

Inside the garage I observed a young man hanging by his neck. He was dead. He was completely nude. There was some rope wrapped around his wrists which were behind his back. My first impression was that the young man had been murdered.

His father and mother were distraught and seemed sure that someone had, indeed, murdered their son.

I really do not remember taking any photographs. I do not think that I did. The Chief told me we would wait for the Harris County Medical Examiner to arrive.

A little while later this gentleman arrived and was introduced as Dr. Joseph Jachimczyk. The doctor had his own camera and went about taking his own photographs. I learned later that the photographs were in color. He was the recently hired Harris County Medical Examiner.

We finally let the young man down and put him on a gurney. The ambulance crew was there to take him to the Harris County Morgue in Houston.

I heard Dr. Jachimczyk tell Chief Berry that this was not a murder case. He stated he would talk to the parents and explain the situation to them.

I learned later from Chief Berry that the Medical Examiner had ruled the death as accidental. I did not understand that.

The chief advised this sort of thing was something called auto-eroticism. The person used this type of activity to gain sexual gratification. Sometimes the person would accidentally strangle himself. The person would fashion a loop in a rope, put the rope over a bar, or in this case, an exposed ceiling joist. The person would secure the rope so it would not slip. He would then stand on something high enough to get his head through the loop. In this case he apparently got his head through the loop and began to apply pressure by stooping, since he was standing on a couple of buckets, one on top of the other. Whatever happened, whether he began to lose consciousness, or the buckets slipped out from under him, it is not known. What is known is that in the condition he was in he could not rescue himself and was strangled.

It was a real tragedy because this sixteen year old young man was an exceptional person. He was an Eagle Scout, an honor student and was already studying to be an aeronautical engineer.

I often wondered how a fine young person like this would learn about this deviant sexual act. It was not until many years later that it dawned on me what might have happened to this young man.

Of course there is no way to prove this suspicion. The family involved here were devout religious believers. I do know this young man helped out during the ceremonies at his church.

*In My Lifetime*

In recent days after all the terrible situations brought on by pedophilic church leaders it has occurred to me that perhaps there was a connection between this young man and his church leader while he was serving as an assistant during the ceremonies

At any rate, we will never know for sure.

# THE "WATCH" SALESMAN

When I was hired by the City of Pasadena Police Department, I was not making very much money.

There was myself, Nettie Grace and our oldest son, Timothy. We had just bought a new house and had to really watch our finances.

At the time, I did not have any kind of watch with which to keep time. I needed a wrist watch in connection with my job.

One day I stopped at a jewelry store in the Corrigan Shopping Center and purchased a wrist watch. It was not an expensive watch, but it was adequate.

The watch was financed by the owner of the jewelry store, Mr. Thomason. I had to make monthly payments, because I did not have enough money to purchase the watch outright.

One day when a payment was due, I stopped at the store to take care of that obligation.

When I got out of my car (my personal vehicle) I was immediately approached by an individual, a stranger.

He stopped me and stated that he was hard up for money and needed some cash to buy a bus ticket to make a trip out of town.

He produced a nice looking wrist watch and asked if I would like to buy it. I inquired as to how much he wanted for it. He said only twenty-five dollars.

I asked to look at it and he willingly handed it over to me for an examination. I looked it over and it did appear to be a nice watch. I do not recall if it had a brand name. It looked tempting, but I had just bought a new wrist watch, which I was wearing.

I suggested we go into the jewelry store and let the proprietor examine the watch to verify it's value. He became agitated and said never mind. If I did not want to buy it just forget about it. I immediately became suspicious and now I really wanted to know about the watch.

He reluctantly accompanied me into the store. I still had possession of the watch and besides, I was bigger than him.

We went into the jewelry store and I handed the watch to Mr. Thomason and asked him to examine it to determine its value. He took the back off the watch and examined the inside workings with a magnifying glass. He then replaced the back on the watch. He handed the watch back to me. He said the watch was worth about $2.50.

I asked him to call the police station and request a police unit to meet me in the parking lot out front. The unit arrived and I turned the man over to that officer and told him the story. I told the officer to book the fellow on a charge of Vagrancy, which he did. I followed him to the station and wrote my report on the incident.

The fellow had a pretty good idea where to position himself to approach people to try to sell his worthless watches.

I suppose he figured I was there to buy a watch and he was just the man to sell me one.

In those days the Vagrancy Law had sixteen different things a police officer could charge a person with.

Some lawyer challenged the law in federal court and the federal court declared the Vagrancy Law unlawful and the state had to get rid of it, too bad.

# HITTING THE HIGH SPOTS

During my career at the Pasadena Police Department, I had the privilege of going to Jackson Mississippi on several occasions to compete in the National Police Combat Pistol Matches.

That is an event that every police officer should go to at least one time during his or her career.

Hundreds of police officers from all over the United States and Territories assemble to compete in these matches. Every kind of law enforcement is represented.

The last time I went I believe they had at least 100 firing positions. They needed that many to get through all the contestants during the days of the competition. The matches were put on by the Mississippi Highway Patrol.

I remember winning at least one trophy at these matches. What an honor and a thrill.

On more than one occasion, just me and C. R. Holt went to the matches. It was kind of expensive, because we had to pay our own way. We were allowed to use a police unit for transportation, but we had to buy or own gas. We bought our own ammunition and furnished our own handguns. We usually took either vacation days or holidays to go on this trip. We paid for our own lodging, also.

Even though we represented the Pasadena Police Department, and our team shooting shirts were inscribed as such, the Police Department refused to help out in any way.

Many of the other agencies represented were fully funded by their respective agencies. Their agencies were apparently proud of their competing shooting teams.

The last trip I made to Jackson was with Lieutenant C. R. Holt. We were using the police unit assigned to me, a Chevrolet Nova. When we left Jackson, Charlie was driving. We traveled south until we hit Interstate 10 and headed west, headed home to Pasadena, Texas.

We were not letting any grass grow under those singing tires on that little Nova. That Chevrolet would run. It had 150 mph on the speedometer.

Somewhere west of Hammonds, Louisiana, we were hitting the high spots on that Interstate. I really do not know how fast we were traveling, but we were moving on.

I looked over on the eastbound lane and recognized a Louisiana State Police Highway Patrol Unit. The driver was looking straight at us. I watched him and he slowed, crossed over the median and headed west after us. I told Charlie to go ahead and pull over because I believed that we had been caught on the highway patrol officer's radar.

We pulled over on the shoulder of the highway and waited on him. He pulled in behind us. We were still wearing our shooting outfits, but no firearms. Just the shirts and caps, the police unit we were using was unmarked.

We both got out of our unit as he exited his. He stopped cold and stared at us. He asked, "What the heck is this?" We told him we had just left the National Police Matches in Jackson, Mississippi and were headed home to Pasadena, Texas.

We did not ask him how fast we were going. We chatted a few minutes and shook hands. He said, "By the way, the Headquarters Troop of the Highway Patrol around Baton Rouge are kind of narrow minded, so you better slow down going through there. We thanked him for his courtesy, got back in that Nova and headed on toward Pasadena.

# THE M.E. INVESTIGATOR
## AND THE TRAFFIC COP

During my tour as Patrol Commander there occurred a hostage situation at one of the local apartment projects.

I decided to slide on over there to check on things. There was nothing I could do, except get a verbal report from the officer handling the problem.

After getting the report, I planned to return to the Police Station. I was traveling east on Jackson Street nearing Tatar when I became aware of the traffic backed up for a block or so. This was unusual because there was not a lot of traffic on Jackson.

I worked my way up to the intersection of Jackson and Tatar and discovered there had been a minor collision there.

There was only one officer on the scene. There was a pickup truck sitting in the middle of the intersection with no one in it.

I parked my unit and got out to give the officer a hand. I got the traffic jam cleared out and walked over to the officer and asked him about the truck. He said it belonged to the man sitting in his patrol unit. I did not observe any damage to the pickup truck. There were, however, two vehicles sitting at the curb with minor damage to them.

I asked the officer if the truck had been involved in the collision and he stated it had not been involved.

The officer stated he had some trouble with the driver of the pickup and had to arrest him.

I walked over to the police unit to check on the man who had been arrested. It was a very hot day, with the temperature in the high nineties.

I leaned over to get a good look at the man, who was sitting in the back seat of the police unit. The back door of the unit was open and when I saw who it was, I could not believe it.

The man was a former officer of the Pasadena Police Department and presently working for the Harris County Medical Examiner's Office as a Medical Examiner Investigator.

He was wringing wet with sweat. He was handcuffed with his hands behind his back. He looked at me with a pleading expression on his face asked, "Smitty, would you get that idiot to take these cuffs off me?"

I walked back over to the police officer and asked him if he knew who it was he had arrested. He said he did not know and did not care who it was.

He said the man had refused to obey his directions when the officer was directing traffic around the two damaged vehicles. I told him who he had in his patrol car. It did not seem to bother him.

I got the man out of the patrol unit and told the officer to take the cuffs off. I would be responsible for the man. I also told him to report to my office as soon as he completed his investigation. I also told the investigator to meet me at my office.

He moved his truck from the middle of the intersection and we proceeded to the Police Station.

In my office he cooled down some. He said basically that he had wanted to turn off Tatar onto Jackson and travel west. The officer kept telling him to proceed on south on Tatar and make the block around the collision, which he refused to do.

The officer finally got the man out of the truck, cuffed him and placed him in the patrol car. He never asked for any kind of identification and the investigator never offered any.

In a little while the officer showed up at my office. I went next door and bought a couple of cold drinks. I took them back to the two. I suggested they talk over their problem. I left them and went elsewhere.

When I returned to my office later, they were both gone.

I never asked the officer for a report of the incident. He never mentioned it thereafter and neither did the investigator.

It was a case of two hot-headed individuals butting heads over an insignificant disagreement.

The amusing aspect of this was, when the investigator worked the streets, this would have been exactly the kind of thing he would have done had the roles been reversed.

# THE RAIN FROGS

I remember that Papa did not talk very much, but when he did speak he said some interesting things.

One day we were working on a job near the town of Jena, Louisiana. The weather was hot, humid and oppressive. The atmosphere very subtly changed and suddenly we began to hear a chorus of frogs all around us.

Papa said, "It's going to rain."

I never questioned Papa's remarks. I would wait and he usually explained himself.

In this case he finally remarked that the frogs were calling for rain.

Before long the sky began to cloud up and we could hear distant thunder. We put our tools away and secured the job site, because apparently rain was on the way.

Sure enough, the rain-storm hit and it began to really pour down. Of course, during the rain, we could not hear any frogs!

The rain slacked off some and I thought it was over. Then it commenced again and rained very hard once more.

Finally, the rain began to let up for real and stopped altogether. The frogs were back croaking their chorus. Papa said the rain is over, because the rain frogs are calling for more rain.

The summer when Paramount Studios was filming "Urban Cowboy" here in Pasadena, the weather produced a very heavy rainstorm. I was working off-duty as a security officer for the Studio. I mean it was really pouring down as I made my way to my police unit.

I left the job and proceeded north on Preston, trying to make my way home. I had to find a high place to park my unit because I reached a point where I could not get through the deep water.

I radioed the dispatcher to send one of the city dump trucks to pick me up. These dump trucks were about the only vehicles which could navigate the deep water. Soon a dump truck came by and I climbed into the bed along with some other flood refugees.

The driver drove north on Preston to Southmore and turned west. I knew he was headed for the Police Station. That was okay with me, because I could later get a ride home or back to my police unit.

As we proceeded along Southmore Avenue, I began to hear lots of frogs croaking. I looked up at the sky and saw that it was clearing. I could see some stars shining. I knew then that the rain was over.

At the Police Station the driver dropped me off and I went inside and down to the Civil Defense Center. The Center had been activated because of the heavy rains.

Since I was Patrol Commander of the Police Department, I let the Civil Defense Director know that I was in the building and available if needed. I told her; however, the rain was over. She asked, quite rightly, how I knew that. I replied it was because the rain frogs were hollering.

In a few minutes the National Weather Bureau announced over the television that the storm had moved on toward the north and the rain for our area was over.

As I got ready to leave the Civil Defense Center, I noticed the Director and some of her aides were watching me from the corners of their eyes.

I grinned at them and left.

After I wrote this article, I decided that I would take a shot at writing a poem about the Rain Frogs. The evidence of that effort follows this article.

Even now, when I hear the Rain Frogs hollering, I remember Papa.

# THE RAIN FROGS
## By Herbert Smith

They began while we were workin'
They sent out a mighty chorus.
Was their medley for us?
The old man smiled knowingly,
As if he knew their secrets.
A cool breeze wafted through.
Suddenly the air changed.
Then we heard the low rumble,
The sound of distant thunder.
I wondered.
Did the frogs hear it before us?
The old man spoke.
It is for rain the frogs are beggin'.
The cloudy darkness was pushed away,
The sheet lightening was a startling brilliance.
The rains fell in torrents.
No croaking of frogs could be heard now,
Only the steady rain a-drummin'.
The unladen clouds sailed away.
The blue sky reappeared.
The air was fresh and clean.
What is that chorus we now hear?
The old man spoke again.
'Tis the rain frogs thankin' their Creator.

# THE FISHING POLE THIEF

This case probably occurred in the late 1950's or early 1960;s.

Near the old downtown area of Pasadena, Texas, there was a cluster of low income rental cabins on North Johnson.

The cabins were of the bare necessity type; a bedroom, a small sitting room, a small kitchen and a small bathroom.

These cabins were built in the pre-air-conditioning days. I am sure some of the residents might have used electric fans to keep cool. Windows and doors were left open in the summertime, even at night, to take advantage of any cool breeze that might waft through. The cabins were equipped with screened windows and doors to keep the flies and mosquitos out. The screen doors were usually kept latched.

We began to receive reports of thefts of wallets and purses from the cabins.

There were no obvious signs of forced entry, except for slots cut in the screened windows.

One night the thief slipped up and got caught by one of the residents. The witness stated the suspect had a cane fishing pole thrust through a slot cut in his screened window of his bedroom.

When the police officers arrived and questioned the man, he readily admitted that he was the person doing the stealing. He stated late at night after everyone was asleep, he prowled around the neighborhood looking into the cabins. He could see pretty well by the available light from street lights. He could see where the residents left their wallets and purses. He stated that they were ususally in a location easily attainable by a pole.

He devised a plan of getting these items with a cane fishing pole. He would cut a slot in the screen wire and carefully insert the pole into the room. The bedroom being small he could reach just about any point in the room with the pole. He could manage to get the purse or wallet onto the end of the pole and ease it back out through the screen.

This was certainly a new trick. If this guy had applied his talents to gainful employment, be would have been much better off. As it was, he ended up in jail.

Another weird story in the annals of the Pasadena Police Department.

# THE MUSTACHE CAPER

After many attempts over the years, in 1972 my request to attend the FBI National Academy at Quantico, Virginia was granted.

This prestigious police training academy was established in the 1950's by FBI Director J. Edgar Hoover. Its purpose is to train local law enforcement officers for administrative positions in their respective agencies.

At the time I was approved for attendance an officer had to hold the rank of lieutenant or above. I had been a captain since 1964.

I reapplied for permission every time we changed chiefs, which was often.

If my memory serves me correctly, more than one Pasadena ranking officer was approved to attend the academy before me, but none with more seniority.

When I finally got approved to attend, one of my former patrol officers, was Chief of Police.

Up to this time, the expense of attending the academy was sustained by the City of Pasadena. Under a new program, the FBI was able to obtain funding to cover the expenses for officers to attend the academy. These expenses were the basics, like transportation to and from Quantico, lodging at the academy and meals at the cafeteria.

I was subjected to an intensive background investigation. This was at the height of the "Cold War." I had to fill out extensive forms for the FBI so they could investigate all my relatives.

In another segment I have related the story of my birth certificate. It is entitled "You Have Got to Be Kidding Me! "This story came out as a result of this background investigation.

I was finally approved by the FBI to attend the academy. I left Pasadena for the three month training course at Quantico, Virginia.

I must say that it was not a good time for me to be absent from home. I know that my wife Nettie was not overjoyed about it. We had two teenage sons at home and they gave her some headaches while I was away.

While I was at the academy I decided to write Chief Denson a letter informing him of my progress at the academy. I was not required to do this, but I felt I should out of courtesy.

One day while at the academy I went into the dining area of the cafeteria and discovered, to my complete surprise, the Pasadena Police Sniper Team was there attending a training school. They had apparently been there several days already, because they were leaving the next day to return to Pasadena.

The academy campus is a big place and it is possible that we just never crossed paths until that day. We did have a nice visit and we managed to get a group picture taken before they left.

Of those who were there training, I would say that only one of them could be called a "sniper." He was later a member of our police pistol team. I do not know how the others were chosen to attend.

After the sniper team returned to Pasadena, I received a short letter from the chief. In the letter he remarked that he had been informed that I had become "a real hippie." I presume that was because I had grown longer sideburns and a mustache.

I wonder which of the team of fellow officers snitched on me to the chief about my appearance.

The academy was divided up into five classes. My class was the "C" class. We had an FBI leader for our class and he recommended we elect officers, appoint committees, pick a name for out class, design a logo and etc. This was to promote spirit in the class, because all the other classes were doing the same. One of the things he suggested for our class to do was for every male member of the class grow a mustache, (There was one lady in my class)

There were already quite a few mustaches in evidence in our class, one of whom was my roommate, James Smith, a captain from the California Highway Patrol.

Facial hair was unofficially prohibited in the Pasadena Police Department. Why, I do not know.

*In My Lifetime*

I had been back to work at my duty station at the Pasadena Police Department for about a week, sporting my luxurious mustache.

One day I was summoned to the office of my supervisor, one of my former patrolmen now my superior officer, he was standing behind his desk when I entered his office and without preamble said, "Captain Smith, this is direct order. You are to shave that mustache off." I immediately replied, "Yes, sir. No problem, Inspector.

I exited his office and went to my police unit to go home and shave that offensive mustache off. One of our very good police patrolmen hailed me. He approached me and said, "Allow me to shake the hand of the man on this Police Department with the biggest balls." When I asked him what he meant, he said it was because I had returned wearing a mustache. I told him thanks, but I had been given a direct order to shave it off, which I was en-route to do. He said "A shame, sir." I agreed.

This was from one of our best police officers, a 250 pound former football player. He later left the department and went to work for the Texas Commission on Law Enforcement Standards and Education. The police department lost a good man.

I went on home and shaved the mustache off. I learned later that when I returned from the FBI Academy and the chief saw my mustache, he called a staff meeting to address the problem of Smith's mustache.

Apparently, it was the consensus of the staff that I would refuse to shave it off. That is why Gilbert gave me a direct order to shave it off. I figured that had I refused to obey a lawful direct order, they were prepared to suspend me.

Some of my friends said I should have refused and fought them over it. I did not have the money to hire a lawyer to do that.

What was amusing, within a short period of time, at least one member of the "staff" grew a mustache. By then about half of the men in the department were growing mustaches and letting their hair grow out.

It was apparent that the Police Department had an administrative staff which was living in the past and refused to advance into the new world of law enforcement. Other departments were leaving us behind.

A side note of interest. At the FBI Academy all officers are asked to submit a "term paper" on what the officer would like to see promulgated back at his or her agency, maybe an innovative new program or a fresh new idea concerning law enforcement. This was to be completed and turned in to the instructor prior to graduation.

My term paper was on "Community Policing." Twenty-five years later, after I retired, the new idea in law enforcement was, you guessed it, Community Policing.

Not one of my superiors had asked a single question about my studies at the FBI National Academy. Not a question about what I had learned, if I had come back with any new ideas or recommendations for the Pasadena Police Department, just a staff meeting about my mustache.

# THE EXPOSER

There was a period of time when John Middleton and I were assigned to the Detective Division as partners,

One day Captain Wornick gave us a warrant to serve. It was for "Exposing the Person." The suspect lived across the Houston Ship Channel in a small community named Channelview..

The captain told us the fellow had exposed himself to a lady while driving along Sterling Street, headed east. She alleged the man had pulled his vehicle up alongside her car, raised himself up and exposed himself to her. She got his vehicle license number and reported him, along with a pretty good physical description.

Using the vehicle license number Captain Wornick obtained the suspect's street address.

John and I located the suspect's home and observed the suspected vehicle in the driveway. The house was a neat little frame building in a nice neighborhood.

We stepped up on the small porch and knocked on the door.

John and I were both pretty large men, each of us being over six feet tall, I do not know what John weighed, but I probably weighed about 190 pounds.

The door opened and a very small lady was standing there. She was about five feet tall. We identified ourselves and asked for the man who was listed on the warrant. She said that was her husband. We told her we needed to talk to him. She closed the door and left us standing on the porch.

We had our backs to the door, looking around the neighborhood. We heard the door open again and we both turned around to face the door.

We were astonished. We were confronted by a giant of a man. He filled the doorway up. He was quite a bit taller than me and John and must have weighed in excess of 400 pounds.

He closed the door behind him and we informed him that we had a warrant for his arrest and he would have to go with us. He stated he wanted to tell his wife he was going with us and we allowed him to do that.

He came with us willingly, thank goodness. I do not remember that even handcuffed him. I am not sure we could have gotten the cuffs on his wrists.

When we got to the station, we booked him and I decided to go ahead and fingerprint and photograph him. We had a stall with mirrors arranged to reveal his profile from both sides. The stall was built to accommodate most large men. I could not get him all the way back against the wall so his exact height could be shown. He was a very large individual.

In retrospect, I wondered how he managed to lift himself up behind the steering wheel of his vehicle to expose himself.

We were never subpoenaed for his trial, so I do not know the disposition of his case.

# THE 'ELECTRIC CHAIR'

While I was assigned to the Detective Division, the Police Department received a complaint of a burglary and theft.

The place of business was a combination service station and auto repair shop. They did only minor repairs on vehicles.

There was no sign of forced entry and we surmised that It must have been an inside job.

I do not recall what all was taken. It did not take long to develop a suspect, after questioning all the employees.

The man suspected was confronted with our information and given a chance to confess. Of course he denied the charges.

I offered him a chance to take a lie detector test and he agreed. In those days we rarely referred to this test as a polygraph test.

I made arrangements to have him tested at the Texas Department of Public Safety in Houston.

Upon our arrival at DPS headquarters, I briefed the examiner about the case and turned the suspect over to him.

I figured it was going to take a while, so I went looking for a cup of coffee.

I found a place to wait and made myself comfortable. In a few minutes the examiner, who was a Texas Ranger, came and got me. He said the man was ready to talk. I was surprised and asked him what happened. He told me to go ahead and take a statement and then he would explain what happened.

I took custody of the suspect, found myself an unused office with a typewriter. I sat him down and proceeded to take his confession.

After I got that taken care of, I found the Ranger and he told me what happened.

He said he took the man into the Polygraph Room to prep him for the test. The fellow backed himself up into a corner with a wild look in his eyes. The Ranger began to explain to him the procedure for taking the test, the first of which was to take a seat in the examining chair. At this period of time the examining chair was an imposing looking affair with broad armrests for the person to put his arms. Next to the chair was the apparatus necessary for administering the test. There were some things which had to be attached to the person being examined. These wee to register breathing, pulse rate and heart rate, and etc.

The Ranger told the man to have a seat in the chair. The man refused to sit in the chair. The Ranger asked him why he did not want to sit in the chair. The man said, "I am not about to sit in that chair." When he was asked why not, he said, "You will hook them things up on me and turn that electricity up as high as it will go. No sir! You ain't going to get me in that electric chair. What do you want to know? I will gladly give a statement about what I did, but I am not going to sit in that electric chair."

We had a good laugh about it, realizing the man thought the testing chair was the electric chair used to execute people.

The Ranger said that he did not intend for the man to believe the chair was the electric chair.

The case was cleared and the man was charged with Burglary and Theft.

# THE 'LETTER OPENER'

We were at a departmental picnic one Saturday, the date escapes me. Naturally, I was on call. I had my family with me.

The dispatcher sent a patrol car to find me because there were no walkie-talkies or cell phones back then. I was needed to photograph the victim of a stabbing.

I had to go to the station to get my equipment. I proceeded to the Pasadena General Hospital, using my personal car. A friend took my family home from the picnic.

I found the victim in the emergency room on a gurney, lying on his stomach. He had no shirt on. He appeared to be between 25 and 30 years of age. He was tanned, muscular and smoking a cigarette.

Protruding from the middle of his back was the handle of a knife. The handle was of wood and there was about a half inch of steel visible between the handle and his back. I asked him how he was doing and he said fine. He said he was waiting for the surgeon to come and remove the knife from his back.

As I photographed him I asked him what happened. I was not one of the investigating officers, however, I was curious.

He said that he and his wife had been to the beach at Galveston and began to argue on the way back. They had been consuming adult beverages.

When they arrived back at their home, he lay down on the couch. Having been drinking, he was sleepy and tired. He kind of dozed off and then suddenly he felt something hit him in the middle of his back. He looked up and saw his wife backing away from him with a wide-eyed look on her face. He yelled at her, asking her what she had done. She never answered. He reached back and felt the handle of the knife in the middle of his back. He screamed at her about stabbing him and yelled for her to call an ambulance, which she did.

He was carried to the Pasadena General Hospital to wait for doctors to remove the knife.

The doctors eventually arrived and he was carried into the operating room. I did not stick around. I had my photographs and if the picnic was still going, I wanted to get back there. I found out that the picnic was over. I had missed out on all the goodies. A friend had taken my family home.

I checked later on the case and found out it took the doctors about five hours to remove that knife. The blade came within a fraction of an inch of severing his spinal cord. That was why it took so long to remove it. He was a very fortunate man.

The blade of the old knife was only about four inches long. The kitchen knife had been sharpened so much there wasn't much left of it.

Now that was a very unusual sight, this man lying on that gurney, smoking a cigarette, with the handle of knife sticking out of his back. I wish I had saved a photograph of that.

The officers took the knife as evidence. The man fully recovered and refused to press charges, the knife was not needed as evidence. The couple apparently did not want the knife back, because they never returned to retrieve it

The last time I saw the knife, it was being used by the Patrol Division Secretary as a letter opener. I was told later it was also used to cut cakes.

I do not know what eventually happened to the knife. When the secretary retired, she might have taken it with her. It would have been a nice memento.

# THE MISSING BOY

A recent incident involving a member of our church caused me to recall something that I was involved in back in the 1960's.

The church member had been fishing out in Galveston Bay. A day or two after the fishing trip his left hand began to swell. I saw this condition myself during choir practice and everyone was commenting on it. He was of the opinion that he had been bitten by a spider of some kind. He planned on going to the emergency room right after choir practice.

A day or so later we were informed that this gentleman was in the hospital in critical condition and not expected to live. Our pastor informed us that the man's hand had been infected with flesh-eating bacteria.

What has that got to do with a missing boy?

This boy was in elementary school and always walked home, usually with some others of his age. He lived with his parents on the West side of Vince's bayou. This bayou is quite a large and deep stream which empties into the Houston Ship Channel.

The boy's distraught mother reported he had not come home after school. An immediate search was conducted between the school and the young fellow's home, with no results.

The searching officers talked to some of his friends and discovered he was last seen on the bank of the bayou, near what was then named Sterling Street. Everyone, including the mother, naturally assumed he had fallen into the bayou.

Along with four or five other officers, we decided to wade the bayou to search for the boy. I pulled my shoes off, not wanting to ruin them. I left my socks on and along with the other officers, waded out into the bayou. We formed a line across the stream and started wading downstream. The bottom of the bayou was about knee deep in mud and muck and the going was slow.

We had waded about 50 yards when a shout went up that the boy had been located. I climbed out of the water upon the bank and retrieved my shoes. I had rolled my trouser legs up over my knees, but they still got wet. Upon inspection of my feet and legs I discovered numerous scratches and minor cuts from objects in the mud of the bayou.

I went home and changed trousers and socks.

From there I went to my doctor's office and got a tetanus shot because that bayou was filthy.

Fortunately, none of us suffered any ill effects from our search of the bayou.

The mother of the missing boy had returned home and found him fast asleep on the living room couch.

As far as the church member is concerned, we all came to the conclusion that he got a minor scratch or cut on his hand while fishing in Galveston Bay. This bay catches the runoff from all the bayous and streams in Harris County and is probably pretty unhealthy in itself.

The church member recovered from the infection, but he lost one finger on his left hand and at least two others are permanently disabled.

One more time the Good Lord protected me and the other officers from being infected with some dangerous bacteria as we searched for that little boy.

# THE RECORDS DIVISION SIGN-IN SHEET

I was Superintendent of Identification and Records for some ten years straight.

This period of time started before we moved from 112 North Walters to 1114 Davis.

I was the supervisor over the Identification and Records. The Records Division had about ten women clerks who performed various typing jobs connected with keeping the police records. I think the Chief of Police then was E. R. Means.

When Means decided to do some restructuring, it was reported to me that one Deputy Chief stated, "Give me Smith to supervise." Up until that time he had no one to supervise.

At one point I was directed by my superior, the Deputy Chief to set up a procedure for the civilian records clerks to sign in and out daily. He wanted the women to sign in when they came to work and sign out when they left. We had only one shift, which was the Day Shift. I suppose he was trying to catch someone coming in a little late or leaving a little early, I do not know.

Once this change was made, the Deputy Chief called me to his office. He immediately told me he was changing my working hours. He told me that in the future my working hours would be from 8:00 AM until 5:00 PM with an hour off for lunch.

Naturally, I protested. I reminded him that the other ranking officers came in at 8:00 AM, and left at 4:00 PM. During that time they found time to eat. He literally yelled at me that those men did not work for him, but I did, and my hours would be those he ordered me to work.

He followed this up within an hour with an official signed and dated memorandum directed to me specifically.

From my office I could see out to the front lobby. At 4:00 PM each day I watched my colleagues from other divisions leave to go off duty.

One day I remembered the official sign-in sheet the Deputy Chief instituted. It was on a desk right outside my office. I began to sign myself in and out on this sheet. I also remembered that the Deputy Chief routinely arrived at the Police Department at around 7:00 AM and he would leave around 5:00 PM. So I changed my own hours. I, too, began to come to work at 7:00 AM and of course, stayed until 5:00 PM, signing myself in and out.

Someone must have told him what I was doing, because one day he came to my office, inspected the sign-in sheet, and told me I did not have to use the sign-in sheet. Well, I continued to use the sign-in sheet. When I got called out after hours I would go by the Police Station and log myself in and out.

I want to tell you that it got under my skin to see those other officers leaving at 4:00 PM and I had to stay an extra hour. Included among those officers leaving at 4:00 PM were some patrol level people temporarily assigned to those divisions involved.

Yes, I sat there in my swivel chair, obtained from government surplus, and watched the exodus. I mention the swivel chair because I discovered that all the other ranking officers had been given new executive swivel chairs. Captain Smith deserved only a used surplus chair. The man responsible for this was none other than my boss, the aforementioned Deputy Chief.

For the City of Pasadena budget year of 1980-81, I submitted my usual budget requests.

The new budget went into effect the first day of October, 1980. After the first of October, I typed some memorandums directed to the aforementioned Deputy Chief, wherein I requested some things for which I had put into my budget requests.

On or about October 29, 1980 I received a three-page memorandum from the Deputy Chief regarding my memorandums. Copies of his memorandum are included herein.

Time passed and the Deputy Chief retired and I was reassigned to the new Deputy Chief C. L Ellis, another one of my former patrolmen.

I filled him in on what had happened about my working hours, assuming that he knew nothing about it. He told me to tally up the total number of hours I had worked overtime and submit a memorandum of same to him.

I did this and requested in writing, that I be allowed to start taking that time off in lieu of vacation time and he approved it.

I was approaching retirement and I knew that I would be paid for any accumulated vacation time and sick leave, but I would not be paid for compensatory time. Therefore I was able to save a lot of vacation time and sick leave for which I was paid when I retired.

I often wonder how the Deputy Chief felt when he found out I was paid for that accumulated time when I retired, knowing that he had required me to work that extra hour every day.

# THE "SMITTYS" DRIVER

During the late fifties and early sixties, loud automobile mufflers, or "Smittys," were the thing to have on your sporty car. I never knew much about them except they were very loud when they were "racked back" as the saying goes. I believe the noise was generated when the car accelerated and then the driver slacked off his speed, leaving it in the gear he was using. It was a violation of the Texas State Law to cause an automobile to make that kind of noise

Lots of citizens worked shift work which meant they had to sleep during the day. There were few air conditioners in those days, so windows and doors were left open to let some air circulate through the house.

Someone called in to report a car driving up and down their street making a lot of noise with their mufflers. The street was in my district so I eased on over to take a look.

I arrived in the area and I did not have long to wait. To put everything in perspective, the units we drove were plain black and had no emergency lights on top, only hand operated spotlights on each end of the windshield. The name "POLICE" was painted on the front doors only. When the units were clean, this sign was readily apparent. However, when the car got dirty with road scum, the name was usually pretty well obscured.

I parked on the street and the driver I was looking for came by me, "racking 'em back."

I pulled him over. Now, if I had just on-viewed him I probably would have given him a verbal warning and let him go. However, we did receive a complaint on him and I knew we were probably being observed by the complainant. Furthermore, I knew that he probably made it a practice to commit this offense.

The driver was a young man whom I had never met before. When writing this I considered using his name, because I think he might have been proud of the incident. I am not going to name him. If he reads this sometime, he will know who I am talking about.

So I wrote him a ticket for violation of the specified state traffic law.

Apparently he did not like getting the ticket, because when he took off, he "racked 'em back "again, right there in front of me. So, I pulled him over and gave him another ticket.

I guess the young man was stubborn, because he took the second ticket in hand, took off and yep, he "racked 'em back" again. I have had officer friends tell me that at that point they would have locked him up. Well, I gave him his third ticket in a matter of about fifteen minutes.

This time he was more judicious in his leaving the scene.

We got no more complaints about his driving.

Many years later, about 1996, Nettie and I were car-shopping at various dealers. We visited this well-known Chevrolet dealer in Clear Lake. You know what, up walked this salesman and said "Captain Smith, the only Pasadena Police Officer to give me three tickets in one day. Yep, it was him. He was now a nice well-dressed man of about forty or forty-five.

I sure did not expect to run across him like that. Of course I had been long retired by then, about thirteen years.

He bore no ill will towards me. We talked and laughed about the incident and we went on our way.

# THE BURNING HOUSE

One night when I was working the Night Shift, the Pasadena Volunteer Fire Department received a call of a house fire in what is now called Old Pasadena. This was in my district so I made the scene to assist if I could. I was a one-man unit that night.

Another officer made the scene at the same time, but I do not recall who it was

When we arrived there was only one fire truck at the scene and those men were laying the fire hose. Smoke was billowing from an upstairs window and we could tell there were people in this part of the house.

There was a ladder available, so the other officer and I climbed the ladder to the flat roof near the window from which the smoke was coming.

We crawled into the room through the open window, located the people and helped them get out of the burning house and down the ladder. I think there were three people.

The firemen put the fire out and we went back into service. We made reports of our participation in the incident.

A couple of weeks later I got a nice Letter of Commendation from Fire Chief Gil Bashforth, complimenting me and the other officer for saving the lives of the people in the burning house.

I never received anything from anyone connected to the Pasadena Police Department.

# THE CALIFORNIA MURDER WEAPON

While I was assigned to the Detective Division, we got a call from law enforcement officials in a town in California about a bank robbery in which the suspect shot and killed someone.

Their completion of the investigation hinged upon the recovery of the handgun used in the murder. Their investigation revealed the suspect had mailed the handgun to a lady in Pasadena, Texas. We were not sure at that time if she was a wife or girlfriend.

Apparently they had obtained the information from confidential sources. The problem was, they needed the handgun right away, but they did not want the suspect to know how the officers obtained the information. They gave us the address where the lady lived, so I contacted her. She admitted that she had received a package from the suspect, but had not opened it, therefore did not know what was in it. I told her that we suspected there was a gun in the package.

She was afraid that if the suspect learned that she had turned the gun over to the police, her life would be in danger. She said he was a very violent man.

After considering the situation for a while, I got an idea. I called for a marked unit to meet me at the home of this lady. I told the lady she would not be in any danger if the police found the gun in her car when she was stopped for a traffic violation. She could tell the suspect the police stopped her on a routine traffic stop and found the gun in her car.

She agreed and took the package and left the house. I told the uniformed officers to let her get several blocks away from her home and then pull her over for a traffic violation. When they asked her what was in the box she was to tell them she thought it was a handgun.

Upon learning this, the officers seized the box with the handgun in it. She was released because the box had not been opened and we could not charge her with knowingly carrying a handgun.

The officers turned the box over to me. I carried it to the station and turned it over to Captain Wornick. He called the officials in California and made arrangements to ship the box to them in California. He learned later it was determined the gun was indeed the murder weapon. The suspect was convicted.

I suppose he never knew exactly how the officers ended up with the murder weapon.

I never got an "Atta-Boy" on that case either.

# THE FINGERS FURNITURE ARMED ROBBERY

This was during my first year on the Pasadena Police Department, in 1955.

Officer Glenn Gardner was training me, now days he would be called a Field Training Officer.

Officer O. L. Pillion was the Evening Shift Radio Dispatcher. The radio mike was on a little base and the whole thing was about 15 inches high. It had a button on the base which, when pressed, opened the mike for broadcasting. As long as the button was pressed the mike was open. When it was released the broadcast was over.

Glenn and I were working the #1 District which covered the area from Jackson Street north to the City Limits and east and west to the City Limits.

At the time of this incident, we were westbound on Sterling Avenue, which is now called State 225. Glenn was driving. We were in about the 1000 block of Sterling when the police radio came alive and Pillion was talking. At first we did not know what was going, because he called no unit number.

It sounded like Pillion was talking to someone on the telephone. We realized that he was talking to someone with the radio mike open. He was asking questions about a robbery. He asked which way he was going. Then he would repeat the person's answer over the radio.

In response to the question about the direction of travel, the person on the telephone apparently said west on Shaw, which Pillion repeated over the air. That gave us the direction of travel of the robber. Glenn immediately cut through a parking lot onto Shaw Street about the time Pillion put out the description of the suspect's vehicle.

The suspect's car passed directly in front of us, headed west on Shaw Street. I said there he goes Glenn and Glenn said "Yep."

We pulled the vehicle over in about the 800 block of Shaw Street. We got the suspect out and discovered he was a juvenile of about sixteen. He had robbed Fingers Furniture Store at gunpoint. Fingers Furniture was in the 1000 block of Shaw Street.

We recovered the money and the gun.

Our quick response was due to O. L. Pillion using his head in getting the information out as quickly as possible, resulting in a quick arrest of the suspect.

If he had taken the time to copy all the information down before broadcasting it, we would have missed him.

It was a good piece of work by Officer O. L. Pillion and he deserved a letter of commendation.

# THE FORBIDDEN FIREARM

I do not recall exactly when this happened, but it iis firmly embedded in my memory, because it was one many embarrassing moments that happened to me.

I, and several other officers, had to make a trip up to North Texas to attend a school of some sort. We, of necessity, had to go through Huntsville, Texas. It was generally accepted that when traveling through Huntsville on official police business, the officer(s) could stop at the State Prison (called "The Walls) and eat lunch there free of charge.

I was driving one of the units and I let my passengers out near the main gate. I then parked the unit and followed them in.

I had to go through the front gate and I guess the prison guard, in an elevated guard house, assuming I was with the other officers, opened the gate and waved me on through. I entered the main building and naturally the place was crawling with inmates.

I was directed on toward the mess hall. I suddenly realized that I still had my side-arm on. I walked over to a desk where there was a guard on duty. I opened my coat and asked him where I could leave my firearm. He almost yelled at me to get that thing out of here, no firearms are allowed in here. You were supposed to leave it at the front gate.

I strolled back out to the front gate and yelled up to the guard that I had a firearm to leave with him. He let down a bucket on a rope, I put my firearm in the bucket and he pulled it back up into his guard shack.

On my way in he never mentioned anything about me leaving my firearm with him.

I retrieved my firearm on the way back out, after enjoying a nice free meal.

I do not know where my mind was. I just did not think about there being no firearms allowed inside "The Walls." After all, we wore firearms all the time around prisoners at the city jail.

That was my first and last time to visit "The Walls" at Huntsville, Texas.

# THE KARATE EXPERT

I was working the Evening Shift as Patrol Sergeant. It was nearly time for the shift to change. Shift change was at 10:00 PM and this was about 9:00 PM.

I was proceeding north on Shaver, just south of Eagle Street. At the time Shaver Street was two-way. I observed this individual of small stature staggering along the sidewalk in front of Pasadena High School. He had what appeared to be a whiskey bottle in his back pocket.

I pulled over near the intersection of Shaver and Eagle and got out of my unit. I approached the fellow as he came staggering down the sidewalk. He asked what I wanted and I told him it appeared to me as if he'd had too much to drink. He asked what I was going to do and I said I am going to take you to jail.

All of a sudden the went into this crouch with both hands extended, making chopping motions. Now, I was about six foot two inches, with my full uniform on, including my head cover. With my head cover I probably was about six foot four inches tall. This fellow was about five feet six or seven inches tall. In a crouch, he was much shorter.

He said I was not taking him anywhere, that he was a karate expert.

I tried to talk to him, but he was having none of it and kept backing up making chopping motions with his hands. I realized we must look ridiculous because of the difference in our posture, the big tall cop and the little fellow confronting him.

About that time a car came to a screeching halt nearby and a woman exited the car and began yelling, wanting to know what was going on. This distracted me for an instant as I told her to get back in her car and leave; it was police business, which she did.

The karate guy took this opportunity to take to his heels and flee.. He ran west through the high school parking lot. I was not about to give chase. Maybe I did not want to get my nice clean uniform dirty. I returned to my unit and alerted the district unit to be on the lookout for the man.

I went on to the station to prepare for the shift change.

A citizen came in to the lobby of the police station and reported what looked to him like a dead body lying alongside Shaw Street about three blocks from the police station. The district unit was dispatched and I thought I would slide on down there to see what was going on.

When I arrived on the scene, I immediately recognized the "karate expert." I told the officers he was the man who had run from me and that he was just drunk.

The officers grabbed him and began to drag him to one of the police units. He was dead weight. He was as limp as a rag doll, but when they got near the door of the unit he began to resist. They would back off and he would go limp again. Officer J. B. Kelly arrived on the scene and began to assist. The guy was limp. Officer Kelly poked his finger somewhere behind the suspect's ear and apparently applied pressure to a sensitive nerve. The guy screamed and went berserk. Now the fight was on. I did not see him doing any karate chops during this struggle. The officers got him down on the concrete in the middle of the street, trying to get the cuffs on him. He was still resisting violently.

About this time a car going east on Shaw pulled up close and stopped, with headlights on the struggle. Officer J. M. "Big John" Sandel got out of the car. He was on his way to work the Night Shift and saw the commotion. When he realized the officers were trying to cuff the man, he said move over and let me sit on him. He did and the air went out of the guy. They were able to get the cuffs on him.

# SPELLING AND PENMANSHIP OF POLICE OFFICERS

In another segment I wrote about poor spelling and penmanship by Pasadena Police Officers.

A lot of officers had poor penmanship and I attribute a lot of that to being in a hurry in writing their reports. I include myself in that category. When I get in a hurry, my penmanship goes awry.

We had two officers who were very bad on both accounts. I am not going to name them out of respect for one of them because he is dead, the other one because he is bigger than me.

One of them was assigned to the Evening Shift while he was a Probationary Patrolman. Probationary periods were for six months. The Evening Shift Supervisors were Captain Doug Warren and I as Patrol Sergeant. This fellow was unlucky to have me and Doug as his supervisors. I was very particular about the deficiencies in these areas by this one officer. Doug was very particular also. His handwriting was much better than mine.

We finally called the Probationary Police Officer in for a talk about his spelling and his penmanship. We had talked to him more than once, but he did not improve. We told him that he was in danger of failing his probationary status and would be let go.

He wanted to know what he could do to improve. We told him to find a tutor to help him with his problems.

This man was a high school graduate.

He found a first grade school teacher who was willing to tutor him. She worked with him for several weeks and sure enough, his spelling and penmanship began to improve. He was able to save his job. This officer stayed with the department some 30 years and retired.

The other officer was worse than the one above. I truly believe that he concealed his poor spelling with his sorry penmanship. We all used ballpoint pens to write our reports. This officer put so much pressure on his pen that I was surprised he did not tear the paper. By the time I became aware of his problems, he was already a certified officer and we just had to contend with the situation.

I truly believe this officer was taught under what was called the phonics system. That is where a person is taught to spell a word exactly like it sounds.

He was assigned to the Identification Division and worked under me. Fortunately he did not have to write many reports.

One of his jobs was processing prisoners early in the morning. Every prisoner had to be fingerprinted. The back of the card called for a lot of information, including the prisoner's address. The ID officer filled out the "master" card and later typed up the other cards from this card.

After all the prisoners were processed, the paperwork was carried upstairs to be finished. Sometimes we had quite a number of prisoners and therefore a large number of cards to the typed. A lot of times I assisted in the typing because it was more than one typist could handle, along with the other ID work.

One day I was helping this officer with the typing on my trusty Royal manual typewriter. When I got to this one prisoner's address, I broke out laughing. The officer asked me what was funny. The man's address was on a street named Bayou View. This officer spelled the name of the street Biovu. You understand that is what he understood, under the phonic system. I thought it was hilarious. He did not think it was all that funny.

# SHOT DOWN BY THE INSPECTOR

As previously narrated, I had studied identification techniques through the Institute of Applied Science of Chicago, Illinois, at my own expense.

The officer working in the Identification Division during this period of time was Captain A. O. Laster. He was the only officer in the division.

I was talking to him one day while I was working the Dispatching Desk, a job which I disliked very much. Allen told me he had been accepted by the FBI National Academy and would be leaving in a couple of weeks for the three-month school. He further stated that Chief Schamerhorn would be looking for someone to take over the job in the Identification Division.

I had told no one about studying identification, except Nettie.

I figured at that point it would be a good time to reveal this information. I told Captain Laster about my study courses in that field. Well, Allen was not too impressed by the fact that I was studying identification "by mail-order" as he put it. Captain Laster was a self-taught identification officer, and he was very good at it, especially the photography part of it.

Apparently, Captain Laster told the chief about me and the first thing I knew I received a transfer from patrol to the Identification Division.

We had about two weeks for Captain Laster to train me in the basic duties of an Identification officer for the Pasadena Police Department.

Before he left for Washington, D. C. Captain Laster urged me to join the International Association for Identification and also the Texas Division of the same organization, which I did.

These organizations had, and still do, annual conventions. I was fortunate enough to get time off to go to some of the International

Conventions. These conventions were attended by identification officers from all over the world. Of course, I only got to attend when these conventions were held in the USA.

I was also fortunate enough to be allowed to go to the State Conventions. This was under the administration of Chief A. J. Schamerhorn. Chief Schamerhorn was very pro-identification. He readily approved my requests to attend these conventions and urged me to get to know as many of the other ID officers as I could. The chief knew the value of meeting other people in the same profession.

Because I was a regular attendee at these conventions, I got appointed to committees in the TDIAI and got to work with identification officers from all over the State of Texas.

I really enjoyed making these trips because they were family oriented. I was able to take my family with me, at my expense, of course. The City of Pasadena paid my expenses and gave me time off to attend.

I was appointed Regional Vice President of the Texas Division of the IAI. This was quite an honor, because it was the first step to becoming president of the organization.

The Board of Directors met quarterly in various parts of the state to make it convenient for all the board members in that area to attend.

By this time, Chief Schamerhorn was no longer in that office. If I remember correctly, a former sergeant was the Chief of Police.

My supervisor at the time was an Inspector. When I requested time off and expenses to attend the quarterly meetings of the Board of Directors, the inspector denied my request. He told me if I wanted to go to these meetings, I would have to pay my own way and use my vacation time and my own vehicle.

# FORBIDDEN LOVE

There were times, when I was a detective; I worked with Juvenile Officer on cases.

One such case involved a very pretty 14 year old girl, mature for her age, who was a student at one of our junior high schools.

The Juvenile Officer stated the girl's parents had reported to him about a problem they were having with their daughter.

It was revealed that a nineteen year old young man had taken a liking to their daughter and they could not discourage him or their daughter.

With the parents' permission we picked the girl up at school to talk to her about this problem. All she would say was "I love him." We were able to get the guy's name, but not where he lived.

We counseled her best we could and took her back to school, knowing we probably wasted our time.

Sure enough, the next day the parents called to report the girl missing. Naturally, they were very upset.

We finally were able to locate the place where the man was living, which was with his parents.

We went to this house and talked to the fellow's parents and got no cooperation at all. They kept asking us to just leave those kids alone. It did no good to tell them the girl was under-age and her parents were worried about her.

The Juvenile Officer got a warrant for the man's arrest on a charge of Contributing to the Delinquency of a Minor.

We located him at his place of employment and arrested him. During our questioning of him we were able to determine that the girl was staying at his parent's house. As a matter of fact, she was there the day we went there looking for her. His parents hid her from us.

The man got a lawyer, got out on bond and he and the girl disappeared.

I had other cases to work, so the Juvenile Officer carried on through with this case.

He told me later that the man's lawyer had helped the couple go to Florida, where they got married.

The Juvenile Officer immediately filed a complaint with the Bar Association against this lawyer. She was subsequently charged in the case and very nearly lost her license over it.

It is not known what happened to the lovers. They may be still married, who knows?

I know one thing; those parents were very frustrated and angry over this situation. I hope they sued the lawyer.

# A MURDER MOST FOUL

The mother was standing at her kitchen sink, looking out toward the street in front of her house. She observed a vehicle stop in front of her house and a man got out. He was nude. There were some children playing nearby and the man moved toward them, exposing himself to them.

She called to her grown son, who was in another part of the house. The son came and looked out the window at the man exposing himself. He told his mother he would go talk to the man. She said she would call the police, which she did. She went back to the window with the telephone in her hand.

She observed her son approach the nude man and could tell words were exchanged. To her horror, the man reached inside his vehicle and pulled out a rifle. As the police answered her call, the man shot her son.

Her son turned and ran back into their garage. The man followed her son and as she began to scream to the dispatcher that this man was shooting her son. She heard additional gun-shots from the garage.

The dispatcher could hear the gun-shots over the telephone. The mother watched as the suspect went back to his vehicle, entered it and drove off.

In response to the emergency call from the dispatcher, a patrol officer was nearby and spotted the truck leaving the area. The officer stopped the truck and held the driver. Other units made the scene.

The young man was lying in the garage. He was dead, having been shot again where he had collapsed.

The weapon the man used was recovered from his vehicle. He was arrested and subsequently charged with murder.

Investigation revealed he was a local business man.

His goal apparently was to expose himself to the young girls who were playing near the scene. When the young man approached him, it infuriated him. He grabbed his rifle and began shooting.

The accused was able to make bond and was released. He immediately jumped bond and disappeared.

A nation-wide search was conducted and no trace of him was found.

Some years later the case was profiled on a national television program. As a result of this publicity, the suspect was spotted in a Central American country. The authorities were notified. He was located, arrested and returned to the United States and Harris County, Texas.

He was later tried and sentenced to life imprisonment.

# THE DRY "WATERING HOLE"

Not long after I became a Pasadena Police Officer, I discovered "off-duty" employment. Admittedly, off-duty jobs during my early years with the department were few and far between. Therefore, when I had the opportunity to work one of these, I jumped at it. My salary as a patrolman was not something to write home about. During these years Nettie and I already had three sons.

So, when I was approached by the owner of an all-night restaurant about working there in uniform, on Friday and Saturday nights, I took it.

I soon learned why he needed a uniformed "bouncer," if you will. I did not consider myself a "bouncer" and I never bounced anyone from the restaurant.

In the southern part of Pasadena there were several establishments which served adult beverages, these places having been voted out of the old part of Pasadena, and then known as "dry-Pasadena." These places were commonly called "watering holes" for the confirmed drinkers, hence the term "The Dry Watering Hole," for this all night restaurant. This is strictly my name for it. Actually, it was a very popular restaurant and frequented by many of the Pasadena residents, mostly during the daylight hours.

The "wet watering holes" were required to close at 1:00 AM.

After closing, their clientele, having worked up appetites, adjourned to the nearest restaurant, which was the one where I was employed. Shortly after the closing of the "wet watering holes," this restaurant's business increased dramatically.

This, of course, was good for my employer's business, but presented a certain amount of problems for me. Almost all of these men and women had been drinking adult beverages and a good percentage of them could be considered drunk. I was not there, however, to arrest drunks, but to keep order and allow these people to consume their late-night meals.

I will add here that in those days I had more nerve than sense. But, I was over six feet tall and weighed probably around 180 pounds, not including my uniform, sidearm and etc. I did not have sense enough to be afraid of any of these people, and some of them had very rough reputations.

I do not remember having any serious problems with any of the restaurant's customers.

Beginning about midnight until around 2:00 AM - 2:30 AM, the place would be very crowded and boisterous. After eating, a number of the male customers would congregate out front along the sidewalk and do what tipsy men are prone to do; make loud, suggestive remarks to passing women and threatening behavior toward male clientele. This was the reason I was there; to prevent this activity.

I did not know it at the time, but apparently I was being observed by a couple of ranking Pasadena officers, who were parked nearby. It was my custom to go outside and stroll through the middle of these groups to let them know of my presence. I learned later my behavior was looked upon favorably by these ranking officers, one remarking, "He walks right through the middle of them and they move aside for him," meaning me. Like I remarked earlier, I guess I had more nerve than I had sense.

A positive thing about working there, the owner had a top-rate "short-order" cook. Every night I worked there he would fix me my favorite late night meal, which was a great cheese omelet, on the house of course.

# THE FROZEN FELON

The officers of the Pasadena Police Department were required to attend in-service training schools.

Instructors from within the department were routinely used. However, sometimes the department utilized instructors from other fields.

On one such occasion a local attorney was asked to teach some classes. These classes were intended to help the officer's testify in court.

The attorney in this instance was a long-time resident of Pasadena and was well known by all the officers of the department.

I am not going to name the attorney out of respect for his family, because he is deceased. While teaching his classes he would sometimes tell of his experiences as an attorney and as a federal law enforcement officer.

After he graduated from law school he obtained a position with a federal law enforcement agency and worked for them several years.

This particular story evolved while he was employed by this agency, and stationed in the territory of Alaska. I feel sure this probably occurred in the early 1950's, while Alaska was still a territory of the United States and before it became a state.

The attorney stated his agency was actively involved in investigating and searching for an individual. This subject had been charged with a felony, the nature of which the attorney did not divulge. Their leads led them into the great frozen wilderness of Alaska.

With his partner, they obtained dogs and a sled, equipped the sled for winter traveling, dressed them appropriately for the environment and set out on the subject's trail. Naturally, he said, everything was frozen solid.

The conditions for trailing were excellent, though, and they soon tracked the individual to an area where they suspected him to be.

Diligent snow-shoe work soon led them to a shelter where it was said the man was holed up. Indeed, they did find the individual waiting for them.

He offered no resistance. He was lying on a cot, frozen solid!

They brought their sled to the "shelter," loaded the man onto the sled, yelled "Mush," and headed back to home-base.

It was not smooth-sledding, though. On the way back the weather changed and a blizzard blew in. They were fortunate to find a "line-camp" with a small cabin. They discovered the previous occupant had left some food, some fire-wood and etc. There was a small enclosed lean-to on the back of the cabin. Being concerned that their sled-dogs and/or local wolves would consume their suspect, they decided to put him in the lean-to. They carried him into the small enclosure and to quote the attorney, "We leaned him up in a corner to protect him from the varmints, since he was still stiff as a board. We opted for this because we did not want him to thaw out by keeping him in the warmer part of the shelter."

After the blizzard blew on through, they reloaded the "stiff" (excuse the pun) and proceeded on back to their home base.

Mission accomplished.

# SCOBY

Dave Scoby graduated from the 15th Pasadena Police Academy in 1967. I have no information about his standing in the Academy, except he was (and is) an excellent pistol marksman. Later in his career he became a member of the Pasadena Police Pistol Team.

As far as I know, Dave was involved in two shooting incidents during his career as a Pasadena Police officer. Dave is retired now.

I see Dave occasionally and we reminisce about our careers with the Pasadena Police Department.

On one occasion, July 4, 1970, Dave stated he pulled into a service station on East Southmore to clean up his patrol unit. While doing this, the service station attendant approached him about a suspicious circumstance. He told Scoby the customer he had been helping was trying to purchase some gasoline, but did not know there was a lock on the gas tank.

When the vehicle left, Scoby followed it and called the plate number in to the dispatcher. In those days, the dispatcher had to enter the plate number on the teletype and wait for a response from the state.

In the meantime, Scoby followed the vehicle as it turned on Strawberry. He decided to stop the car. The vehicle pulled over to the curb with Soby's unit right behind it.

Scoby exited the patrol unit and approached the suspect vehicle. He asked the driver for his license. While he was waiting for the driver to produce his license, Scoby observed the passenger get out of the car on the other side. This individual was watching Scoby intently as he walked toward the rear of the car. As he rounded the back of the car, Scoby noticed the suspect had something in his right hand. As he walked toward Scoby, he brought the hand up and Scoby saw that the suspect had a handgun.

Scoby immediately drew his weapon and began firing at the suspect before the suspect could bring his weapon to bear upon Scoby. The suspect dropped to his knees and let go of his weapon. Scoby returned to his unit, called for an ambulance, a backup and a supervisor.

The man was rushed to a hospital. Scoby had hit him five times before the man could get a shot off.

The man survived the shooting, recovered and was sentenced to prison. Years later he was released. He made the mistake of going to the Police Station looking for Scoby. He did talk to Scoby, telling him he was sorry about the incident. Scoby told him what a sorry individual he was, that the department knew all about the things the suspect had said in prison concerning Scoby and what he was going to do when he got out of prison. Scoby suggested he leave Pasadena and not return.

Scoby knows where the suspect lives in East Texas.

I do not have the date of the other shooting incident.

Scoby was working off-duty as security at First Pasadena State Bank. A teller told him that a businessman had come in, withdrew a large amount of cash and told the teller a man with a gun was holding his wife hostage at the back of the bank. The money was withdrawn for the man with the gun.

Scoby went to the back door of the bank and without revealing himself, observed the situation. The businessman was driving and there was a woman and another man in the front seat. The vehicle left the bank and Scoby followed in his unmarked police unit.

The suspect and hostages traveled back toward the North end of Pasadena. They did not stop at the business place, but pulled around on the block behind the business. Scoby exited his unit and followed on foot.

The vehicle stopped near the corner, a block or so away from the businessman's office.

Scoby stopped behind a large light pole and observed the suspect get out of the vehicle, walk around the front of the car, pause at the driver's door and then proceed to the rear of the vehicle.

At this point, Scoby stepped out from behind the light pole and yelled at the suspect "Police, freeze!" Scoby stated the man whirled immediately and fired a shot at him. The bullet hit the light pole near Scoby. Scoby fired one shot and the man went down.

Scoby went to the man, removed the suspect weapon from near him, and checked on the business man and his wife.

Scoby then notified the dispatcher waited for the ambulance and other officers.

The suspect was dead. He was wearing two sets of clothes and had other items with which to disguise himself.

He had been a bad dude out of Louisiana.

# THE POLICE ASSOCIATION AND THE POLICE ATHLETIC LEAGUE (PAL) BUILDING

After I joined the Pasadena Police Department I found out there was a Pasadena Police Officers Association. All the members of the First Pasadena Police Academy were asked to join the association.

I do not recall how many members there were in the association at the time, nor how many our group brought the number up to.

We had one member of our academy who was very ambitious and he began right away to campaign to be president of the association.

When the election for association officers was held, all us new members voted for him as the new president. He and another new officer were elected to the positions of president and vice president. I do not recall who the vice president was. I do remember they asked me to be the Secretary and Treasurer of the association.

The association at the time was in the process of building a gymnasium for young people to play basketball in. All they had done was the foundation of the building.

The association raised money by selling tickets to Policemen Balls (called dances these days). They generally sponsored two each year and they were very popular.

Since the department was small, it was convenient for the association to contract with a promoter to sell the tickets for these dances.

Before the new regime took over the Police Association, a particular officer ran the show, getting the promoter signed up, finding a place for their telephone banks and etc.

*In My Lifetime*

We found out the promoter received better than fifty percent of the proceeds of the ticket sales. We knew guys and began to plan our strategy and figured we could get a better deal with the promoter.

One day at our meeting the police chief showed up and announced that any business dealings with the promoter would be conducted by this particular officer.

The way the promoter operated, he would hire a number of people to man the telephone banks to call all over the United States and sell tickets to these police dances. There was no way we could have got all the people in one of those dances who bought tickets.

As soon as the calls started, the mail began to come in, paying for the tickets sold over the telephone.

This officer had charge of the mail. He went to the post office, picked up the mail, took it to the promoter's office, opened the mail, tabulated the money coming in, and worked with the promoter on paying the workers and so forth. What was left he gave to me to deposit in the association's bank account. Figuring what the association received, we became aware there was a large amount of money coming in. This particular officer was solely responsible for that part of the fundraising.

I am not alleging that anything unlawful was going on. It was just peculiar that this officer was so interested in this situation that he went to the Chief of Police to request he be in charge of the money coming in.

I helped out in a number of ways while I was a member of the Association. I think I served only one term as Secretary and Treasurer. We put on several dances, some at the famous Shamrock Hilton in Houston and they were very popular.

When I went to these dances, I seldom danced, because my lovely wife Nettie did not dance. What I generally did was carry the departmental camera and take pictures.

Over the years the Police Athletic League building was completed. I went there often; helped keep it clean, sweeping the floors, cutting the grass outside, and playing some basketball.

New administrations in the Police Association came and went. The building became a problem and the members feuded over the handling of it.

It became such a problem that one year the president of the association announced that he was padlocking the thing.

He did not know, I guess, that under our contract with the City of Pasadena, which gave us the land to put the building on, he was in violation of the contract.

The City of Pasadena immediately filed papers to take over the building, and the courts granted that request.

The association had a $100,000 title guarantee on the building. The association sued to collect that money. They lost that case also.

That is why today the City of Pasadena owns the PAL building.

*Captain Herbert Smith - While at the FBI National Academy Photo*

# QUINCY JAMES

Quincy James was a local attorney. He ran for a position on the Pasadena City Council in 1963 and was elected. His area of responsibility was the Police and Fire Departments.

As soon as his election was official, he notified Chief of Police A. J. Schamerhorn that he was being replaced. The Chief of Police served at the pleasure of the Councilman who was over the Police and Fire Departments.

Apparently, in this case Mr. James did not specify exactly when Chief Schamerhorn's term ended. So, I presume that Chief Schamerhorn assumed that he would be working until the end of his pay period.

What resulted was, Chief Schamerhorn moved his office into the Assistant Chief's office and the Assistant Chief, John L. Gaines, whom Mr. James had appointed as the new chief, moved into the chief's office.

Between the time of the new appointment, and the end of Chief Schamerhorn's term, there was approximately two weeks. Chief Schamerhorn was adamant. He was staying on as long as he was being paid.

For about two weeks, we had two Chiefs of Police. Schamerhorn was not reduced in rank to Assistant Chief. He was just fired, but stayed on for the remainder of his pay period.

I was Patrol Commander at the time. Something came up one day which I needed the advice of my superior, which was a chief of police.

I was headed toward the Chief's office when I met Chief Schamerhorn in the hallway. I had been working under him for some seven years. I presented my problem to him and he answered my question.

I do not know how Mr. James and/or Chief Gaines found out I had talked to Chief Schamerhorn, but shortly, I received a summons to Chief Gaines office, where I was confronted by none other than Mr. Quincy James, the Police and Fire Commissioner.

He wanted to know why I had gone to Chief Schamerhorn instead of Chief Gaines. That upset me. I immediately stated, "What was I expected to do, with two chiefs running around here?"

He looked at me for a moment and told me I was dismissed.

I think Mr. James served only one term on the City Council. I would see him around town occasionally and I wasn't sure he remembered me, especially when I was out of uniform.

One day, shortly before he died, I saw him in Wal-Mart. I asked him if he remembered me, and he said, "Yes, Captain Smith, you were the best captain the police department ever had."

I appreciated that and I thanked him for the remark.

# AMBULANCES

There was a period of time; I believe it was during the 1960's, when there was a serious problem with ambulance service in Pasadena.

There was an ambulance service company in the city. This company began to have financial problems, caused mainly, I think, by people who would not pay for the ambulance service. Naturally, the company had to have employees, qualified EMT's, dependable ambulances and so forth. They were required to respond when someone called for an ambulance, whether it was to an auto collision, a residential call or a business call. The company would bill the appropriate people for the service, but a lot of times they got no response.

Eventually, the company announced it was going out of business. This resulted in a sense of emergency among city officials. The city had to have an ambulance service.

The decision was made for the city to take over the ambulance service, same service to be operated by the Police Department.

All police officers who graduated from the Pasadena Police Academy had to undergo and complete an advanced course in first aid. They knew how to use the basic techniques to save lives. They were not qualified as EMT's.

Along about this same time, Chief of Police made the ill-advised decision to rotate the three captains in the police department. This meant Captain J. A. Middleton was transferred to the Detective Division, where he wanted to be, Captain R. E. Rhodes was transferred from the Detective Division to the Identification Division, where he did not want to be, and I was transferred to the Patrol Division, where I did not want to be. I had been in the Identification Division some ten years and that was my line of work. Captain Rhodes had never worked in the Identification Division and knew practically nothing about that area of expertise.

So, overnight I was responsible for supervising a police-operated ambulance service. The officers involved were not in favor of the program either.

To begin with, we kept the ambulance on the parking lot, presumably ready to make emergency runs. The police unit assigned to the district wherein the police department was located had the responsibility of responding when an ambulance call was received. It was the Shift Commander's responsibility to see that this unit was always a two-man unit. They were required to test the ambulance at the beginning of their shift, to make sure it would start; all the equipment was operable and so forth.

It was a plan doomed for failure.

One night, right at shift change, a call came in requesting the ambulance. A man was suffering from an apparent heart attack.

The dispatcher begins trying to locate the officers who were assigned to operate the ambulance. He did not know right at that time whether they were still in the building or already in their unit. He began calling their unit, with no response. He paged them over the public address system in the building, still no response. He was receiving additional calls about the person who needed the ambulance. One person who called was a Ham Operator, who said he had picked up the request on his ham radio.

The dispatcher finally got a response from the unit, which had hit the streets. The unit was not, however, near the police building. He dispatched them to the parking lot to pick up the ambulance. We'd had some cool weather and the ambulance was difficult to start.

They received the address where the ambulance was needed and preceded in that direction. Witnesses later reported the ambulance missed the street where it was needed and a citizen had to chase it down and get it turned around.

By the time the officers got the man into the ambulance and to the hospital, he had died from a heart attack.

I do not know if the time lost would have saved him. I do know I had a very difficult time explaining to the widow why the ambulance did not make it there quicker.

Everything that could have gone wrong did go wrong.

As soon as I could, I went to Inspector Gilbert and told him, "We need to get into this ambulance program with both feet, or get out of it completely." He agreed with me and we changed the whole program.

In the future the ambulance would be manned 24/7 and would patrol just like a police unit. It was qualified success.

Later another ambulance service started up and the police department was able to get out of the ambulance business.

# JOHNNY, WHERE ARE YOU?

The time was September, 1961. A very large hurricane was in the Gulf of Mexico, moving slowly northwest toward the Texas coast. The name of the storm was Carla.

Practically all of the Texas coast would be affected. I remember seeing an aerial photograph of the storm and it covered the whole Gulf of Mexico.

Our daughter Amy Lou was about six months old. All officers of the Pasadena Police Department were called in for duty. We were put on two shifts, twelve hours on and twelve hours off. I was assigned to the Night Shift, working from 6:00 PM to 6:00 AM. I was a Sergeant at the time and we were working two-man units. My partner was Probationary Officer J. A. Alspaw. He was a graduate of the 7th Pasadena Police Academy.

The eye of the hurricane made landfall down the coast near Port Lavaca, Texas on September 11, 1961. Our area was on what they call the "dirty" side of the storm. We had very strong winds, approaching 100 miles per hour and torrents of rain. The winds blew out many store-front windows, blew over many trees and broke many electrical power lines.

The power lines were hot, of course, and when they struck things, sparks would shower like a fourth of July celebration.

One night while we were on "hurricane" patrol, during the height of the storm, a citizen called to report their teenage daughter missing. The dispatcher was told she disappeared while they were all trying to get some rest. They found the screen gone from her bedroom window and the window was left open. The family did a search of the immediate neighborhood, but could not locate her. They asked for the Police Department's assistance in locating their daughter.

The dispatcher broadcast the situation and several units responded to the area to search for the girl, to no avail. She was not to be found. One by one the units went back into service to their assigned districts.

Since I was a Sergeant, I was able to roam all over the city to respond wherever we were needed.

After all the units gave up and returned to service, I suggested to Officer Alspaw that we go to the area and have a look around. Officer Alspaw was driving.

We had just arrived in the area and was driving south on Richey Street when we observed a figure of a woman walking down the middle of the street. The wind was howling, lightening was flashing, and electrical sparks were flying everywhere.

We pulled up to the figure walking along in the middle of the street. She did not notice us, she just kept walking. She was calling out, "Johnny, Johnny, where are you?"

We stopped the patrol car and got out to approach her, one on each side. She seemed oblivious to us. She was dressed only in a thin nightgown. She and it were soaked thoroughly.

We took her by the arms and led her back to our patrol unit, placing her in the rear seat. We were not equipped with a blanket to cover her, so we checked in with the dispatcher and headed for the police station.

At the station, someone found a blanket and put it around her to keep her warm. She was placed on a bench in the lobby of the station and the dispatcher called her family to come pick her up.

If she told us who Johnny was, I do not remember. Once we wrote up our report, we hit the streets and resumed patrol.

I have read that storms affect some people like that. It may be the low barometric pressure that causes the problem.

# THE ANN WILLIAMS MURDER CASE

March 1955, in Pasadena Texas two Pasadena Police Patrolmen, Officer Glenn Gardner and Probationary Officer William H. Smith, responded to an assignment to investigate a possible missing person.

The call came from a person living in a small trailer court. The officers made contact with the reportee and was told that the lady and her two small boys had not been seen for several days, and all the neighbors were worried about them.

The missing woman's car, a 1950 Cadillac, was parked near the trailer, but she and the boys had vanished. With the neighbor, Glenn Gardner and I entered the trailer to look around. There was a photograph of the lady in the trailer and in the photograph she was wearing a new style of glasses popular at the time. However, laying on the television set were the glasses which the lady was wearing in the photograph. Alongside the eyeglasses were the keys to the Cadillac. This did not look good.

The neighbor told us the lady's name was Ann Williams, and her son's names were Calvin, age 9, and Conrad, age 8. Mrs. Williams worked at a discount store and the neighbor worked there also.

Glenn and I reported back to the station and at his request, I wrote up the report on what we found out, careful to point out the information about the woman's eyeglasses.

After this incident, I more or less forgot about it. We had other calls and reports to write. Nettie and I had just moved to Pasadena and I was very new on the job. At that time we did not subscribe to any newspaper, so most of the time we did not know what was going on around us. We had a TV, but it broadcast only three stations. Their main news broadcasts were in the evening and at ten o'clock at night. As a general rule, I missed both of these broadcasts.

However, later I did learn that the missing woman case had made all the news venues. All the news items mentioned the eyeglasses in their reports. No one had seen the woman and the boys.

Various law enforcement agencies were involved in searching for the missing woman and the two boys.

In charge of the Pasadena Police investigation was Chief of Police Vareece Berry. The department had no detective division at the time. As a matter of fact, we had only about 32 officers, total.

It was revealed later Ann Williams showed up at an acquaintances place near Alvin. These people had a large place and the man worked on cars, including Ann's Cadillac. She told the lady there she had some spoiled deer meet she needed to get rid of. She borrowed a shovel and drove to the back of the property. She was joined there by the owner of the property and his grandson. The owner dug out a trench for the "spoiled deer meat."

When Ann left, the grandson asked for a lift into town to see a movie. She dropped him off near the theater. After the movie he was looking for a ride home. He found a friend who agreed to give him a ride. The grandson told the friend about Ann and the spoiled meat. The friend had read a newspaper account of the missing woman and told the grandson about it. The grandson told the friend that the woman was not missing, because she had been at their place most of the day, burying spoiled meat. The two agreed they had better go see what had been buried.

They found the two boys which Ann Williams had buried. She had killed both boys, cut up their bodies, called them spoiled venison and buried them on this man's property.

She was located at an address in Houston. She had been driving a different kind of car. She was arrested, charged with two murders, tried, found guilty, and given two life sentences.

She never did give a good reason for killing the boys. She told conflicting stories, everything from "I don't remember: they accidentally took some of my medicine and died; to I don't know why I killed them. I loved them."

The medical examiner testified the boys died from blunt-force trauma to their heads.

This was the first major case that I was involved in during my 28 year career at the Pasadena Police Department. I had been a police officer about four months at the time.

# THE LAWNMOWER THIEF

Back in the 1950's, the City of Pasadena was plagued with numerous lawnmower and edger thefts.

Many were reported to the Pasadena Police Department and all officers were alerted to be on the lookout for this thief.

All the thefts were from driveways and garages left open. These items simply vanished with no trace, no witness, nor any evidence.

I was working in the Identification Division, but I did have knowledge that these items were being stolen.

Along about this time, I had to buy a lawnmower. The grass in our new yard had finally gotten high enough to mow. We went to K-Mart and bought a new mower. We paid some $39.00 for it. Not having enough money to pay cash, we charged it, with the obligation to pay it out monthly.

Well, you guessed it! I had left it sitting in my garage with the door open and it disappeared. You talking about agitated. Man, was I agitated. A brand new mower gone and we still had to make the payments on it.

We had to go get another one, and our payments doubled.

One day a vigilant citizen observed this elderly fellow loading up his neighbor's lawnmower into the back of his old pickup truck. He got the license number off the truck. When he talked to his neighbor about what he saw, he gave the neighbor the license number. The neighbor reported the theft, along with the license number of the truck. Officers soon located the truck and the suspect.

The fellow cleared up about a hundred thefts. Surprisingly, he remembered a lot of them, including mine. He told the officers he got a good price off that new lawnmower.

From then on, I kept my mower behind closed doors or in the back yard.

Now days, a lawnmower thief would be hard to spot. About every-other pickup truck and/or trailer driving around neighborhoods are loaded with lawnmower equipment.

# THE MOTEL LOVERS

After I had some experience behind me, I was always on the lookout for things out of place, or people doing things different from "norm."

I was working the Night Shift, a one man unit, patrolling District l, or the Old Downtown Area. A motel had been built in the 700 block of what was called Sterling Street. It has changed ownership so many times; I do not recall the original name of it.

The office of the motel was facing Sterling. As I drove by, at about 1:00 AM, I noticed a vehicle pull into the driveway. The driver did not, however, park at the front door, but pulled in beside the office, where his vehicle could not be seen by the clerk. I turned around, cut my lights and watched him. He got out and went into the office. He stayed long enough to register, came back and reentered his car. He then drove around into the motel parking lot and stopped in front of a room. I watched as he and a young girl got out of the car and went into the room.

I went to the office to check on the registration of this fellow. The clerk showed me the card. He put on the card that he was alone. He also put his vehicle license number on the card, and this number did not agree with that on the vehicle.

Because the girl appeared to be underage, I called the juvenile officer and requested his assistance. When he arrived I briefed him on my suspicions.

We went to the motel room and knocked. The fellow came to the door and we entered. We got his identification, which did not agree with the name on the motel registration card. The Juvenile Officer asked him where the girl was and he stated there was no girl in the room with him. The Juvenile Officer went to the door of the bathroom and yelled for the girl to come on out, and she did. We did determine that she was in fact, a juvenile. We checked under the pillow on the bed and found material which proved the man's intentions.

The Juvenile Officer carried both of them to the Police Station. I wrote my part of the report and left them with the Juvenile Officer.

I do not know what, if anything was filed on the man for his actions. If I remember right, he was about 19 or 20 years of age.

Many years later, I was in my office in the Identification Division and the Juvenile Officer came to see me. Not the same one, naturally. This one was a captain. The Captain told me there was a DPS trooper in his office with a request. The trooper told the Captain that when he was 18 or 19 years of age, he got arrested by the Pasadena Juvenile Officer for being in a motel room with a juvenile girl. The trooper was curious whether there was still a record of this incident. Of course, I remembered the incident well, but I did not tell the Captain. I got the trooper's name and checked our files. Sure enough, there the information was.

The Captain told me the trooper was going to apply to become a Texas Ranger and he knew he would not be accepted if a record was found of his arrest. I told the Captain I could find no record of his arrest.

I sincerely hope the trooper was able to become a Texas Ranger.

# THE HIDING PLACE

The police department was always getting notices from the military regarding personnel who were absent without leave from their units.

This incident involved a local man who was absent without leave. I cannot confirm that the department had a notice on him. I was not involved in the case.

The department got a call from a citizen regarding a possible AWOL military man. When the officers contacted the citizen, they were told a neighbor of the reportee was harboring an AWOL military man and pointed out the house. The neighbor did not know the name of the man.

The officers went to the house to check it out. They talked to the people there and they were told there was no such person there. The officers left.

They had not been gone long when the neighbor called again to inquire why the officers did not detain that AWOL subject. The neighbor was told the people there denied having such a person there. The neighbor said as soon as the police car was out of sight, the subject walked out on the front porch.

The officers were dispatched back over to the house. This time they requested permission to look through the house for the subject. They did not find him and left again.

Once again the neighbor called, sighting the subject over at the house and wanted to know what was going on.

On this trip the officers were more thorough, even looking under the beds. One officer noticed that one of the beds was sagging in the middle! He grabbed the mattress and pulled it off the bed. There was the AWOL person.

The man and the people there had cut out a section of the mattress just his size. When the officers showed up they would place the mattress over him for concealment, very innovative, for a while. I don't know how he kept from sneezing, though.

He was taken into custody, the Military Police were called and he was returned to his base and confined.

# THE RODEO "QUEEN"

Every year there is The Pasadena Livestock Show and Rodeo. Lots of business people support the show. The City of Pasadena, of course, is always heavily involved in the show. One year all the Pasadena Police Officers had to wear bow-ties which had "Pasadena Rodeo" on them, I may still have mine somewhere.

Even though it is an event to benefit young people, there is quite a bit of consumption of adult beverages there.

Occasionally, when some of these imbibers leave the show, our officers come into contact with them.

One day I was working the Evening Shift as Patrol Sergeant. The time was in the early evening. One of our patrol units requested a supervisor at a violator traffic stop. I figured that was me, so I slid on over to see why my presence was needed.

I arrived at the designated location on Red Bluff Road and observed the police unit had a vehicle stopped. They were about a half mile north of the Rodeo area. When I exited my unit, I saw the violator vehicle was a pretty, new, baby blue Cadillac and said to myself, "Uh-Oh!"

I approached the vehicle and observed the driver to be a middle-aged lady, all dressed up in her cowgirl outfit, "to the nines" as the saying goes, including all the associated sparkling jewelry.

The officers told me that she had been driving all over the road and they pulled her over. They were of the opinion she was inebriated, in other words, drunk.

They could not, however, get her to even acknowledge their presence. They shined their flashlights in her face and knocked on the window of the vehicle. Her doors were locked. She just sat there, looking straight ahead, motor idling, and ignoring them.

I decided to try my hand, thinking surely she will acknowledge a Sergeant of the Pasadena Police Department. No dice, nothing. Being smart enough to have attained the rank of sergeant, right away I made a command decision. I called for my Captain.

In a little while said Captain appeared with an annoyed look on his face. He was apprised of the situation and striding forward to the baby blue Cadillac, he took over. He approached the vehicle and proceeded to use the same unsuccessfully tactics yours truly and the patrol officers had tried, same results.

The Captain stated there was one thing we were not going to do and that was breaking a window out. Besides, he said, he knew the lady. She was the wife of a local well-known business man and a long supporter of The Pasadena Livestock Show and Rodeo.

Another situation developed which required my presence and I had to leave it with the Captain. WHEW!!

A check with the patrol officers later revealed the Captain told the lady to drive on home and the officers would escort her there to make sure she made it alright.

I do not know who the lady was, and the Captain never mentioned the incident thereafter.

I wonder, if any of those young people at those shows back then are now the ones running the show and consuming their share of adult beverages, getting ticketed, and maybe even getting locked up for driving under the influence?

# "WITHOUT A TRACE"

This is how I got involved in the case of a missing police officer.

During the 1960's I was elected as president of the Pasadena Municipal Federal Credit Union (PMFCU).

The credit union had a lady who took care of the credit union books, and did a very good job of it. She was a city employee and worked for the credit union in addition to her job with the city.

When a member of the credit union needed to borrow some money, said member had to fill out loan papers and get three eligible co-signers before the loan could be approved by the loan committee.

As a back-up security against the loan, the credit union had an agreement with the City Comptroller regarding the city employee's "drag-up" pay. If the city employee had sick leave, vacation or holidays accumulated on the records of the City, the employee could be paid for those accumulated days upon his or her departure from City employment, either through termination or retirement.

So, when the employee left the employment of the city, the Comptroller would contact the credit union about any outstanding loans before issuing the employee's final check.

If there was an outstanding loan, the credit union would inform the Comptroller of the exact amount of money owed by said employee. The Comptroller would then withhold that amount from the employee's final check. In that arrangement, the credit union was always assured of getting its money back when the employee left.

In the case at hand, a police officer named David, a graduate of the 25th Pasadena Police Academy, failed to show up for work on his assigned shift. The police department had a policy that when an officer was absent more than three days, he or she had to bring a doctor's statement confirming the officer had been ill and under the doctor's care.

When Officer David had been absent without authorization for three days, his pay was suspended, pending receipt of termination papers from the Chief of Police.

When the Comptroller's normal paperwork was forwarded to the credit union and his name was not on the list, the credit union secretary called me, with the question, "What are we going to do about this officer's outstanding loan when it comes due?"

She stated if the Federal Auditor found out we had an unresolved outstanding loan, he would write up the credit union. I told her I could do nothing right then except go against David's co-signers. The co-signers would be obligated to pay off the loan since they had co-signed the note. I told her we would wait and see what the Chief of Police would do about terminating Officer David.

The Chief of Police had been very active in the credit union during his career with the police department. It was not like he did not understand the situation. I had contacted him more than once about the problem, but he procrastinated.

Time passed and she would call me every few days about the situation. I eventually decided the Credit Union would have to notify the co-signers about their obligation. I did so with letters to each of them.

WOW! Talking about a hornet's nest! Did I stir one up. All three of the officers contacted me in an upset manner. I reminded them of their obligation. I also told them that everything would be resolved if the Chief of Police would terminate David. Several weeks had passed since he had disappeared and his case was being investigated by officers with our department.

David had enough termination pay coming to pay the loan off. Once again, I contacted the Chief of Police to bring him up to date on the situation, and still he waited.

I guess the three officers caused such uproar about the situation that Chief of Police Wornick finally sent David's termination papers through and he was officially terminated. His money was released, the loan was paid off, and the three co-signing officers were off my back.

Now, where was David? After he had been absent about a week, an investigation was began to find out what happened to him.

He had been training to be a K-9 officer. He had a dog pen in his back yard and his dog was in the pen. One of the neighbors finally called the police department about the dog, since it had not been fed or watered for several days. A K-9 officer took custody of the dog.

David had also been taking flying lessons at a local airport. He lived alone and I am not sure about any next of kin. David was a close-mouthed individual. When he worked the front desk, he was always reading Soldier of Fortune magazines.

The investigation revealed that he'd had only a few hours of flying lessons. The officials at the airport told the investigating officers that the plane which David had been taking lessons in was also missing. The key to the plane was still in the office, however. His flying instructor stated it was doubtful that David could successfully fly the plane solo and navigate it to fly any great distance.

No other person of David's acquaintance was missing, as far as could be determined.

Did some other unknown person with flying qualifications leave with David?

As far as I know, as of this writing, neither Officer David, nor the airplane has turned up anywhere.

He and the airplane are still classified as missing, vanished without a trace.

# TOMMY

These days the yards of new houses are sodded with San Augustine grass. It was not always so, especially in Red Bluff Terrace where Nettie and I bought our first house.

Our front yard, mostly covered with sand, was "sprigged" and not sodded. Until those sprigs began to cover the dirt, the yard was mostly sandy and pretty poorly looking. I watered it most every day to get those little sprigs to start spreading. I did not have a sprinkler; I used the water hose with my thumb over the end of it.

The yard was far from needing mowing. One day while I was watering it, this young boy came by on the sidewalk pushing an old lawnmower and carrying a small gasoline can. He stopped to watch me for a minute and then asked if I wanted my grass mowed. I looked at him and back at my "sprigs" and told him I did not think the grass was ready for mowing. He thanked me and walked on down the sidewalk, pushing his old lawnmower and carrying gas can.

I noted that his hands were very dirty and greasy looking and his clothes were dirty also. It appeared to me like he had been working on that lawnmower. I had not seen him in the neighborhood before and did not know where he lived. We had not lived there very long. I guessed the young boy's age at about eight or nine.

I began to see him around the neighborhood from time to time. I learned his name was Tommy. He lived with his family on our street, about a block or so from us. He never asked me again to mow my yard.

I lost track of him over the years after he began to grow up. If I were to make a guess, I would venture he probably dropped out of school at an early age.

I actually heard more about his dad than I did Tommy. His dad was prone to drink too much.

As for Tommy, I do not know what he ended up doing for a living or what kind of life he was living.

The next time I heard his name was from a police report. During this time the Pasadena Police Department had a very active and successful narcotic division. We had several very good undercover narcotic agents.

After a state law was changed to allow private clubs in "dry "areas, a private club started operating in Pasadena.

One night our narcotic undercover agents were in there to do their business. One of the officers made a narcotic buy and signaled to his backup and walked away. The backup attempted to arrest the narcotic pusher and a fight ensued. The supervisor, who happened to be present, moved in to assist in the arrest, the supervisor reported later that he was jumped from behind by a big burly man who got a choke hold on him. The man was choking him down and the officer could not break the hold. The officer had to resort to deadly force. He pulled his firearm, pointed it around under his left arm and pulled the trigger. The man released him and dropped to the floor. The fight was over.

The identity of the dead man turned out to be Tommy.

The shooting was ruled justified and no action was taken against the officer.

# THE COP AND THE BURGLAR

Most of the time when an officer is working the night shift, he is cruising through alleys behind shopping centers and other stores, checking for open doors and other things of a suspicious nature.

The officer involved in this incident had been on the department the same period of time as yours truly.

I have been out there, doing the things I just described. The problem was, sometimes things got so ordinary that one let his guard down.

That was the case with the officer involved here.

He was easing through a back alley behind a shopping center in the dead of the night. His lights were off and he was driving very slowly. Ahead of him in the alley was an automobile parked behind one of the stores. Finding an automobile in an alley like that was unusual, especially one with the trunk lid up.

As the officer eased upon the automobile, a man came out of the store with an arm load of suits. The store was a man's store which sold suits, shirts, ties and etc.

The officer got out of his unit and walked up to the fellow putting the suits in the trunk of the car. The officer asked the man what was going on and the man replied that he was transferring some suits from this store to another store. The officer offered to lend the man a hand and the man accepted.

The officer then began to assist the man in carrying out loads of suits, shirts and etc., placing them in the man's automobile.

The man then closed the door of the store, thanked the officer for his help and drove off while the officer watched.

The officer was very surprised the next night to learn that a clothing store in his district had been burglarized and a great amount of suits and other clothing items had been stolen.

This was quite embarrassing tor the officer. He had to report what had happened. He said the fellow was very personable and polite.

I have to add that the fellow was one cool customer, also.

The thief was caught, though, because the officer had logged the automobile license number when he rolled up on him.

The officer endured the situation and stayed on to take his well-deserved retirement.

# THE CUBAN ARMS CASE

In the late 1950's or early 1960's, the country of Cuba was in a turmoil involving one Fidel Castro.

The Houston office of the FBI asked our department's assistance on a case they were working on. Apparently, some individuals were putting together a cache of military arms to be sold to a group involved in the situation in Cuba; this was a violation of federal law.

The suspects were staying at a local motel and the FBI had them under surveillance. The men at the motel were allegedly waiting for the "money-man" to show up with the cash for the arms.

Somehow, a reporter for one of the Houston newspapers found out about the situation and requested a statement from the FBI before printing the story.

The FBI agreed, but asked the reporter to hold off for twenty-four hours so they could catch the man with the money. The reporter agreed and the FBI gave him the full story.

Mistake!

The next morning the whole deal was on the front page of that newspaper.

The FBI immediately raided the motel room and arrested those who were there, but they missed the "money-man."

At the time I was working in the Identification Division. The chief called me to grab my camera and go with him.

We traveled down Red Bluff Road to a new sub-division back in the woods near Clear Lake. In the house we went to there was a stockpile of all kinds of guns and ammunition.

283

With my trusty black and white camera I took a lot of photographs of this cache of arms.

Back at the station I developed the film and made 8 by 10 black and white prints of the exposures I made. I turned over one set to the Houston office of the FBI.

I kind of forgot about the case.

Many years later, after I retired, I was able to go through my personal file at the Police Department and make copies of various items I thought might be of interest to my family.

In my file I found a Letter of Commendation from J. Edgar Hoover, the Director of the FBI, complimenting me on the quality of the photographs I had made of the so-called "Cuban Arms "case.

I do not remember anyone telling me about this letter. Apparently, someone had just filed it away and kept their mouth shut.

Of course everyone knows what happened in Cuba. Castro did not, however, get the arms which I photographed.

It was an interesting case and I was honored and proud to have received an "atta-boy" from the Director of the Federal Bureau of Investigation J. Edgar Hoover.

Sometimes I wonder who arbitrarily decided to withhold from me the knowledge of that letter from the Director of the Federal Bureau of Investigation, J. Edgar Hoover.

As far as I know, during my career at the Pasadena Police Department, no other officer had every received a commendation from Mr. Hoover.

UNITED STATES DEPARTMENT OF JUSTICE
FEDERAL BUREAU OF INVESTIGATION

WASHINGTON 25, D. C.

October 23, 1959

PERSONAL

Mr. W. Herbert Smith
Police Department
Pasadena, Texas

Dear Mr. Smith:

      I have recently learned of your part in the location and apprehension of Fredrick Davis and Robert Dick Kellner.

      The efficient and cooperative action of you and Captain Wornick brought this case to a prompt and successful conclusion. My associates join me in expressing our sincere appreciation for your efforts in this matter.

Sincerely yours,

J. Edgar Hoover

*Letter from J Edgar Hoover to W H Smith Photo*

# "TARZAN'

This Pasadena character's last name will not be mentioned. He crossed the paths of various Pasadena Police Officers back in the sixties. I don't know where he picked up the nickname.

He lived not too far from the old Police Department building which was on N. Walters.

We got a call one day from Tarzan's dad. He told the dispatcher his two sons were fighting in their back yard. Both sons were of legal age. This call came in on the Evening Shift. It seemed the Evening Shift was always getting these types of calls. Our Evening Shift supervisor at that time was Assistant Chief John L. Gaines.

I do not remember what unit responded, or who the initial officers were. I do remember they called for the supervisor.

The officers reported to Chief Gaines they observed the two brothers on the ground in the back yard of the residence. The older brother was sitting on Tarzan and holding him down. Both were very sweaty, dirty and appeared to be exhausted.

The officers stated the only thing Tarzan could do was spit. He had spit in his brother's face until it was dripping off. The officers got them separated and put the cuffs on Tarzan because he was still violent.

Chief Gaines arrived on the scene and talked to Tarzan's father. The father agreed to have Tarzan locked up. Chief Gaines called for the departmental strait-jacket. When this item arrived, delivered by yours truly, we managed to get Tarzan de-cuffed and into the strait-jacket.

The Evening Shift was short on men and units that day, so Chief Gaines made a command decision. He looked at me and said "We'll take this man to the lockup, you drive."

So, the Chief and I placed Tarzan in the back seat of the Chief's unit and away we went toward the lockup. Chief Gaines smoked, but I did not. Having had a cancer on his lip removed, he opted to use a long cigarette holder with a filter, kind of like FDR.

We were headed toward our destination and Tarzan was very quiet. The Chief and I were conversing about various police topics. Chief Gaines lit up a cigarette and began to puff.

Suddenly, we heard a voice from the back seat, a voice real close. The voice asked for a cigarette. I looked around over my right shoulder and Tarzan was leaning forward on the back of our seat. He did not have the strait-jacket on.

Chief Gaines looked around and grunted, as was his habit, and gave Tarzan a cigarette. There on the back seat lay the strait-jacket. Tarzan sat back and enjoyed his smoke while we transported him to lockup. He gave us no more problems. We turned him over to the personnel at the lockup and returned to Pasadena. We did not know how he got out of that strait-jacket.

I don't think I ever saw Tarzan again. The usual course at this hospital was for them to keep a person of this sort for three days, examine him, question him, observe him, and if he exhibited no further radical behavior, they would release him to his parent or guardian.

# THE MARINE "SUSPECT"

Even now, after all these years, I find this hard to believe.

I was Superintendent of Identification and Records. My office was on the second floor of the old police station at 112 N. Walters.

I do not remember the exact date this happened, but it had to be about 1972. Neither do I remember the position this officer held at that time. He was either an inspector or deputy chief, which were basically the same.

He called me to his office for a conference. I do not think he was my superior. I think at that time I was answering to the Chief of Police.

It was obvious he was very agitated about something. He wanted to know what my son was doing in the Records Division talking to one of the clerks. I told him I had no idea. He ordered me to call "that boy of yours," immediately and find out what he was doing in the Records Division.

At this time our oldest son Timothy was in the U. S. Marines. He was stationed in California.

Of course Wilson did not call my son by name. He just said "that boy of yours."

Tim had been in the marines for over a year. He came home on a surprise visit. He came to the Police Station and arrived while I was away from my office on police business. This I already knew.

When I got home I got on the phone and finally got in touch with him at his duty station.

I told him that it had been reported he was in the Records Division talking to one of the clerks. He admitted he did go into the Records Division. When he arrived at the police station and found out that I was away from my office, he walked down the hall to the Records Division counter. There was a young female clerk typist at her desk. Tim began to talk to her. She eventually stated that she was having trouble with her electric IBM typewriter. Tim said he hopped over the counter to determine if he could fix it. He did manage to get the typewriter going again. Tim was an Avionics Technician in the Marines and pretty well knew what he was doing. He said nothing else transpired and he hopped back over the counter and left to try to find me. He was in his marine uniform.

Tim was a year and half old when I went to work at the police department. He practically grew up at the department. All the older officers knew him on sight.

Tim made a mistake by hopping over the counter the way he did and I told him so. I do not know who the clerk talked to about the incident. She did not mention it to me. She must have known who Tim was, otherwise she would have told me. Obviously, she told someone and the word got back to this officer and he hit the ceiling. He knew all my children and he knew Tim, otherwise why he would order me to call him long distance to get a report.

Had the shoe been on the other foot, as the saying goes, and one of his sons had been in the Records Division, I would have said "so what, he is a police officer's son. He can be trusted."

Tim still is a kind of a "fix-it" guy. He has a history of fixing various kinds of machines, electronic devices and etc.

I don't know what this guy suspected Tim of doing. Sure, the clerk was young and pretty, but Tim was more interested in working on her typewriter than flirting with her.

After I talked to Tim on the telephone by long distance, at my expense, I reported back what I found out. I think he still suspected Tim of flirting with the clerk. All the single police officers flirted with her. This guy gave me the usual dire warnings about unauthorized people going into the Records Division.

As far as security goes, the department used a jail trustee to clean up the offices and I guess he was more trustworthy than Captain Smith's marine son. Go figure!

Our son Timothy served honorably. He was a career marine, serving twenty years and retired a Gunnery Sergeant.

Unbelievable!

# A COUPLE OF PROMOTIONS

Allen O. Laster graduated from the FBI National Academy and returned to the Pasadena Police Department.

He was immediately assigned to the newly formed Detective Division. This lasted for a year or so and he was transferred back to the Identification Division and I took his place in the Detective Division. There is an undated photograph which I am including with this article. In the photograph there is, left to right: Richard E. "Dick" Rhodes, yours truly, Captain G. W. Wornick, Kenneth Green, John A. Middleton, and D. L. Wilson.

In 1959, the new chief of police, A. J. Schamerhorn, called me into his office and asked me if I would like to be a sergeant. I asked him to let me think about it. I walked over to Captain G. W. Wornick's office and told him about the offer. He said, "Take it. You might not get another chance." I walked back over to Chief Schamerhorn's office and told him he had himself a sergeant. He said okay and I was subsequently promoted. Chief Schamerhorn told me that if anyone asked me if I took a test to tell them he had tested me and I passed. Later, an officer did ask me that very question and I told him what the chief had said. I also asked the officer what he would have done if the chief had offered him the job, and he said he would have taken it. After all, it meant a small pay raise, which Nettie and I needed badly.

After I was promoted I was assigned to the Evening Shift as Patrol Sergeant. I was a brand new sergeant and did not know what I was doing. Some of the officers I was supervising had seniority over me in employment. In other words, they had more experience than me in police work. I did, however, struggle through and with God's help, I made it.

At some time later the announcement was made by the Civil Service Director that a promotional test was going to be given for the position of captain. The department had no lieutenants (officially, that is). There were a couple of officers who called themselves lieutenant, but I never saw any official document verifying this.

I signed up for the captain's test and was told what books to get to study. Two other sergeants were eligible to take the test. The civil service rules required time in rank of two years, so, since all three of us were promoted at the same time, we were eligible.

I took the test and passed it. It was said the older sergeant beat me on the test. At that time we were not allowed to examine the test results. Later on it was revealed that the tests were supposed to be graded in the presence of the person who took the test. The Civil Service Director handled the whole thing and posted his results of the test. The older sergeant came in first, I was second and the other sergeant came in third.

On this test there were a number of questions regarding identification work. As far as I know, the older sergeant did not know a loop from a whorl, as the saying goes in the identification field. I don't know for sure how he beat me and the same went for a number of my colleagues.

The older sergeant was promoted to Captain, the other sergeant resigned from the department and that left yours truly the only person on the eligibility list.

Later one of the captains resigned (Captain D. T. Warren) and I was promoted to the rank of Captain, where I remained for the rest of my career, in spite of my best efforts. If my memory serves me correctly, this particular test occurred in 1963.

*Pasadena Police Detective Division Photo*

# FILMING OF THE MOVIE "URBAN COWBOY"

I had been assigned to the Identification Division for approximately ten years and was quite satisfied, working in my chosen field of law enforcement. I held the rank of Captain and my title was Superintendent of Identification and Records.

There were two other captains in the police department at the time. One was supervisor of the detectives and the other supervisor of the patrol division.

The patrol division supervisor, Captain John A. Middleton, became dissatisfied with his assignment and appealed to Chief C. W. Denson for a transfer. Middleton's choice of assignments was the Detective Division. I had no argument with that. John loved detective work and I loved identification work.

For reasons which were not clear to Captain Rhodes and me, Chief Denson decided to rotate all three captains. I went to the Patrol Division, Captain Rhodes went the Identification Division and Captain Middleton went to his choice, the Detective Division.

I had not worked patrol for some ten years and Captain Rhodes had never worked the Identification and Records Division. As a result, Middleton was perfectly happy. Me and Dick Rhodes were unhappy campers.

Fortunately, I had three good lieutenants in the Patrol Division. Lt. C. R. Holt was on the Day Shift, Lt. Charles Hilborn on the Evening Shift and Lt. H. D. Costilow was on the Night Shift.

Things worked out in my favor though, because off-duty jobs became available to me as Patrol Commander. I was already working a good off-duty job at First Pasadena State Bank. Other short-term off-duty jobs opened up for me, also.

My immediate supervisor was one of my former patrol officers when I was Patrol Sergeant. This was Inspector Lee Gilbert. (He was one of the officers who bailed off the front porch when I was confronted with a man who had a gun pointed at me. That story is told under the title "He Had the Drop on Me.")

One day while I was in conference with Inspector Lee Gilbert, his secretary ushered in an individual who introduced himself as a representative of Paramount Studios, out of Hollywood, California. The gentleman informed us that Paramount Studios was about to begin filming a movie at Gilley's, the world's largest beer joint and dance hall. This establishment was located on Spencer Highway and owned and operated by one Sherwood Cryer.

The object of the gentleman's visit was to get help in setting up security at the site of the filming. Gilbert told the man that I was the Officer to talk to about that. The gentleman and I adjourned to my office to discuss the particulars of what was going to be needed. I saw right away this was going to be an awesome undertaking. I called in my lieutenants and we discussed the project. What was needed was a list of officers who would be able to work off-duty at the filming. I put out a memorandum to all interested officers and directed them to sign up with the Patrol Division Secretary if they wanted some of the work. By the time the filming started, we had plenty of officers signed up to work.

The stars of the movie were John Travolta and Debra Winger.

Over the next three months I worked many off-duty hours handling the job out there.

I found out that it usually takes three months of filming to make a 90 minute movie. I got to meet some other "stars" who came by to observe the filming.

Nettie told me later that I was paid more in three months by Paramount Studios than she was paid for a whole year at Graybar Electric. We needed the extra money. We always had to scrimp and save to get by, even with my off-duty jobs.

I did not let my regular off-duty job at the bank go. If I could not get someone to fill in for me at the bank, I worked both jobs

Obviously the Lord smiled on me with that transfer to the Patrol Division. I feel that Mr. Denson never expected that turn of events. After all, I did not have my mustache any longer, thanks to him

I could not have done this security job at the filming without the able assistance of Kaye Cole, the Patrol Division Secretary. I put her on my Paramount payroll and she got paid for her work. She kept all my schedules, the officers' schedules and the hours they worked.

It was an interesting three months, but I would not want to do it again.

*Captain Herbert Smith and John Travolta Photo*

# A MOTHER'S PERJURY

I was working the Night Shift at the Pasadena Police Department. It was in the late 1950's. I was assigned to the "accident unit." It was the only patrol unit which was solid white and the only one with an emergency red light on the roof.

A call came in from a citizen who lived in the unincorporated area known as Golden Acres. This area was under the protection of the Harris County Sheriff's Department. At times we backed them up and assisted them in any way we could. We were all shorthanded in those days.

This citizen reported that someone had just stolen his old work car. The car was sitting in his driveway with the key in it. He had a bad muffler on it, so when the thief started it, he woke up. It was about 12:00 midnight. He told the dispatcher he last seen his car headed west on Spencer Highway. Spencer Highway was only a block or so south of where he lived.

When the dispatcher put out the call Officer Don Turner was westbound on Spencer, but east of where the citizen last saw his car, the citizen gave the dispatcher the license number on the car and also described it as being a multi-colored old model Ford.

Don Turner advised he would head west on Spencer and try to catch the suspects.

At the time the call came in I was sitting in front of the Police Station at 112 North Walters. I told the dispatcher I would head south on Shaver in an effort to head them off.

I proceeded south on Shaver at a high rate of speed with my little red light whirling on top of my unit.

About three or four blocks south of Southmore, Shaver curves slightly to the left and merges with Main Street. This was years before the City made Shaver and Main Streets one-way from where they merged.

There was practically no traffic on the streets at that time of the night. As I rounded that slight curve on Shaver, I observed a pair of headlights coming my way about a half a mile south of me. I immediately shut off my emergency light when I saw those headlights. I continued on south on Shaver at pretty good clip. The approaching vehicle had caught the red light at Allendale and Shaver. Allendale ran west off Shaver. I caught the red light at Garner Street, which ran east of Shaver about a half a block north of Allendale.

When the traffic lights turned green the vehicle facing me turned left, or west on Allendale. When it proceeded under the street light I observed that it was an old model multi-colored Ford. The vehicle traveled west on Allendale and I fell in behind him.

I called the license number in, but it was not the same number the citizen had reported. The driver pulled up in a driveway on the south side of Allendale. We were about two blocks west of Shaver. I pulled my unit in behind their vehicle; put the car in neutral with my foot on the brake. I was waiting for the dispatcher to call the citizen back to confirm the license number.

My headlights were shining on the old Ford, illuminating it and the inside of the car. All of a sudden, both car doors on the car flew open and men jumped out of both doors. The driver ran around the front of their car and joined the other man. They both disappeared down the side of the house.

When they bolted from their car, I bailed out also. I ran around the front of my unit to try to give chase. As soon as I saw down the alley between the houses, which was kind of dark, I saw these two men going over the chain-link gate of the back yard. Neither of the men had looked back, even from the time when I pulled in behind them in the driveway.

Suddenly, I found myself standing there looking at the dark area, with my weapon in my hand and the smell of gun powder in my nose. I realized that I had fired one shot at the suspects. I do not remember drawing my weapon. I ran forward to the gate to try to see them. It was all dark in the back yard. Everything happened so fast I had forgotten to grab my flashlight! I did not see the suspects anymore. I turned and ran back to my unit to get my flashlight. I discovered my police unit had rolled out of this driveway, across the street and into the yard across the street. Breathless, I ran to my unit to report the suspects had run from me and was now on the ground in the neighborhood.

While I was talking to the dispatcher, Don Turner came off Shaver at a high rate of speed. I told him what happened and he took off to check the neighborhood for the suspects.

I removed my unit from the yard of the neighbor across the street and waited for my supervisor. Captain Wornick arrived on the scene and I related everything that had happened. The dispatcher revealed that the citizen had given the wrong license number of the car. That was the reason the numbers did not agree.

The Captain and I walked back toward the gate where I had last seen the suspects. I now had my flashlight. The first thing we found was a cigar box lying on the ground. It had some papers in it, some savings bonds and a little cash. Apparently one of the suspects dropped the box when my weapon went off. The papers had the name of a small grocery store on Spencer Highway.

Captain Wornick kept looking through the grass with his flashlight. He spotted a place on one of the fence posts where my bullet struck. The spot was dead center on the metal post. Looking down at the base of the post, Captain Wornick found the flattened bullet which had struck the metal post. The spot on the post was about belt-buckle high. My shot must have gone right between the two and hit the post. No wonder they dropped the box!

The Captain told me if I'd had my shotgun, I would have gotten them both.

In retrospect, I am glad that missed them. All they were doing was running from me.

While the area was being searched for them, Sergeant Doug Warren and his partner were looking around in the area from where the car was reported stolen. This was probably a couple of hours later. The sergeant pulled his unit up to a stop sign and while they were sitting there, a car drove in front of them on Spencer. As the vehicle passed through, their headlights they observed a subject climb over the seat into the back seat.

They stopped the car, thinking this was unusual activity. They got the men out of the car to question them. One of the men was wearing a jacket and protruding from the pocket of the jacket was what appeared to be a savings bond with the name of a local grocery store on it. They checked the store and found it had been burglarized. The two men were arrested

The City of Houston had annexed a strip along the north side of Spencer and the grocery store was in this strip. The Houston Police Department was notified and two burglary and theft detectives soon arrived on the scene. They took over the investigation and the two suspects were turned over to them.

Further investigation revealed the two men had driven over from the north side of Houston with the intent and purpose of burglarizing this store. They tried to get into the safe, but failed.

They carried a load of cigarette cartons out to their car which was parked behind the store. They had taken some savings bonds which they found in the store office and also a small amount of cash in a cigar box. When they attempted to turn the car around, the driver backed it off into the ditch and got it stuck. Being unable to get it out, they decided to find another car and steal it. They found this old multi-colored Ford sitting in a driveway with the key in the ignition. The driver started the car, which made a lot of noise, backed it out and drove off toward Spencer Highway. Apparently, they did not stop to try to get their car out of the ditch. They turned west on Spencer Highway, made it to Shaver Street, which they knew led through Washburn Tunnel and on to the north side of Houston.

They proceeded north on Shaver and as they approached the intersection of Allendale and Shaver, they observed a police unit coming toward them, which was my unit. When the light turned green, they turned left on Allendale with the police unit right behind them.

They pulled into a residential driveway and the police unit pulled up behind them. They decided to run for it.

As they bailed out and ran around to the back of the house, they said the police officer shot at them. They climbed over the fence, ran through the back yard, climbed another fence and ran.

They found another car which they stole. They drove it back to the neighborhood where they lived, they abandoned it, got another car and went back to recover the car which they had stuck behind the store. That car could have been traced to them that was why they tried to recover it. When they arrived back at the scene of the burglary, they got pulled over by the police.

The Houston Police Department filed on both of them for Burglary and Theft of the grocery store. I am not sure if they were filed on for the theft of the old Ford. That would have been a Harris County case. I do believe they were filed on by our department for the theft of the car they stole right after I jumped them out of the old Ford.

One of the suspects pled guilty to all charges and was sentenced to a number of years in the state prison.

The other suspect pleaded not guilty and was tried by two different juries. One trial was for burglary and the other was for theft.

I testified at both trials.

The mother of the suspect was a defense witness. She testified her son had been at home most of the night. She said the other suspect came to their house to get her son to help him get his car out of a ditch.

She said it was a cool night and her son borrowed the other man's jacket, the jacket which had the savings bond in it. The savings bond was in the pocket when he borrowed it, according to her.

The suspect's lawyer put him on the stand and of course he denied all charges.

The testimony in district court in those days was taken in shorthand by a court reporter and backed up by a new device called a wire recorder.

The jury asked to review the defendant's testimony regarding what he said about the officer shooting at him.

One of the jurors heard something none of the other jurors heard during the suspect's testimony. He wasn't satisfied with what the court reporter had read from his notes and wanted to hear what was on the wire recorder.

The controversy over the testimony was what the defendant testified to about being questioned by the Pasadena Police.

He had maintained all along that he was not with the other suspect when that man burglarized the store and stole the car.

If it was not him with the other suspect, who was the other man?

Here is where it gets weird. What this one juror heard was one little word. That word was "said."

When the court reporter read the defendant's testimony, that portion in question was read like this: "The officer who shot at us said so and so."

When the recording from the wire recorder was played back for the jury, it went like this: "The officer who said he shot at us said so and so."

The first statement implied that he had been present when the gun was fired.

The second statement implied that he was not present when the gun was fired.

Apparently, based on that one discrepancy, the jury found the defendant not guilty on all counts and he was released from custody.

The prosecution failed to call the other defendant back from prison to testify.

We later learned from the Houston Police Burglary detail that this suspect was shot and killed at a beer joint on the North Side.

I believe that had that mother not committed perjury on behalf of her son, he would have gone to prison, but he would have probably been alive.

# A COMMUNICATION BREAKDOWN

In order to successfully accomplish their task, law enforcement agencies must maintain good communications. There are times, however, when there is a communication breakdown. The following is an example of what can happen when the most basic of communication rules are forgotten.

During the course of one of their investigations Big City Police Department developed a prime suspect, Hubert Elbert Didit, hereinafter referred to as H. E. Didit.

In their search for the suspect the Big City officers received information that he could be located at 1234 First Street in Small City. They also ascertained that he was armed and stated he would not be taken alive. The community of Small City lies adjacent to Big City. Armed with an arrest warrant for H. E. Didit and a search warrant for the house at 1234 First Street, the Big City officers arrived enmasse at that location around 1:00 A.M. After arrival they surrounded the house then contacted the Small City Police Department and requested assistance. The supervisor in charge, along with several officers, responded to assist the Big City officers. Upon presentation of proper identification by the Big City officers and an explanation of their presence there, they asked for help in arresting H. E. Didit.

The house at 1234 First Street was drenched with floodlights and a megaphone was brought into use. The supervisor of the Big City group repeatedly demanded, over the megaphone, the suspect's immediate surrender. He told the suspect to come out with his hands up because the house was surrounded. The noise and lights aroused everyone in the area except those in 1234 First Street. Getting no response, he ordered teargas be fired into the house. The officers reacted promptly and the windows of the house wee penetrated with several teargas projectiles. This obtained quick results, but the wrong kind. When the house disgorged its occupants there was no H. E. Didit. As a matter of fact the weeping disfranchised people had never heard of him. They informed the officers that they had been standing inside the house watching the activity outside, unaware that it was their house which was under attack until the teargas came crashing in.

A closer examination of the search warrant revealed that the house described was one street further over, namely 1234 Second Street. A grave mistake had made by officers of both departments.

The mistake made that night could have been avoided had there been better communication between the two departments. The Big City officers should have called first and then stopped at the Small City Police Department headquarters. This would have given the supervisor more time to review the search warrant and double check the address. He could then have assigned officers to take the Big City group directly to the right street. When he arrived on the scene that night he assumed the Big City officers had the right house.

During the ensuing investigation it was determined that the suspect had been in the house on Second Street and had escaped during the raid on the house at 1234 First Street.

It was further revealed that the man and woman forced from their home by the teargas were the parents of a young Big City police officer. Their house was saturated with the teargas. Even after being completely renovated at the expense of the Big City Police Department they were still unable to live in it.

The incident was the subject of news media headlines and comments for several days, resulting in bad publicity for both police departments.

The fiasco also resulted in civil lawsuits by the outraged family against the officers and cities involved. When these suits are finally settled no doubt both departments will experience an additional monetary loss.

# JOHN RAY HARRISON

I know I have mentioned a man with whom I worked at the Pasadena Police Department. His name was John Ray Harrison.

John Ray Harrison was hired by the Pasadena Independent School District and the City of Pasadena as a Youth Counselor. He worked out of my office when I was Juvenile Officer. I was instructed by the Chief of Police to check John Ray's reports before he turned them in. I did just that and often found misspelled words. I chided him about and he said spelling was not important. I told him that spelling was important to me and to correct the misspelled words, which he did.

John Ray already had a teaching degree when he was hired here. He had also some experience as a police officer. It was my pleasure to work with John Ray while he was performing the duties he was hired to do.

John Ray went back to college part time and obtained a law degree. He later got into politics and was elected to the Pasadena City Council. I think it was at this point he severed his relationship with the school district and the city..

Attorney at Law John Ray Harrison ran for and was elected to the Texas State House of Representatives. After a term at that position, he ran for and was elected as Mayor of Pasadena. Later, he ran for and was elected to the bench in Harris County as a Civil District Judge. He subsequently returned to Pasadena politics and was elected as Mayor again.

Now, I may have some of these events mixed up, but he did serve in those capacities.

The Pasadena Police Department got into the helicopter business and at one time had three choppers. One in the air, one as a backup and the other having maintenance done.

An amusing incident occurred one night during the Evening Shift of the Police Department. It involved Mayor John Ray Harrison. Please be advised that it was always my opinion that John Ray was a little bit eccentric. You had to know him to understand him. He had a small problem trying to be humorous when the situation did not call for humor.

Our helicopter did some routine aerial patrolling. There were times when the ground patrol units requested the assistance of the helicopter.

On this night, a clear night, the helicopter was circling an area of Pasadena in which the mayor lived. The helicopter made a distinctive noise, of course, so everyone in that area was aware of the presence of the aircraft.

John Ray grew curious about it and decided to call the police dispatcher to determine what was going on. Now, the dispatcher did not recognize his voice when the mayor asked about the helicopter. Unfortunately, John Ray was trying to be humorous and he asked the dispatcher what "fox-trot" was doing flying around his area. The dispatcher did not know what the man was talking about. The helicopter's radio call sign was Fox, as in "This is Fox Seven" or something like that. When he could not get any satisfaction from the dispatcher, he asked to speak to a supervisor. The dispatcher referred him to his sergeant. The sergeant asked the dispatcher who was calling and the dispatcher told him "John Ray." So, when the sergeant picked up the telephone he asked "What can I do for you Mr. Ray?" Wrong kind of question, by the time John Ray got through with the sergeant, the sergeant was saying "Yes, sir, Mayor Harrison," and so on.

It was never revealed whether John Ray found out what the helicopter was doing.

Years later, after John Ray appointed Leroy Mouser as Chief of Police, another amusing incident occurred.

Mouser was a retired Deputy Chief from the City of Houston. I was Patrol Commander at the time and that included the jail. I knew we had been getting complaints from people who had been in jail about how cold the jail was.

I feel sure that some of the complaints made their way to the Chief's office. Rest assured, if the people could not get satisfaction from the Chief, they would go to City Hall. My lieutenants had investigated these complaints and determined that indeed, the jail stayed rather cold in the summer time. At first we suspected a jailer was purposely adjusting the thermostat to make the inmates uncomfortable. Such was not the case, though.

We were having a conference in the Chief's office. Present were two inspectors in addition to myself. The chief's hall door was open. I was facing this door and could see the people passing back and forth in the hallway.

Lo and behold, there went Mayor Harrison down the hall without even glancing into the Chief's office. Now John Ray knew exactly where the Chief's office was. I cleared my throat and told the chief that the mayor just went down the hall. The chief jumped up asked "Where do you think he is going?" I said I did not know for sure, but I think he is headed for the jail whereupon the chief wondered why he would be going to the jail. I said I believe he is headed for the jail because he had a thermometer in his hand.

John Ray had purposely gone down that hall so the chief could see him on his way to the jail. The shortest route to the jail was down the other hallway. Like I said, John Ray was a little eccentric.

He never revealed what the temperature reading was in the jail. If he did it was between him and the chief.

By the way I do not know how he managed to gain entrance to the jail because the door leading into the jail stayed locked and could be opened only from the jail side.

When John Ray and I were working together, he was always after me to go back to college and get a degree. I did not have the time or the money to do that.

After John Ray retired from politics, he started having problems with his neck. He finally agreed to surgery to correct the situation.

Suddenly, one day I heard that he had died.

I knew a couple of his sons and one day I asked a son what happened to his dad. He said that the operation on his neck was a success. He was in recovery. They had put a neck brace on him and told him to not turn his head for any reason. The son said there was a telephone in his room and the phone rang. John Ray reached over for the phone, turning his head to do so and immediately expired by injuring the surgery that had been performed on him.

John Ray Harrison was a good friend of mine and I really hated to hear that he had died under those circumstances. He had a large family and a lot of grand kids.

# THE OLD POLICE UNITS, CIRCA 1954

I want to describe some of the equipment we used when I first joined the Pasadena Police Department. Mainly, I am going to write about the police patrol cars.

The department had seven cars assigned to it. The chief and assistant chief had take-home cars. The shift supervisors had one unit which they rotated from shift to shift. There were three district units and an accident unit. Take home cars for patrolmen were unknown in those days.

The accident car was able to roam over the whole city. It was colored white and the only unit with an emergency red light on the roof. The light was a "bubble-gum" type with a rotating red light inside.

The regular patrol units were solid black. These units had only hand-operated spot lights. Some of these had factory installed red lenses. Others had regular plain lenses, but were equipped with removable red plastic lenses which fitted over the spot light and could be removed when necessary.

The sirens were of the kind operated with two buttons on the dash. One button would cause the siren to wind up and peak. To make it "warble" the officer would activate one button until the siren peaked and then let off on it to drop the sound down. Then he would do that all over again. To stop the thing he used the other button.

After I got some experience, I was assigned to one-man units. If it was the white accident unit, I would flip the switch to turn on the rotating red light on the roof, push the siren button and away I would go to my assignment.

All the cars had stick shifts, so when I was chasing someone, or making an emergency call, it got kind of hectic.

In the black units, operating under emergency conditions, the officer had to (1) use the two-way radio; (2) clutch and shift gears; (3) operate the siren; and (4) operate the spotlight.

These cars had no consoles, no bucket seats and no seat belts. Therefore, in a one-man unit, the officer tended to slide across the seat when turning left at an intersection, shifting and accelerating. He sometimes ended up sitting in the center of the front seat. All he had to hold onto was the steering wheel. Usually the driver quit trying to use the radio and spot lights and concentrated on driving and using the siren.

There were some items you had to keep on the front seat with you, your clipboard and your flashlight. These usually ended up on the floorboard.

Speaking of floorboards, these old cars had many hard miles on them. It was not unusual to get muddy water splashed on your shoes from holes in the floorboard. The engines never cooled down, except maybe when they were serviced. When I patrolled what was called the number 1 one district it was not unusual for me to put one hundred miles on my unit and never get out of my district. Number 1 district was from Jackson street north and extended to the city limits east and west.

By the way, there were no air conditioners in those old police units. The summer temperature in Pasadena was about the same then as it is now, very hot.

The Lord was good to me for I never wrecked one and I did get into a few chases. Did I mention the brakes were never all that good?

I always looked forward to driving the accident car because I could roam all over the city and respond to calls the other units were making.

I see the fine police units our officers are driving now and I tell you the department has come a long way in regard to its rolling stock.

It would be a pleasure to drive one of the new units these young police officers are driving in a take-home situation.

1961 (left to right) Jack Linn, Sgt. Herb Smith and Insp. G. Wornick

*The Old Police Units circa 1954 Photo*

# WHERE'S THE MONEY?

There was lots of police activity in Pasadena, Texas in the 1960's.

Right at the Evening Shift change one day, the dispatcher received a call of an armed robbery. I was a Patrol Sergeant at the time.

We hit the streets on the run, headed toward the area where the offense occurred. I directed units to specific points to be on the lookout for any possible suspected vehicle.

The robbery had occurred in the Weingarten Shopping Mall on South Street. I headed east on Sterling Avenue, now known as State Highway 225. It was my intention to advance toward the Mall by driving south on South Avenue.

The robbery had taken place at a record shop in the mall.

I pulled up onto the parking lot at the mall to watch for any suspects, driving, running or walking away from the scene.

There was a tow truck sitting on the parking lot and the driver honked his horn at me. I drove over to see what he wanted. I knew the driver. His shop was nearby and apparently he had heard the broadcast over his police scanner.

He told me he thought the suspect was walking East on Cedarcrest away from the scene. The suspect had been described as a white male wearing a topcoat.

I preceded East on Cedarcrest and right away I saw the suspect walking along the sidewalk. I pulled to the curb behind him and got out of my unit. He never looked around. I stepped up on the sidewalk about twenty feet behind him. I said "Hey, Buddy, wait up." In the meantime I was walking rapidly toward him. When I was just a few feet behind him he whirled around to face me. The topcoat was open in front and he had a revolver stuck down behind his belt. I continued walking up to him and reached out and took the firearm from his waistband. I asked him, "Where's the money?" He reached into the pocket of his topcoat and handed me a roll of currency.

I put the pistol in my waistband, the money in my pocket and told him to get into my police unit. I put him in the front seat with me. I did not handcuff him, nor did I shake him down for other weapons.

I turned my unit around and drove back to the scene. We got out of the car and walked into the Mall to the records shop. The employee immediately yelled. "That's him!"

The young man was physically the size of a grown man, but he was a juvenile.

I turned him and the roll of currency over to the police officers making the investigation at the scene. They subsequently turned him over to the Juvenile Officer and returned the money to the clerk at the store.

At the end of my tour of duty that day, I wrote my report concerning the arrest just another day in the life of a Pasadena Police Officer.

No "atta-boy" on that case either and none was expected.

# THE HOSTAGE CHILDREN

I believe it was in the 1960's when this incident occurred.

The call came in to the police dispatcher that a husband and his wife were involved in family disturbance. The first two officers who arrive at the scene were C. R. Holt and Chester Fincher.

They reported later that when they arrived all looked quiet at the house. An ambulance was on the scene. It is not known who called the ambulance.

Chester walked up to the door and Charlie Holt stopped just short of a set of double windows. Chester rang the doorbell. A shotgun blast tore through one of the windows near Charlie, between the two officers. I think some of the shot hit the ambulance and the vehicle left.

The officers had been advised by the estranged wife that their children were in the house with the suspect. The house was completely dark, no lights showing. It was not known right then where the children were, or their condition.

Holt and Fincher took cover and began to try to reason with the man, to no avail.

I was the ranking supervisor on the street and so I went to the scene. By that time the Captain of Detectives. G. W. Wornick was on the scene along with the Chief of Police and the man's pastor. I think the wife must have called their pastor.

I checked with some of the patrol officers on the scene about the possibility of gaining entrance to the house through the back door. They all said there was a dog in the back yard and they did not want to go into the yard.

I finally went to the back gate to check out the dog situation. I was amazed. The dog was a small "house-dog" or "lap-dog." Probably did not weigh more than a few pounds. I opened the gate and, followed by Chester Fincher, entered the yard. The dog retreated to the back of the yard.

I saw that the back door was the same kind of door I had on the back of my house, which could be opened with a pocket knife. I used my knife and slipped the lock on the door, being very quiet about it. We could hear the man up front talking to all the negotiators on his front porch.

Chester and I pulled our shoes off and got down on our hands and knees, we began to crawl up toward the front of the house. We could see the silhouette of the man against the back-drop of the lights outside. We could not at first determine where the gun was.

Fincher was apparently wearing a brand new sam-brown harness and it squeaked every time he moved. I kept whispering "Shhhh" to him and we kept crawling.

We were able to get within a few feet of him and he did not realize we were there. At my signal, Fincher went for the man and I went for his gun.

Then it was all over. We rescued the children, who were in another room and unharmed.

The man was arrested and locked up, just another day in the life of a Pasadena Police Officer.

No "atta-boy" on that incident either.

# DROP THAT KNIFE

I was serving as Patrol Commander when this happened.

A call came in to the police dispatcher about a man with a knife.. Jerry Alspaw and Kenneth Crawford took the assignment

I eased over to check on the situation.

The incident occurred at one of the old duplexes in what was named Walter Williams Court.

I pulled up to the scene and observed my two officers on the porch of the duplex. Both officers had their guns drawn and were yelling at a man in the yard. I exited my unit and realized the man in the yard had a large knife in his hand.

Both officers were yelling at the man to drop the knife. The man was backing up into the corner of the yard. I took a few steps toward the scene and also yelled at the top of my voice, "Drop that knife!" The man looked over at me and dropped the knife on the ground. Jerry and Kenneth jumped off the porch and grabbed him. They handcuffed him and placed him in their patrol unit.

What made him obey my command and not theirs, I do not know. Maybe it was because a third officer had arrived on the scene. Anyway, the situation was resolved and no one got hurt.

By the way, I did not draw my weapon during this incident.

# THE COWBOY BOOTS

There was a rape and murder case in the Harris County jurisdiction.

The time period was probably in the early 1960's. The Harris County Sheriff's Department investigated the case and promptly developed a likely suspect.

A search began for this suspect, but he could not be found. As was usually the case in those days, the Sheriff's Department was assisted by a representative of the State of Texas investigative agency.

In this case, the sheriff was ably assisted by one of those agents. Exhaustive investigation revealed the suspect had fled the area. Months passed and the trail was going cold. Leads were developed which lead the investigators northward.

The story from here was related by the suspect. He had traveled up north and subsequently found a job, apparently with a home remodeler.

He said he was on the job doing some painting. A lot of houses up north are built with basements. He was in the basement of this house doing some painting. Usually, these basements are built in such a fashion that there is a small narrow window right at ground level. This allows a certain amount of light into the basement. The windows can also be opened to ventilate the basement.

The suspect was painting near one of these windows. He looked out through the window and saw the legs of two men standing on the walkway near the house. Right away he noticed both men were wearing cowboy boots. Knowing that very few men in that area wore cowboy boots, he realized these were strangers, and furthermore he knew why they were out there.

He stated he put his paint brush down, went up the stairs to the ground floor, and out the side entrance near where the men were standing. When he walked out, he had both hands in the air, because he knew the Texas Law had found him.

He was arrested and eventually returned to Harris County, Texas to answer to the charges for which the Texas Lawmen had found him.

# SERGEANT ROBERT K. LYON

Robert K. Lyon graduated from the 20th Pasadena Police Academy in 1971.

I do not know the length of this academy, nor do I know what Robert's standing was in the academy.

I do know he began night school early on to further his education. He worked patrol and was eventually promoted to sergeant.

I do not recall when he was assigned to the Identification Division. He learned the craft of identification work and I am sure attended various schools along that line.

As Superintendent of the Identification Division I had attempted for a number of years to up-grade the division to modern standards. Each year my requests were denied. During these years we had to ask the Houston Police Department and the Texas Department of Public Safety to process evidence which required the services of a forensic crime lab.

After I retired the city finally purchased the equipment necessary to set up a modern crime lab. (Probably because the Houston Police Department finally refused to process anymore of Pasadena's evidence.)

My friend and colleague Sergeant Robert K. Lyon had by then obtained his degree in chemistry. He was able to begin processing evidence for the Pasadena Police Department. This was evidence involving paint samples, blood stains, hair samples, firearms evidence and etc.

Robert attended night school for some ten years to obtain his degree in chemistry. I admired his tenacity and dedication to achieve his goal, and I still do.

It was my pleasure to work with him during our careers at the Pasadena Police Department and I am proud to acknowledge him as my good friend.

# EPILOUGUE

This effort has taken longer than I had anticipated. Over this extended period of time and through the use of two computers, I had the able assistance of the love of my life, Nettie Grace Coleman Smith, who continued to encourage me in spite of my period's procrastination.

My friends and colleagues Charles R. Holt, Tommy Lucas, Fred Ratliff, Jack Johnson, Al Humphreys, Don Jones, Rudy Ramirez, and many others who urged me on.

Certain members of the Pasadena Police Department indicated an interest in my efforts which encouraged me.

I want to include the members of the Pasadena Inspirational Writers Alive! They were always eager to give me their sage advice about how to develop a manuscript and I am eternally grateful.

I am particularly grateful for the able assistance of Ms. Pat Vance who did a line-by-line editing of the manuscript.

I could not have done this successfully without the treasured assistance of our beloved daughter Amy Lou Smith Beaty. Her 31 years in the San Jacinto College Computer Department enabled her to give me valuable help learning how to utilize this new lap-top and the new printer she and Larry bought me.

I have enjoyed sitting down at the keyboard and putting on record my memories of my childhood, my life and especially my career at the Pasadena Police Department.

I insert this paragraph at a point after I had finished the manuscript and forwarded it to the publisher. My efforts were reviewed by these folks and I was notified there were certain issues in the manuscript which needed to be taken care of to avoid being sued. Therefore I have spent

*Herbert Smith*

the last week or so going over the thing and changing names, deleting names and outright deleting articles. Some of these articles made very interesting reading and it is regretful that the will not be in the book. I appreciate the people at the publisher who gave me the good advice. After all, they have a world of experience in this sort of thing. I hope the second submission will be successful.

There are some people I want to pay tribute to as "They would do to 'Ride the River With:' Gus Vance Austin, James Westbrooks, Quitman T. "Pete" Smith, Charles R. Holt, Allen O. Laster, Roy Satterwhite, Dave Scoby, Ray Wiggins, Robert K. Lyon, and my son-in-law, Larry Joe Beaty.

Made in the USA
San Bernardino, CA
20 December 2014